Communists Like Us

New Spaces of Liberty, New Lines of Alliance

SEMIOTEXT(E) FOREIGN AGENTS SERIES

Jim Fleming and Sylvère Lotringer, Editors

IN THE SHADOW OF THE SILENT MAJORITIES
Jean Baudrillard

NOMADOLOGY: THE WAR MACHINE
Gilles Deleuze & Félix Guattari

DRIFTWORKS
Jean-François Lyotard

POPULAR DEFENSE AND ECOLOGICAL STRUGGLES
Paul Virilio

SIMULATIONS
Jean Baudrillard

THE SOCIAL FACTORY
Toni Negri & Mario Tronti

PURE WAR
Paul Virilio & Sylvère Lotringer

LOOKING BACK ON THE END OF THE WORLD
Jean Baudrillard
Gunter Gebauer
Dietmar Kamper
Dieter Lenzen
Edgar Morin
Gerburg Treusch-Dieter
Paul Virilio
Christoph Wulf

FOUCAULT LIVE
Michel Foucault

FORGET FOUCAULT
Jean Baudrillard

BEHOLD METATRON, THE RECORDING ANGEL
Sol Yurick

BOLO'BOLO
P. M.

SPEED AND POLITICS
Paul Virilio

ON THE LINE
Gilles Deleuze & Félix Guattari

SADNESS AT LEAVING
Erje Ayden

REMARKS ON MARX
Michel Foucault

69 WAYS TO SING THE BLUES
Jürg Laederach

INTERVENTIONS
Michel Foucault

ASSASSINATION RHAPSODY
Derek Pell

Communists Like Us

New Spaces of Liberty, New Lines of Alliance

Félix Guattari
& Toni Negri

with a
"Postscript, 1990"
by Toni Negri

Translated by Michael Ryan

SEMIOTEXT(E) FOREIGN AGENTS SERIES

Main text originally published in French
in 1985 as *Nouvelles espaces de liberté*.
This is the original publication of the
"Postscript, 1990" by Toni Negri.

Special thanks to Jared Becker,
Jim Fleming, Jeff Fort,
Michael Hardt, Sylvère Lotringer,
Michael Ryan, and Tom Yemm.

Semiotext(e)
522 Philosophy Hall
Columbia University
New York, NY 10027 USA

Printed in the United States of America

Communists Like Us

The project: to rescue "communism" from its own disrepute. Once invoked as the liberation of work through mankind's collective creation, communism has instead stifled humanity. We who see in communism the liberation of both collective and individual possibilities must reverse that regimentation of thought and desire which terminates the individual.

Bankrupt: the collectivist regimes have failed to realize socialist or communist ideals. Capitalism too has played fast and loose with promises of liberty, equality, progress and enlightenment. Forget capitalism and socialism: Instead we have in place one vast machine, extending over the planet an enslavement of all mankind. Every aspect of human life — work, childhood, love, life, thought, fantasy, art — is deprived of dignity in this workhouse. Everyone feels only the threat of social demise: unemployment, poverty, welfare.

Work itself defaults on its promise of developing the relations between humanity and the material environment; now everyone works furiously, to evade eviction, yet only hastening their own expulsion from the mechanical process that work has become.

Indeed work itself — as organized by capitalism or socialism — has become the intersection of irrational social reproduction and amplified social constraints. Fetters — irrational social constraints — are thus at the foundation of all subjective consciousness formed in the work process. And establishing this collective subjectivity of restriction and surveillance is the first imperative of the capitalist work apparatus. Self-surveillance and doubt prevent any intimations of escape, and preempt any questioning of the political, legal or moral legitimacy of the system. No one can withdraw from this capitalist legality of blindness and absurd goals.

Each instance of work, each sequence, is "overdetermined" by the imperatives of capitalist reproduction; every action helps to solidify the hierarchies of value and authority.

And yet — why is it that the discussion of communism is taboo? This discourse is defamed and banished by the very people it pretends to liberate from their chains. Could it be due to the seductive, "progressivist" rationality of capitalism and its organization of work?[1]

After all, capitalist work arrangements have succeeded in appropriating the discourse of communism — an analysis of labor and its liberatory power — and reduced it to techniques of manipulation: "Arbeit Macht Frei." Even the socialist varieties trumpet recovery and reconstruction as though these were instrumental goals attainable through technical means. The "ethic" of social revolution has become instead a nightmare of liberation betrayed, and the vision of the future is freighted with a terrible inertia...

Not so long ago, the critique of capitalism was directed at its destructive, penetrating market. Today we submit to its traumatization of our souls, passively assuming that reinvestment strategies are the least oppressive form of planning — and socialism or capitalism becomes a moot point.

So now everything must be reinvented: the purpose of work as well as the modalities of social life, rights as well as freedoms. We will once again begin to define communism as the collective struggle for the liberation of work, that is, at once, an end to the current situation!

*****

Empty-headed economists dominate all over the globe — and yet the planet is devastated, perhaps inexorably. We must affirm first of all that there is more than one path: the path of capitalist imperium and/or socialist/collectivist work forms whose persistence and vitality depend to a large part on our own incapacity to redefine work as a project and a process of liberation. We will define communism as the assortment of social practices leading to the transformation of consciousness and reality on every level: political and social, historical and everyday, conscious and unconscious. Recognizing that discourse is action, we will forge a new discourse in such a fashion as to initiate the destruction of the old way. But our communism will not for all that be a spectre haunting the old Europe...We rather envisage an imaginative, creative process at once singular and collective, sweeping the world with a great wave of refusal and of hope. Communism is nothing other than a call to life: to break the encirclement of the capitalist and socialist organization of work, which today leads not only to a continuing surplus of repression and exploitation, but to the extinction of the world and humanity with it.

Exploitation has advanced, on the basis of nuclear accumulation, to become a threat of execution; the cycles of war and the danger of destruction are well known. Now we are not determinists — but today it is not only determinists who recognize that the end is, if not near, certainly close by, especially if we abandon power to the capitalist and socialist juggernauts of labor. Preventing catastrophe will require a collective mobilization for freedom.

Continuing...

Why does everyday life tremble with fear and loathing? This fear is not the state of nature as described by Hobbes — that old excuse of the war of all against all, individual wills fragmented in a thirst for power. Rather what we have now is a transcendental, yet actually manmade fear which seeps into every mind with immobilizing, catastrophic dread. Indeed hope itself has fled this hopeless, hapless, grey world. Beyond malaise, life sinks into sadness, boredom and monotony, with no chance to break out of the morass of absurdity. Communication — speech, conversation, banter, even conspiracy has all been taken in by the "discourse" of mass media. Interpersonal relations likewise have spoiled, and are now characterized by indifference, disingenuous disgust and self-hatred — in a word, we're all suffering from bad faith.

Amazingly, the fabric of human feelings has itself come unraveled, since it no longer succeeds in connecting the threads of desire and hope. As a result, this pseudo-war has passed over the world for 30 years without its key features being noticed; the Cold War escapes unrecognized as the true culprit.

During that whole time, human consciousness has been ground down into something more manageable, even complicit. As the individual sinks into isolated despair, all the built up values in the world collapse around him. Fear breeds impotence and paralysis of every sort. Only this collective stupefaction prevents onrushing despair from reaching its logical conclusion in collective suicide; apparently there's not enough passion left for such a crisp transformation. But the real tragedy is that exploitation masquerades as fear: individual extensions — of desires and hopes for the future — have been simply prohibited, but under a metaphysical, rather than political guise.

And yet. And yet all the developments in the sciences and in the productive capacities of labor point to the existence of an alternative. Extermination or communism is the choice — but this communism must be more than just the sharing of wealth (who wants all this shit?) — it must inaugurate a whole new way of working together.

Real communism consists in creating the conditions for human renewal: activities in which people can develop themselves as they produce, organizations in which the individual is valuable rather than functional. Accomplishing this requires a movement — to change the character of work itself. And redefining work as creative activity can only happen as individuals emerge from stifled, emotionally blocked rhythms of constraint. It will take more than the will to change, in the current situation; to resist neutralization itself demands desire.

Paradoxical as it seems, work can be liberated because it is essentially the one human mode of existence which is simultaneously collective, rational and interdependent. It generates solidarity. Capitalism and socialism have only succeeded in subjugating work to a social mechanism which is logocentric or paranoid, authoritarian and potentially destructive. By means of progressive struggles, workers in the advanced industrial countries have succeeded in lowering the threshold of direct and dangerous exploitation; but this has been countered by changes in the character of that domination. Modern exploitation accentuates the disparity between rich and poor countries — now it is unfree workers in underdeveloped nations who bear the brunt of exploitation through violence and the threat of hunger. The relative improvement in the situation of the "Metropolitan Proletariat" is balanced by extermination in the Third and Fourth

Worlds. As contradictions built into work have proceeded to their limit, it is not an accident that the liberation of work can now be accomplished by workers in the most advanced sectors of science and technology. What is at stake is the fundamental ability of communities, racial and social groups, indeed minorities of every kind to conquer and establish autonomous modes of expression — not just lifestyles, but the work process itself.

There is nothing inevitable about work — no destiny leads work into ever greater repressions. In fact, the potential for liberation inherent in work itself is more visible than ever. How can Capital continue to present its work process as natural and unchangeable, when for technical reasons it is changing every day? This unexamined gap in the logic of work is the opening through which new movements of social transformation will charge pell mell.

Traditionally, the refusal to work, as an instance of struggle and as spontaneous action, has aimed at those structures which are obstacles to the real liberation of work. From now on, that struggle involves appropriating a new capital, that of a collective intelligence gained in freedom, the experience and knowledge that comes from breaking down the one dimensional experience of present day capitalism. This involves all projects of awakening and building towards liberation; in short, anything that helps reclaim mastery over work time, the essential component of life time. All the current catchwords of capitalist production invoke this same strategy: the revolutionary diffusion of information technologies among a new collective subjectivity. This is the new terrain of struggle, and it is not utopian to believe that consciousness itself is the "swing voter" deciding if capitalist or non-capitalist roads are taken. Once, knowledge and power were stockpiled like so many canon or missiles; now the empowering of a collective consciousness, part of the turmoil of the workplace, threatens to unite small arms into a mass revolt.

From this perspective, communism is the establishment of a communal life style in which individuality is recognized and truly liberated, not merely opposed to the collective. That's the most important lesson: that the construction of healthy communities begins and ends with unique personalities, that the collective potential[2] is realized only when the singular is free. This insight is fundamental to the liberation of work. Work as exploitation has completed its development of the general, the mass, the production line; what's now possible is to tap into the potential of individual creative energies, previously suppressed. Nothing less than a genetic breakthrough, this "rhizome"* of autonomy in the workplace can establish itself as a productive enhancement — and a serious challenge to the dead weight of bureaucratic capitalism with its "over-coded" and de-individualized individual.

Make no mistake about it: communism is not a blind, reductionist collectivism dependent on repression. It is the singular expression for the combined productivity of individuals and groups ("collectivities") emphatically not reducible to each other. If it is not a continuous reaffirmation of singularity, then it is nothing — and so it is not paradoxical to define communism as the process of singularization. Communism cannot be reduced in any way whatsoever to an ideological belief system, a simple legal contract, or even to an abstract egalitarianism. It is part of a continuous process which runs throughout history, entailing a questioning of the collective goals of work itself.

Glimpses of these new alliances are already available. They began to form and seek each other out at the time of the spontaneist and creative phase, which of course developed parallel to the big break-up and realignment in capitalist society to which we have been witness over the past three decades. To better locate and appreciate their importance, one can distinguish:

✷ "molar antagonisms": struggles in the workplace over exploitation, criticisms of the organization of work, of its form, from the perspective of liberation;

✷ "molecular proliferation" of these isolated instances of struggle into the outside world, in which singular struggles irreversibly transform the relations between individuals and collectivities on the one hand, material nature and linguistic signs (meanings) on the other.

Thus the maturing social transformations, which in turn affect productive work arrangements, are induced, piecemeal, by each and every molar antagonism: any struggle against capitalist and/or socialist power formations contributes to overall transformation. Social, political and workplace advances condition each other. But, and this is our point, the revolutionary transformation occurs in the creation of a new subjective consciousness born of the collective work experience — this moment is primary, all stakes are won or lost here, in the collective creation of subjectivity by individuals. We need to save the glorious dream of communism from Jacobin[3] mystifications and Stalinist nightmares alike; let's give it back this power of articulation: an alliance, between the liberation of work and the liberation of subjectivity.

Singularity, autonomy, and freedom are the three banners which unite in solidarity every struggle against the capitalist and/or socialist orders. From now on, this alliance invents new forms of freedom, in the emancipation of work and in the work of emancipation.

2
THE REVOLUTION BEGAN IN '68

I. SOCIALIZED PRODUCTION

It is not necessary to sit reading in a café to realize that the cycle of revolution reopened in 1968, and indeed achieved its high water mark of intensity. What was only an indication in 1917, and which subsequent wars of national liberation failed to achieve in any lasting way, was brought to light by the events of 1968 as the immediate possibility of collective consciousness and action.

Yes, communism is possible. It is true, more now than ever, that it haunts the old world. 1968 revealed the fragility of the social contracts installed successively to contain the revolutionary movements of the beginning of the century, those which followed the big crisis of 1929 and the movements which accompanied and followed the second great imperialist war. However one views the events of 1968, it is undeniable that they revealed the failure of this social compromise to eliminate or supersede the antagonistic contradictions of the capitalist systems.

We will now examine the three series of material transformations which concern the quality, the dimensions, and the form of capitalist "producing", and by doing so, highlight those new objective starting points from which any effort to change society will have to begin.

The quality of producing. The struggle between the working classes and those of the capitalist and/or socialist bosses had resulted in a system of production that was more concentrated and "massified." The impossibility of rationally overcoming crises, which revealed the social polarization of power, led to the efforts at managing the strongly centralized, planned economies, both capitalist and socialist. In this new environment, the classical law of value no longer operated as an expression of the relation between concrete real labor and amounts of money needed to secure an existence. The new version of the law instead related huge masses of "abstract" or undifferentiated labor to the ethereal information machines which supplant industrial production. Labor is "deterritorialized" — without foundation or meaning, it neurotically succumbs to a process which deprives working people of knowledge even as it is essentially knowledgecreating activity in the first place. Modern work was creating a global, infernal disciplinary apparatus, in which the constraints were invisible: educational and information constraints which placed the worker at all times under the sway of capital. No longer an eight hour wage-slave, the worker now produced and consumed continuously for capital. Capital in the process became more socialized, advancing social cooperation, integrating the collective forces of labor even as it turned society into a giant factory, in which the pacified consuming classes were organized into unions.

Deterritorialized production signifies that work and life are no longer separate; society is collapsed into the logic and processes of capitalist development. The consequences of this assimilation of society to work are profound: All the guarantees and resources of the welfare state — (wage systems, unemployment insurance, family assistance, pensions etc. — were intensified, but now they became part of the production process itself, rather than social defenses against capitalist dislocations. Social welfare in fact became a social dream: as the production process remade society in its own image, that high degree of abstraction was transferred to social life. Production now conferred membership in society. As the independent variable, production stamps society with its characteristic, leaving no region untouched. An equation is established, in which capitalist advancement and exploitation are seen as essential features of social machinery — that this is the meaning of society, and of course it has become true...

The political consequences of this transformation are equally profound. A high degree of political mobilization, evident in the demand for political participation growing out of a century of revolution and class consciousness, has expanded but then dissipated into a social consciousness. All the efforts of the bosses, who are conscious of this new socialization, consist of maintaining it — either through democratic or totalitarian means — within the framework of institutions and of rules for dividing the social product, which permit them to reproduce and thus to reinforce their commanding positions, in a manner that transforms economic into political power.

Before examining the consequences of this transformation of command, it is important to recognize another essential aspect of the changing character of production. The emergence of socialization as a crucial component of production has naturally affected the production process itself. Socialization, typically viewed as a formal quality, mutates into a substantive one: One may observe, for example, how the socialization of rural peasants accompanies their loss of independence, or how service sector workers lose social cohesion as they are functionally absorbed into rigid, mechanized production processes.

Up to this point, however, the industrial modes of production associated with capitalism and socialism had only taken possession of social inequalities from the outside, so to speak. The great conflagration of 1968 demonstrated that the new economic techniques now implicated the domain of social reproduction. Before then, the world of production was based on exchange values (commodity production) and the reproduction of use value (utility). All that is over. In this regard, one could consider the movements of that period as necessary preliminaries...

Now the remaining private sphere — family, personal life, free time, and perhaps even fantasy and dreams — everything from that point on became subjected to the semiotics of capital. This transformation took place regardless of political climate: democratic, fascist, socialist. Socialized production succeeded in imposing its law, its logic, on every facet of social life on earth, vampiristically appropriating free time, the life blood of humanity.

The events of 1968 posed themselves as an antagonistic recognition of this transformation of the social quality of production and work procedures. In a chaotic but nonetheless convincing way, they revealed the fundamental contradiction at the base of these transformations, that of conferring an immense productive capability to humanity while at the same time imposing a new proletarian destiny. This destiny originated in permanent expropriation, in the deterritorialization that allows no home base, no solidarity, no recourse, no guarantees, and extends not only throughout social life but into the unconscious.

Generalized exploitation, at all levels of society, had the effect of redefining production as the source of new, "supplemental" sources of unhappiness, and correspondingly new forms of political, even micro-political conflict. The new modes of production — integrative, totalizing, subtly totalitarian — effectively transformed the old modes of economic slavery into thinly disguised cultural and political subjection. A struggle ensued, which attempted to reduce all resistance against the supposed economic necessity to powerlessness. But it is precisely this transfer of "totalitarist" objectives to the minute, molecular levels of everyday existence which gives rise in turn to new forms of resistance on these most immediate levels, throwing into relief the entire problem of individual and collective isolation.

In 1968, this new "reactivity" expressed itself in the form of a tremendous shortcircuit. It would be useless to try to mystify these events, as the softheads of recovery have tried. It would be useless at this point to stigmatize the return of the great monsoons of irrationality. And what would such references to rationality signify anyway, in a world in which functionalism is strictly geared toward Capital, which in itself constitutes a maximization of irrationality? The question which remains posed since 1968 is rather that of knowing how to establish a creative and liberating relation between happiness and instrumental reason.

From '68 on, we have also witnessed an inversion of the cycle of struggles against colonialism and underdevelopment, and some attempts at internal modernization have appeared, on the part of the more dynamic sectors of the capitalist and socialist bourgeoisies. But there is a big difference between these ideological efforts — lip service, basically — and the realities of exploitation and new forms of concrete resistance.

1968 expresses the actual reopening of a critical consciousness, itself the crystalization of objective changes within the work force and production generally. This recognition appeared at first as rebellion, and as a new opening itself made possible by economic growth, its impasse, crisis, and the consequent reflexes of rejection. The essential force of 1968 resides in the fact that for the first time in the history of human revolts against exploitation, the objective was not simple emancipation, but a true liberation, extending beyond the removal of obvious, individual chains. The movements attained a global level reflected in a heightened consciousness of the historical linkage of singular struggles. For the first time at that level of intensity, the molar macrocosms and the molecular microcosms — the global and the local — began to combine in the same subversive whirlwind.

The events of 1968 thus mark the reopening of a revolutionary cycle. Not by the repetition of old slogans, but through the intervention of new perspectives on action, and by a redefinition of communism as enrichment, diversification of community and consciousness. Certainly the movement remained inseparable from the development of previous social struggles, and the redeployment of the employers' capacity for resistance and attack, but an important historical qualitative leap nevertheless occurred. At that point of individual radical fulfillment, what was required to generalize revolution among a significant portion of the population? Nothing short of a social cyclotron: the generation of an immense collective energy, the acceleration of ideas and emotions. In 1968, a revolution worthy of the most authentic aspirations of humanity was born.

II. BEYOND POLITICS

At the time of these movements, the refusal by living social labor of the organization of profit-based capitalism and/or socialism began to spread into the political arena. From a multiplicity of singular conflicts a grand opposition arose, directly confronting the political power responsible for administering social production. Traditional politics found itself completely cut off from this mass movement of collective consciousness; it shared no ground with the transformation of subjectivity. Traditional politics succeeded in grasping it only from the outside, by attempting to stall, repress, and finally to restructure and recover on its own. But by this very misapprehension and denial, it merely demonstrated its own powerlessness.

Politics today is nothing more than the expression of the domination of dead structures over the entire range of living production. A short time ago, at the end of the great revolutionary periods, history witnessed similar political restorations, which had no other goal than to "cover" the fundamental absence of legitimacy on the part of the elites who regained power. The princes who govern us seem to have returned, in the most absurd of ways, on the same perverse and empty stages, in the same vicious cycles which appeared in the aftermath of the Great Revolution and the Napoleonic epoch. (It is sufficient here to cite *The Charterhouse of Parma.*)

And Hegel's remark comes to mind: "This temple decidedly lacks religion, Germany lacks metaphysics, Europe humanity, reformism imagination..."

On the other hand, the collective imagination remains alive, but it can no longer conceive of politics outside of the paradigms and avenues of change which began to appear in 1968.

This is true first of all for the traditional left. The historical communist parties, prisoners of antiquated paradigms of production, did not even succeed in imagining the revolutionary force of the social mode of production which was in the process of emerging. Incapable of separating themselves from centralist organizational models deriving from a paradigmatic split between the avant-garde and the masses, they found themselves disoriented and frightened in the face of the unexpected self-organization of a social movement.

Loyal to the one dimensional destiny of the reformist movement, they experienced the explosion of new demands in the workplace, and of new desires in the sociocultural world, as a catastrophe which literally left them in a paranoid state. The same applies to a lesser degree to social democratic forces.

In the "actually existing socialist" countries, the reaction was extremely brutal, while in the West, it was more insidious, maneuverable, willing to compromise.

In all of these instances, one finds the same invariants: — social conservatism, combined with a systematic corporatist effort to channel and co-opt struggles; — political reaction, combining a recourse to State power with an appeal to traditional structures, in an attempt to reestablish the legitimacy of the old "elites"; — the squandering of collective subjectivity, in particular through intense use of the mass media, governmental agencies, and the Welfare State as a whole.

In fact, the left parties have been devastated by the effects of the movement of '68 and, even more so, by the collective-singular movements which have emerged since then as the bearers of social transformation. The left has attached itself even more to the traditional statist structures; and in doing so it has jettisoned its own relationship of conflict and compromise, and thus its own basis of legitimacy. But these structures were irrevocably altered by the counter-attacks of '68; from then on, the old politics could no longer hide its cadaverous face. The constitutional and institutional structures of developed countries east and west find themselves to be doubly undermined: from the inside, by their severe inability to adapt; and from outside, by the new forms of labor protest, reflected in the increase of marginal and part-time "non-guaranteed" workers,[4] as well as other numerous minorities who reject the status quo. This impasse has precluded any possibility of renewal.

All "progressive" capitalist perspectives, which would have involved increased popular participation, were systematically blocked. Constitutional structures, whether they be capitalist or socialist, democratic or totalitarian, have certainly experienced change, but typically in negative terms, always cut off from social movements whose effects they endure, and always by mystifying the actual operation of the system of political representation.

Attempting to respond to this decline in the institutions of popular political representation, power has resorted to techniques of anticipation and substitution, opting for symbolic simulation, adaptation and control. At the moment when the whole of society was finally absorbed into production, and the entirety of working and everyday life was exposed as fundamentally political, that political character was repressed, denied and manipulated. What a gothic sort of society which can maintain as its only ideal a vision of castles and courts completely removed from all real life, these small aristocratic universes which are blind to the new aspirations for freedom, new territorialities striving for autonomy! But how else can one describe these political aristocracies when, from their fortresses, they attempt to impose a stratification of society, devoid of consistency, substituting instead a general arrogance, an indifferent cruelty?

Disease, corruption, plague and madness spread within these closed universes just as they did in the ruling houses of the *ancien régime*. But their time is running out: we are at the threshold between suffering and the moment when history's potential will realize itself. The paralysis of political structures and all the current governmental "difficulties" are both symptoms and specific traits of moribund power formations; they are incapable of adjusting to the movements of society.

There is no doubt that these problems were initiated by the movements of the '60's. In fact, that was the moment when the surging tide of social struggles arrived at history's center stage. Since that time, as we shall see, the attempts to regain control of the situation have been numerous. But they were all short-lived because the political crisis was not, as the reactionary right assumed, the result of simple economic imbalances, having nothing to do with politics, but rather due to the inability of institutions to transform themselves. The roots of the crisis of politics were social. The current silence of the political forms of opposition reflect a curious neutralization: a canceling-out effected by the mutual interference of different components of social production, each of which is itself thoroughly disturbed and undergoing transformation. The so-called "death of politics," of which one hears so much, is only the expression of a new world which is emerging and which employs new and different modes of material and cultural self-valorization — either through entirely external means or peripherally to the dominant power formation, but which, in any event, are antagonistic to it. It is thus a world in the process of change which began its expansion in '68 and which, since then, through a process of continuous mutation, including all sorts of failures and successes, has struggled to weave a new network of alliances at the heart of the multiplicity of isolated singular components comprising it.

This is the new politics: the need to recharacterize the fundamental struggles in terms of a continuous conquest of (new) arenas of freedom, democracy, and of creativity. And, whatever the militants and the intellectuals who have "given up on all that" may say, there is nothing anachronistic or retrograde or anarchist in this way of conceiving things; indeed, it attempts to understand contemporary social transformations — including their contradictions — on the basis of the productive activities, the desires, and the real needs which regulate them. What is on the other hand entirely irrational and mad is the power of the State, as it has evolved since the 60s, into a sort of lunar Stalinism which only multiplies ad nauseam its rigidity and its institutional paralysis. The ferocious will to a "death of politics" is nowhere more dominant than in the Glacial Palaces of power.

Although much of it is empty and mystified, this type of power is nonetheless terribly effective. Moreover, one should not underestimate or overlook the great mass of pain and anguish that lies concealed behind its cynicism and its technocratic indifference: the insecurity of everyday life, the precariousness of employment, the fragility of civil rights, and, perhaps most of all, the impossibility of locating meaning in individual and collective life, the de facto banning of communitarian projects, of all "creative becomings" from establishing themselves on their own terms. This pain, which accompanies the lack of humanity in the capitalist brand of subjectivity, can be converted into an infinite array of reaction formations and paradoxical symptoms: inhibitions, evasions of all sorts, but sabotage as well, the transformation of refusal into hatred. This to-and-fro movement reaches its limit when the fear of destruction articulates a consciousness of the madness of power; then the pain itself becomes the vertigo of annihilation. This monstrous will to death in all its different forms today constitutes the true character of politics and the true cause of human misery.

III. THE NEW SUBJECTIVITIES

Since the '60s, new collective subjectivities have been affirmed in the dramas of social transformation. We have noted what they owe to modifications in the organization of work and to developments in socialization; we have tried to establish that the antagonisms which they contain are no longer recuperable within the traditional horizon of the political. But it remains to be demonstrated that the innovations of the '60s should above all be understood within the universe of consciousnesses, of desires, and of modes of behavior. It is on this level that the changes became definitively irreversible. These new modes of consciousness have literally dislocated the old scenarios of class struggle by invading the imaginary and cognitive roots of productive activity, transforming the consciousness that corresponds to that activity into an act of transformative individual will. Along the way this individuation of desire has thus spread to the realm of collective practices, which now constitute the new political territories. The dramatic and tumultuous affirmation of desire puts our social "living" into question and makes it the basis of a higher subjective expression of the ensemble of material and semiotic systems of production. Its opposition to private property is a radical negation of all forms of blind collectivism in capitalist and/or socialist undertakings, and its refusal of work on command actually expresses the will of a higher level of social production.

All seeming connections between this refusal and the massification of social subjectivity must be broken; the relation must be reduced to a paradox, by virtue of which the poverty of this massification is confronted with the most singular processes of subjective will.

Communism has nothing to do with the collectivist barbarism that has come into existence. Communism is the most intense experience of subjectivity, the maximization of the processes of singularization — individuation which represent the capability potential of our collective stock. No universality of man can be extracted from the naked abstraction of social value.

Communism no longer has anything

to do with any of this. It is a matter rather of manifesting the singular as multiplicity, mobility, spatio-temporal variability and creativity. That today is the only value on the basis of which one can reconstruct work. A work which no longer is crystallized in the form of private property, which does not consider the instruments of production as ends in themselves, but as means for attaining the happiness of singularity and its expansion in machinic rhizomes — abstract and/or concrete. A work which refuses hierarchical command and which in doing so poses the problem of power, clarifies the functions of deception and exploitation in society, and refuses all compromise, all mediation between its own existence and productivity. (All of which implies redefining the concept of work as the transformations and arrangements of production within the frame of immediate liberation efforts.) New modalities of collective subjectivity themselves bring together these qualities and these desires which change relative to productivity. The new production of subjectivity conceives of power from this point on solely as an horizon of the collective liberation of singularities and as work oriented toward that end — in other words, as self-valorization and self-production of singularities.

The social struggles which exploded in '68 and in the years following conferred a tremendous power on the coming-to-awareness of students and young people, the women's movement, the environmental and nature first movements, the demand for cultural, racial and sexual pluralism, and also the attempts to renovate the traditional conceptions of social struggle, beginning with that of workers. All too often these experiences have been described in terms of marginality. Marginality was quickly drawn toward the center, and the minoritarian demands succeeded — with difficulty — in detaching themselves from those of the lifeless middle ground. And yet each of them, by following its own course and by articulating its own discourse, potentially represents the needs of the large majority.

Potentially, but in a way that is not any the less efficacious: By taking hold of society as a whole, productive socialization wanted to confer on individuals, communities, and their reciprocal relations the character of universality. But the universality with which they were decked out didn't suit them in the least! Instead of a well-fitting hat, it is a mask, a cowl which only disfigures the expression of their needs, their interests, and their desires. It is not a paradox to say that only the marginalities are capable of universality, or, if you prefer, of movements which create universality. "Universal" politics are not capable of any transcendent truth; they are not independent of the games of economic valorization; they are inseparable from specific territories of power and of human desire. Political universality cannot therefore be developed through a dialectic of ally/enemy as the reactionary Jacobin tradition competitively prescribes. Truth "with a universal meaning" is constituted by the discovery of the friend in its singularity, of the other in its irreducible heterogeneity, of the interdependent community in the respect for its appropriate values and ends. This is the "method" and the "logic" of the marginalities which are thus the exemplary sign of a political innovation corresponding to the revolutionary transformations called forth by the current productive arrangements.

Every marginality, by placing its stakes on itself, is therefore the potential bearer of the needs and desires of the large majority. Before '68, the problem of reproduction remained marginal in relation to production. The women's movement has made it central. Although the questions relating to the preparation of the abstract and non-material labor force remained lateral in relation to the factory labor force, the student movements made them central in the same way as the new needs which the theoretical and aesthetic imagination proposed. The emerging collective consciousness came thereby to see itself as the nodal articulation of a multitude of marginalities and singularities; it began to confirm its power on the scale of a significant social experience, which did not close back on itself or "conclude," but which opened out onto further struggles, the proliferation of processes of collective singularization and the infinitely differentiated phylum of their ongoing transformation.

This imagination of liberation thus undertook, with more or less success, to superimpose — and to impose itself — on the fiction of the dominant realities. Its lines of collective feeling, its "new softness," its capacity to bring together the most immediate preoccupations with the broadest social dimensions demonstrated that the emerging forms of production were not the enemy of desire, liberation, and creativity, but only of the capitalist and/or socialist organization of work for profit. Human goals and the values of desire must from this point on orient and characterize production. Not the reverse. During this period, the production of liberation became the foremost goal. It will probably take some time before one can grasp the full significance of what was then at stake. To repeat, it had nothing at all to do with utopianism, but with the intrinsic reality of that historical period's social movement. It was probably the women's movement, with its extraordinary power of development, which, after '68, most advanced the new synthesis of the concept of production and of social liberation. For the first time, with that degree of lucidity, production for profit and work for the reproduction of the species were overturned, revolutionized on the basis of the most extreme singularity, that of the total "conception" of the child and of generating a new softness to life.

But this incredible experience was also a symbol: the revolution was understood as an optimization of singularities, as the beginning of a mobilization against the disaster of the current situation and its forms of command. The corporeality of liberation became primary. Insurrection of bodies as an expression of subjectivity, as incarnating the materiality of desires and of needs, as promising in the future the impossibility of separating the collective character of economic development from the singularity of its ends. Insurrection of bodies, meaning the successful liberation of those immense productive forces which humanity, up to this point, only turned against itself. 1968 represents the subjective side of production; this is an "interpretation," on a large scale, of its social texture, which displaces the previous political problematics onto the terrain of representation considered as a singular project of liberation.

1968 is also a magnificent reaffirmation of democracy. The fact that it was crossed by a certain naive "Rousseauism," that through it a few last champions of Jacobinism and of a disfigured Leninism came to shine forth for a few moments, doesn't in any way detract from the power of democracy in the movement considered in itself. It showed that the proletariat, from this point on, socialized and singularized, would not be able to "comprehend" a political movement except on the condition that it is founded on democratic arrangements in action. This was not only a theoretical truth but also a concrete historical affirmation: there is no specific form of freedom which is not attached to the group goals of the movement and lived, "experienced," by its members. This new "given" was underscored in a certain way, ontologically, in the generation which came after '68. And which wants today to send us back to the school of Anglo-American liberalism and its ideas of the marketplace! Anti-capitalism and anti-socialism have become the only forms which permit a renaissance of democracy.

3
THE REACTION OF THE '70S: "NO FUTURE"

I. INTEGRATED WORLD CAPITALISM

A restructuring of power helped to restore the command mechanisms in the 70s, and to restart the process of capitalist and socialist productive accumulation. Politics and economics, capital and the State, were now completely integrated. The process developed in two directions.

In the first place, as the international integration of national economies on an increasingly world scale, and their subordination within a polycentric and rigorously planned project of control. We call this figure of command which coordinates yet exasperates the unity of the world market, submitting it to instruments of productive planning, monetary control, political influence, with quasi-statist characteristics, Integrated World Capitalism (I.W.C.). In this process, World Capital integrates, besides the developed countries and directly dependent on them, the ensemble of real socialist countries, and controls, in addition, the means by which the economies of numerous Third World countries are absorbed, putting in question their previous position of "peripheral dependence." Indeed, statist command and the national States thus undergo a veritable deterritorialization. Integrated World Capitalism is not limited to recomposing, using new forms of unification, the flux and hierarchies of statist powers in their traditional sense. It generates supplementary statist functions which are expressed through a network of international organizations, a planetary strategy of the mass-media, rigorous taking control of the market, of technologies, etc.

It is certainly important to avoid an ingenuous or anthropomorphic conception of I.W.C. which would entail describing it as the work of a Leviathan or as a one-dimensional macro-structure of the Marcusean variety. Its planetary expansion, as well as its molecular infiltration, occur through mechanisms which can be extremely flexible and which can even take contractual forms. Each one engages legal forms that rely on continuous procedures rather than constraining substantive law. But it is no less true that it is this very procedural and regulatory continuum of relations which consolidates the centripetal tendency of the system, by diluting and "negotiating" the effect of crises in time and space and by relativistically reterritorializing each singular process.

In the second place, and conditioning the constitution of this global integration, the restructuring aims at the mode of production and the ensemble making up the collective labor force which relates to it. This deterritorialization and this integration was facilitated by rendering the social into data form, i.e. on the basis of the fundamental computerization [*informatisation*] of society. Exploitation could thus be articulated scientifically over the entire arena of the social, extending the control of profit creation mechanisms. Under these conditions, the assembly line of commercial and industrial production spreads its fabric over the social, not in its symbolic sense but materially. Society is no longer merely subsumed by capitalist command; it is absorbed entirely by the integrated mode of production. Differences in productivity and in levels of exploitation can then be articulated in a smoother, more diffuse way within each geo-political segment according to region, country, or continent. Competition, the key link in the bourgeois market, is no longer very important for this process of capitalist retraining.

The transnational computerization of the social is concerned with only one form of competition: that which it can provoke between workers and between the different strata of the working class and of the proletariat. It thus becomes possible for Integrated World Capitalism to activate specific techniques of analysis and control of social classes — which now make struggles erupt, now pulverize their power at those points where their level of politicization is significant, or, on the contrary, unleash them in a controlled way at those points where the problems of economic "take-off" and of political reform are posed most urgently.

As it has always been in the history of capital, this renovation of the forms of command by Integrated World Capitalism goes hand in hand with a redefinition of the ways surplus-value is extracted (computerization of the work process, spread of social control through mass media, subjective integration by governmental apparatuses, etc....).

And as it has always been in the history of the exploitation of workers' struggles, this leap forward of the organization of work and of the State was "anticipated" by the movements of the class struggle. The forms of social subjectivity which emerged in 1968 gave rise to a "weaving" of molecular struggles for liberation which are concerned with objectives that are at once immediate and long-term, local, everyday, trivial, yet engaged nevertheless with the future of humanity on a global scale. This operation was of course very complex and, in many respects, impossible to "sum up" within the framework of a single historical sequence.

It is no less true that the pseudo-progressive dialectic of capitalism which triumphed after the second world war was thus completely blocked. After '68, the dynamic between the different functions of capital (constant and variable) and the interaction between the class of capitalists and the social work force has radically changed context; this is a result of the emergence of increasingly important, heterogeneous arrangements of subjectivity and sensibility. The law of value has ceased to function — if it ever worked in the manner in which it was described — along with norms of economic proportionality and even the ordinary modalities of simple class exploitation. The social hegemony of the new proletarian subjectivities, once it was affirmed, had to acquire the quality of irreversibility: no longer would anything be able to prevent it from revealing itself, regardless of the prevailing relations of force, "the highs and the lows;" indeed, particularly on the "front" of their affirmation in the mass-media, no longer can anything prevent these subjectivities from being basic reference points for future struggles. Capitalist and/or socialist restructuration does not automatically refer to relatively rational laws. It is not "scientific" — no matter how sophisticated the theoretical devices and the instruments of prediction which it employs: it is essentially repressive. The computerization [*informatisation*] of the social is inseparable from its mechanization and its militarization, in such a way that the systematic production of information tends to be substituted for the search for it. Such are the zones of strategic importance that the circuits of reproduction which support life and the struggle are more and more controlled, ordered, and, ultimately, repressed in a preventive fashion. Life time thus finds itself tightly fastened onto the military time of capital.

The time of capital, or the capacity to translate every sequence of life into terms of exchange, and of overdetermination with the urgency and the necessity of the operations of economic quantification and of political command; terror, or the capacity to annihilate all those who refuse to submit to it: this is what the reshuffling of the traditional functions of the state, and their unlimited penetration of people's attitudes, sensibility and minds, amounts to. By threatening the very foundations of being, the state manages to control the singular flow of our lives, subjecting it to the rhythm of capitalistic time. Once it became clear that no law, nor other norm, could ever mediate between the capital and the proliferation of collective subjectivities, terror became the only way to secure the resumption to capitalistic and socialistic accumulation in the 70's. It is under the impetus of this terror that the nuclear state became the central figure of Integrated World Capitalism.

At present the club of nuclear powers subjects on a large scale all nations and peoples to its multicentered networks; but it also dictates in details the countless conflicts and local strifes which poison life on this earth, repressing or fueling them at will. In the Third World, since the so-called period of "decolonization," all these conflicts make up some kind of world war that doesn't dare call itself by that name. Nuclear terror is at the root of every kind of oppression and overdetermines the relationships of exploitation between social groups at both political and micro-political levels. Thus threat and intimidation seep through all the pores of the thin skin of nuclear deterrence, which doesn't exclude more direct forms of intervention. The ultimate goal, as always, is to force people to condone their misery and political impotence. Capitalism answers: "No future" to the rise of new forms of proletarian subjectivity, countering their offensive with state terror.

At this juncture the word "democracy" begs redefinition. The word "communism" has clearly been defaced, but the word democracy itself has been trashed and mutilated. From the Greek *polis* to the popular uprisings of the Renaissance and Reformation, from the proletarian rebellions that coexisted with the great liberal revolutions, democracy has always been synonymous with the legitimation of power through the people. This legitimation, always concrete, punctual, material, took specific forms, breaking away from a divine or absolute tradition.

With democracy, legitimacy is primarily human, spatially and temporally defined.

We're all subjected to Integrated World Capitalism because it is impossible to locate the source of its power.

If we try to go back to its source, all we find is subjection to the second, third, n^{th} degree.

The origin of power recedes higher and higher up and can be sized up in relation to the depth of our own impotence. Political relationships — called "democratic" — as we experience them on a daily basis, are at best *trompes-l'oeil* when they don't throw us straight into pain and despair. This is the common feature, the unavoidable axiom of the capitalist or socialist restructuration of the political powers.

II. NORTH / SOUTH: TERROR AND HUNGER

As we have begun to see, the capitalist and/or socialist reaction of the 70s integrates the world market according to a design for the exploitation of work and for political control which evolves in a homogeneous manner. The fundamental transition, in this sense, begins with the phase of nixonian initiative in the monetary and international political arenas. Between 1971 and 1973, a series of operations lent a political character to the multi-national network of exploitation which was already implanted in the world market. The take-off of the dollar relative to the gold standard and the petroleum crisis articulated, under the same monetary command, (subtracted from all questions of value) the rules for the organization of work and those of the productive hierarchy on an international level. The petroleum crisis emptied the treasuries of countries and pushed financial centralization and unification to the point of paroxysm. Initially, this operation appeared, during the Kissinger era, as a great shock. The divisions within the capitalist and/or socialist political personnel reverberated successively in the Trilateral Commission, then through the agreements and the cooptations within Integrated World Capitalism, that is, in the new arrangements of the political will of domination. It is on this foundation that the effective political cartography of exploitation on a world scale is sketched out. Capitalist integration determines certain fundamental polarities around which move dependent sub-systems, in partial rupture with the hierarchies of power which overcode the struggles for liberation and the class struggles, — that permit capitalist integration to allow itself the luxury, on the level of these subsystems, of large scale modifications. At the heart of this complex play of multicentered systems, which disjoin the flows of struggle and carry out destabilizations and/or strategic stabilizations, a transnational mode of production is consolidated. Throughout these systemic ensembles, one finds the immense enterprise of the production of cybernetic subjectivity [*subjectivité informatisée*] which regulates the networks of dependence and the processes of marginalization. The working class and the socially productive proletariat of the central metropolitan countries are by virtue of this fact subject to the exponential competition of the proletariat of the large metropolises of under-development. The proletariats of the most developed countries thus are literally terrorized by the spectacle of the extermination by hunger which Integrated World Capitalism imposes on the marginalized (and often limotropic) countries. The industrial reserve army, dominated by a new law of absolute pauperism, is currently constituted on a continental basis. Capitalist and/or socialist command, multiplied into polycentric subaltern sub-systems, brings together the highest rates of exploitation with areas of poverty and death. For all that, the struggles for liberation have not been militarily or politically strangled. But, within the frame of these different sub-systems, Integrated World Capitalism has not ceased to stimulate fratricidal wars for the conquest of intermediary degrees of participation in integration. The enemy has become the poor, those poorer than oneself. If theory has ever had the need to evaluate the basis of power and of command over human life, it finds in this a convincing example, in that the essence of the problem turns out to be in production and in the organization of work, in the frightening capitalist voraciousness which structures them on a world scale and which subjugates them within the frame of the generalized mass-mediated, cybernetic [*informatique*] integration of poles of domination.

To a certain extent, the poor find themselves produced twice by this system: by exploitation and by marginalization and death. Terror, which in the metropolitan countries is incarnated as the potential for nuclear extermination, is actualized, in the marginalized countries, as extermination by famine. Let it be clear, nevertheless, that there is nothing "peripheral" in this last design: in fact, there are only differences of degree between exploitation, destruction by industrial and urban pollution, welfare conceived as a separating out of zones of poverty, and the extermination of entire peoples, such as those which occur in the continents of Asia, Africa, and Latin America.

It is worth taking proper note the newness of the forms of control implemented by I.W.C. [Integrated World Capitalism]. The strategies of terror and of repression tend to be more and more transversal, punctual, and sudden.

Each piece of earth, each geo-political segment, has become a potential enemy frontier. The world has been transformed into a labyrinth within which one can fall at any moment, at the will of the destructive options of the multinational powers.

A practice of piracy, corresponding to the current phase of over-maturation of capital, has been substituted for the politics of power of the period of maturity of imperialist capitalism. Flotillas of hyper-power [surpuissances] plow the oceans and the seas the same as Morgan and the Dutch.

We should prepare for the settling of accounts between the submarines of the capitalist and/or socialist nuclear buccaneers. But it is not just in the explicitly military earthly, maritime, and aerial arenas that the permanent war of I.W.C. against world society takes place. It is also in the ensemble of civil, social, economic, and industrial domains. And, there as well, according to infinitely differentiated, transversal filiations of operators of power, who are beyond the control of common humans, beyond union or political control — at least in the traditional sense — and in the middle of which can be found mixed up: multinationals, the Mafias, the military industrial complexes, the secret services, even the Vatican. On all levels, on all scales, everything is permitted: speculation, extortion, provocations, destabilizations, blackmail, massive deportations, genocide... In this virulent phase of decadence, the capitalist mode of production seems to rediscover, intact, the ferociousness of its origins.

All these modalities are inscribed within the same continuum of integration: of information, command, and profit. If it is true that for a long time, the global struggles of "communist liberation" will develop — at least in the imagination of revolutionaries — along the East–West axis, one must also acknowledge that the fundamental contradiction which runs through the Integrated Capitalist mode of production today on a world scale is distributed emblematically between the North and the South. If Red Square ever represented a light of hope, the socialist system has currently become the supreme stage of the degeneration of capitalism and is an integral part of the multivalent axis of North-South exploitation. Capitalist and/or socialist restructuring in the '70s has stitched together the old modes of production, redistributing the functions of the players, and reorganizing on a world scale the division of exploitation.

It is respectable to say, among the western intelligentsia, that, for strategic reasons or for old maoist memories, the countries of really existing socialism and, in particular the Soviet Union, constitute a greater threat to Europe and the countries of the Third World than the U.S.

This is not at all our point of view; we do not believe that the West can be preferred to the East. In the sense that we consider ourselves "citizens of the world," we are not concerned with the existing antagonism between the two super-powers. Perilous, debilitating, dramatic — this antagonism is no less in certain regards factitious and mystificatory, in the sense that it is overdetermined by a fundamental functional agreement relative to the subjugation of the productive force of the european proletariats and to the appropriation of a quasi-gratuitous area of expansion and provisioning in raw materials and in labor force on the other continents.

Without calling on, in the "last instance," a final marxist referent, but simply in the light of good sense and of a perception of everyday international relations, it seems to us that the current rise in East-West tension has above all as an object the masking of the destruction by hunger of entire peoples, in an equal fever of reproduction through profit, which torments the dominant castes, as much in the U.S.A. as in the U.S.S.R.. In the long term, therefore: complementarity and complicity in order to assure a common domination on a world scale over the division of labor and its exploitation.

And it is precisely on this scale that the "civilizing mission" of capital has demonstrated the extent of its ferociousness and its absurdity. On that scale, poverty, marginalization, extermination, and genocide are revealed to be the ultimate consequences of a mode of production which set itself up in a till-now peaceful symbiosis with the struggles of the working class of the metropolitan countries. But, faced with the crisis of its own system of profit and with the degradation of its own principles of legitimation, capital is now constrained to have recourse (and to theorize that recourse) to the most extreme measures. The era of the over-maturity of capitalism reveals the violence of its origins in a climate of panic due to the weakening of its motivations. The capitalist restructuring of the world market, undertaken since the 70s, has entailed an extraordinary acceleration of the process of integration, while separating out its effects under the form of paradoxical crises. The capitalist integration of the world market, if it has not crowned the dreams of the promotion of a more humane civilization, has shown, on the contrary, to what level the cruelty and cynicism of the capitalist mode of production can be raised. The attempts to overcome the internal contradictions initiated by the emergence of new collective subjectivities founded on the widening of the market, despite the caution of political personnel of the Kissinger or Carter type, have not only put an end to the internal crisis of the central metropolitan countries, but have pushed it to the point of paroxysm and have spread its devastating effects over the entire globe.

The space dominated by capital, which is subdivided, fragmented, segmented, and functionalized according to the ends of capital's command, is opening as a new terrain of resistance and of conquest. The extreme weapons of extermination and marginalization will not succeed forever in blocking the process of recomposition, whose vitality one can already detect. It is important to underscore the correlation between the level attained by capitalist restructuring and the unprecedented dimensions of the crisis of the past decade. One can thus note, on the one hand, that even in the most terrible of tests, the new social dissidence has not stopped weighing on the situation and accelerating the crisis, and on the other hand, that the capitalist instruments of control are proving to be less and less adapted to their end, more and more ineffective.

It was no doubt beginning in 1982 that the cycle of restructuration, which began between 1971 and 1973, launched a first decisive barrage, when the most indebted countries of the Third World threatened the consortium of banks with the possibility of declaring bankruptcy, in response to the unprecedented politics of deflationary strangulation which they were undergoing. It seems that in an irreversible fashion, a new type of process of liberation and of largescale self-organization came into being. We will return to this point.

III. THE RIGHT IN POWER

The temporal and spatial mechanism for controlling struggles, put in place during the capitalist and/or socialist restructuration of the world of producing, invested new figures of class struggle. In those places where the Right triumphed, Integrated World Capitalism succeeded in institutionalizing these new figures and in making them act as a motor of restructuration. As the reactionary cycle of the 70s puts them on display for us, the instruments set in motion by Integrated World

Capitalism in order to channel and even produce class struggle within the frame of institutional integration reside: 1) in its ability to put in place systems of transnational competition between class sectors; 2) in the utilization of deflationary monetary politics which increase unemployment; 3) in the reconversion which it effectuates in the politics of welfare, toward a "controlled" increase of poverty. This politics is accompanied by a pulverizing, molecular repression of all attempts at resistance and at the free expression of needs. It is essential that the control that it promotes succeeds in becoming effective in the collective imaginary,[5] thus initiating a situation of diffuse crisis within which it will attempt to separate: 1) that part of the proletariat with which incumbent power relies on negotiating a guarantee of reproduction and 2) the immense mass of those excluded or "non-guaranteed."

This division is multiplied infinitely and hierarchized in the labor market, in which the competition between workers makes itself felt, and beyond, on the "social and institutional market" in which all the other sectors of the population are constrained to "make themselves valuable."

The revolutionary events of '68, as well as the material transformations of the mode of production, have shown the determining weight which the working class continued to possess on the social stage. The spirit of competition between workers was thus weakened in favor of a recognition of revolutionary objectives concerning a growing number of categories of oppressed people. But with the return of the Right to power during the '70s, a resegregation of the working class, which falls back on "already attained advantages," its guarantees, and its corporate privileges, has taken place. We have seen the paradox of an institutionalization which preforms the working class into its own enemy (this time, one can really speak of a "new working class"). In this context, the struggles were condemned to remain institutionalized, to be piloted by Integrated World Capitalism; frequently they even revealed themselves to be the best supports for political and social conservatism. (In particular, on the molecular terrain of capital's subsumption of social work and against the social diffusion of revolutionary needs and transformational desires.) It seems to us essential to insist on this point: today, Stakhanov, the superior dignity of the worker with calloused hands, (for whom Reagan has a certain nostalgia) a certain conception of worker centrality, and the entire old imaginary manipulated by the unions and the left, in a systematic misapprehension of the great majority of the "non-guaranteed" proletariat, has irredeemably gone by the wayside.

"Really existing socialism" has become a privileged instrument of the division of the metropolitan proletariat, a weapon directly manipulated by capitalist conservatism. Which does not mean, nevertheless, that the working classes, in themselves, can no longer in the future develop decisive struggles within the dynamic of social transformations. But only on the condition that they are radically reshaped by the molecular revolutions which run through them.

In fact, capitalist and/or socialist structuration in the '70s directly confronted the new revolutionary subjectivities, constraining them to interiorize their potential consciousness and obliging them to be under the thumb of systems of technological control and a battery of government apparatuses which are more and more sophisticated. The fundamental objective of Integrated World Capitalism was to attain a maximal expansion of the integrated productive dimension on the social level and on the geo-political level, segregated from the reintroduction of poverty, of hunger, and of terror as an instrument of division. The victory of the right was based on its ability to neutralize the recomposition of that revolutionary subjectivity which found itself exposed to the great difficulty of reconstituting unitary lines of attack against exploitation. This reactionary turn-around succeeded in assuming, in reversing, and in exploding everything which, since 68, was revealed as a new power of the proletariat — that is, the ensemble of social components and of collective capacities for articulating the molecular multiplicity of its needs and its desires. The division imposed through instruments of economic and institutional violence was consolidated through the promotion of a symbolism of destruction pushed to an extreme. "Exterminism" became the referent value par excellence. Extermination by submission or death, as the ultimate horizon of capitalist development. The only law of value which capitalism and/or socialism recognizes today: it is the blackmail of death. We will not let ourselves be taken in by this deathly realism. "It is right to revolt."

The responsibility of the traditional organizations of the workers' movement, which remained prisoner to the illusory choice between capitalism and socialism, was thus decisive. It is necessary to recognize that the fact that the development of the mode of production and the maturation of collective consciousness completely passed them by does not in any way eliminate the consequences of their drift, mystification, and paralysis of all initiative in the workers' movement. The inertia of the social movements, which revealed itself in numerous situations, the inability of the revolutionary movement to reconstitute itself on politically new foundations, the incapability of the transformation process to impose itself in its entirety — all are essentially conditioned by the monopoly of political representation and of the imaginary, which the alliance between capitalist and socialist personnel has sealed for decades. This alliance is based on establishing the model of the double labor market: that of guaranteed workers and that of the non-guaranteed — with socialism legitimizing only the first. From this has resulted a frozen society, comparable to that of the *Ancien Régime,* but, in the end, a society equally untenable because it is undermined by innumerable molecular forces expressing its productive essence. This is the source of its nagging thematics of security, of order, and of repression and of its imaginary of urgency, its obsession with crisis, the impression it gives of being able to act only a step at a time, without retreat and without a coherent project. Caught in the same drift, capitalism and socialism now constitute the two pillars of conservatism and in certain cases of quasi-fascist [*fascisante*] reaction.

It is no less true that a new revolution took off in '68. It is not the fantasms of the "death of the political" or of the "implosion of the social" which will change anything. Beginning in the '70s, capitalism and/or socialism was constrained to make a parade of its failure on questions of social progress, of the coherent management of economic and social relations on an international scale, of impulsion in the vital domains of technico-scientific creation. It was revealed for what it is, that is, a ferocious and irrational system of repression, which is an obstacle to the development of collective production arrangements and which inhibits the movements of the valorization and capitalization of wealth which it engenders. The world market, far from responding to the principles which liberalism attempts to reestablish, is only an instrument "blocking" for poverty and death, "chaining-up" for marginalization and planetary discipline, supported by nuclear terror. We inevitably return to the point: the ultimate "reason" of capitalism and/or socialism is its impossible tendency toward a sole paradigm: that of a passion to abolish everything which is not in accord with maintaining its power.

But this passion also threatens instrumental reason itself, from inside. In effect, the will towards exclusion and segregation in Integrated World Capitalism tends to turn against itself, by threatening the consistency of its own systems of political communication and reducing to near zero its ability to objectively gauge relations of force. Thus one can beware that before us opens an era of the great paranoiacs of power.

If this is so, the task of reconquering the meaning of work, begun in 68, is identical to the liberation of life and the reconstitution of reason. For everyone and everywhere: promote the potential carried by the new singularities!

4
THE REVOLUTION CONTINUES

I. RECOMPOSITION OF THE MOVEMENT

In the context of Integral World Capitalism's restructuring of production, undertaken since '68, the new revolutionary subjectivities are learning to recognize the ruptures imposed by the enemy, to measure their consistency and their effects. The first fundamental determination of Integrated World Capitalism is that, independently of sociological segmentations, it produces a model of subjectivity that is at least tripolar, synchronically cutting across all sorts of unconscious collective levels, personal consciousnesses, and group subjectivities (familial, ethnic, national, racial, etc).

These three poles are: an elitist pole, which comprises both the managerial and technocratic strata of the East and of the West, as well as those of the Third World; a guaranteed pole, cutting across the different specifications of class; and a non-guaranteed pole, which runs through each social stratum equally.

Under these conditions, the new revolutionary subjectivities proclaim, from their point of origin, a desire for peace, collective security, and minimal safeguards against unemployment and poverty. One finds a fear of the hell of the absence of guarantees at the heart of the three poles of subjectivity: among entirely deprived groups, among proletarian groups already somewhat guaranteed by wage labor and welfare, as well as among certain sectors of the elite whose status is made systematically precarious. Thus the essential basis of contemporary production is constituted by this fluctuating mass and continuous mixture of "guarantism" and "non-guarantism." The non-guaranteed constitute a fundamental point of support for the constitution of capitalist power: it is in terms of them that the institutions of repression and marginalization find their consistency. But in counterpoint, they assume a social role within the new framework of power and exploitation, because of the values and productive potential of which they are the bearers. They are also focal points of imagination and struggle which are capable of catalyzing singular becomings, of bringing to light other references, other praxes, appropriate for breaking the immense machine of discipline and control of the collective force of production.

The history of the struggles of the '70s has already sketched the process of recomposition and of social liberation. A number of matrices of rupture were opened then by the new proletarian movements. Whatever their diversity, they all originated in the tremendous mutations of an increasingly complex, over-powering, and deterritorializing social productive force, and they all affirm themselves with reinforced clarity against the repressive normalization and restructuration brought about by social segmentation and stratification. These phases of struggle were most significant for workers as an experience of discovery and comprehension of the cesuras and corporatist overcodings imposed on the proletarian socius, and as an experience of internal struggle against the violence by which Integrated World Capitalism has constantly tried to interdict processes of innovation wherever they are involved. Internal struggles thus recuperate the tripolar segmentation of Integrated World Capitalism within the struggles of each subjective component. Since this always occurs at each phase in the emergence of a new social subjectivity, their quality, force, and cohesion is self-composed [*auto-agencée*], the result of a collective self-making. Need, consciousness, and production are fused at the heart of such a process. The '70s were thus marked by the continuous emergence of moments of rupture punctuating the capitalist and/or socialist attempts at restructuration, all of which are characterized by new subjective problematics and by a special collective effort to redefine their perspective.

From 1977 in Italy to the "Great Break" in Central Europe (Germany, Switzerland, Holland), from the Iranian revolution to the period of Solidarity, to the renewal of revolutionary struggles in Central America, to the enormously important liberation movements that are beginning to erupt in the Southern Cone... wherever we turn, we find these principle characteristics of the project. The struggles that are internal and antagonistic to the politics of reactionary restructuration are mobilizing, either against their repressive texture, or inside these processes of subjective development as a unifying tension and as a self-liberating perspective. Revolutionary struggles have never "targeted" to this extent the theoretical definition and the practical realization of an orientation resting intrinsically on collective subjectivation and implying, in consequence, the destruction of all ideologies of an external vanguard. Autonomy has never appeared with more force as a primary objective. We repeat: there is nothing anarchic about this, since it essentially has to do with a qualitative autonomy, capable of apprehending the social complexity of movements, and of grasping it as a process of subjective convergence, centered on the quality of life and on the communitarian restructuring of production goals, and since it is equally a matter, by virtue of this reconstruction, of assuming peace against all forms of terrorism and of imposing mass negotiation as a basis of mobilization and of organization.

It is obviously necessary to be very

careful when we broach the question of the experiences and the initiatives of the new subjects. Frequently, during the course of the events we have just evoked (from 1977 in Italy forward), the action of these new subjects has been presented, from a theoretical point of view, as a hypostasis and, from a practical point of view, as a linear function. Once again, one risked falling into the old mythology of "mass action." This has to do with illusions that probably inevitably result from deception and regression. But it would be difficult to determine the stakes of the theoretical elucidation of this question. The theoretical struggle against such illusions leads to patient acceptance, without reservation, of the real situation, that is, of the fact that the universality of the proposition of transformation must necessarily be diluted in the multiplicity of movements, the contradictory moments which characterize them and in the "long term" of the movement of collective imagination.

Before developing this point, we must first insist on the constructive effort that the new modes of subjectivation have already accomplished on a stage profoundly changed in relation to the history and the traditions of the revolutionary and workers' movements, because of expanded competency and performance in the arrangements of subjectivity at work on that stage. Confronted by the amplitude of the production of totalitarian subjectivity by the capitalist States, the revolutionary arrangements pose the problem of the quality of life, of reappropriation, and of self-production in an equally sizable dimension. Through a movement with multiple heads and a proliferating organization, their episodes of liberation will be capable of investing the entire spectrum of production and reproduction.

Each molecular movement, each autonomy, each minoritarian movement will coalesce with an aspect of the real in order to exalt its particular liberatory dimensions. It will thus break with the schema of exploitation that capital imposes as the dominant reality. It is this new consciousness of the modern proletariat — deterritorialized and fluctuating — which will permit envisaging the rupture of capitalist segmentation and the reformulation not of "commands," not of programs, but of "diagrammatic propositions" of communism and of liberation And it is capitalist restructuration's hyper-reactionary character that explains the positively catastrophic acceleration which the movement has experienced since the beginning of the 80s. Nonetheless this restructuration has not damaged the emerging points of new proletarian subjectivities; it has simply reduced their elasticity. Numerous signs indicate to us that once again the movement is on the verge of stepping forward to undo the repressive obstructions which have successfully blocked its force during this last period.

If we return to the tripartition proposed earlier and if we examine how the process of recomposition runs through the elitist pole, the guaranteed pole, and the non-guaranteed pole, we can discover the forcefulness with which the movement of new alliances has posed its premises. This is immediately evident once one takes into account the fluidity of relations that the crisis has introduced and continues to accentuate between the guaranteed and the non-guaranteed sectors. But this is no less evident when one considers the articulations which the elitist pole has with the two others. Many individuals who evolve in management and at the highest levels of the institutions of knowledge were, during the past ten years, not only implicated in the process of "precarization" that is coterminal with their role and function, but also introduced to an elaborated critical consciousness regarding the legitimacy of their status. The irrationality and the madness of the extended reproduction choices of I.W.C., the obsession of the arms race and of nuclear war, the vertigo of famine and genocide which deepen the differences and engender cleavages, to the point of pushing certain managerial elites to the point of refusal and dissidence. This process, which is all too frequently disfigured and made ridiculous when it is reported in a propagandistic way, nonetheless demonstrates the expansion of resistance in the new forms of subjectivity. Previously, one of the slogans of the communists was the proposed importation of the class struggle into the institutions: today we note more modestly that the new subjects are capable of exporting their values and their antagonistic recommendations to the highest levels of management and of the institutions of knowledge. The true processes of dissidence are not recuperable; it is not a commodity that can be sent to the enemy as a gift.

In point of fact, the revolution continues. The irreversible character of the hitherto completed processes affirms itself. The new subjectivities rearrange their political identity by "assimilating" (that is, semiotizing and smothering) the obstacles posed by the adversary — including those that the adversary has made them introject. The changing characteristics of the collective force of labor, the living forces of the non-guaranteed urban proletariat, the transfinite network of dissident discursive arrangements set themselves up as so many protagonists of the new cycle of struggle.

II. THE TERRORIST INTERLUDE

The development of new subjectivities has undergone deep internal breaks during the course of this process which result primarily from the capitalist mode of production that we have just described and from the internal convulsions of the movements.

Each historical period can be affected by the birth of elitist poles and by extremist surges of self-exaltation which develop to the detriment of the interests of the movements whose interests they pretend to represent. That was particularly evident during this period when Integrated World Capitalism worked to defend and reconstitute the model of a systematic segmentation of both social movements and ideologies.

Terrorism was perhaps the deepest and maddest cesura that revolutionaries experienced during the entire course of the '70s. In the face of reactionary pressure exercised by the State and by I.W.C. to block the liberation movement, faced by attempts to divide and force competition between different exploited groups in order to freeze constitutional and social relations at regressive levels, and faced with the deathly rigidity of the dominant power's formations, whole sectors of the movement were seized by rage and frustration. In the context of the molecular effervescence and maturation of new revolutionary subjectivities, the State has an interest in imposing a molar order of return to a reinforced social dichotomy; it thus undertakes to make a parade of its power by adopting drastic measures and in deploying highly sophisticated mechanisms of control and repression. For the same occasion, State terrorism undertakes to destroy without distinction all political and existential dissidence.

On this terrain, I.W.C. has carried out a veritable mobilization of State functions and set going a new type of civil war: not only by military and police means and by states of emergency, but also by means of a psychological and informational war and by corresponding cultural and political strategies.

During the '70s, this sort of civil war created a favorable basis for the development of the most extreme reaction. In order to understand what happened then, it is necessary to bear in mind the sizable stakes of the contest of force between, on the one hand, the new desires and needs of the collective subjectivity, and on the other hand, the different components working for the restoration and restructuration of production and command. It is true that the civil war frequently gave the State the chance to give itself powers and the instigation to "react" against a situation that it no longer controlled. The new revolutionary movements also have everything to gain from clearly recognizing the realities within which they operate. All the more so because certain groups can have the illusion of having some measure of control by their own means over this sort of situation, by taking the risk of placing themselves on the molar terrain of confrontation hoped for by the enemy, by identifying in some sense with him, by entering fully into the imaginary traps of political domination which are dangled in front of the movement.

The '70s were thus years of a civil war whose direction, imposed by I.W.C., led to pure and simple exterminations, like those of the Palestinians. One cannot deny that within this context, a terrorism of worker and proletarian origins sometimes managed to take the initiative, but nevertheless without ever stepping out of that vicious circle of capitalist over-determination. Rather than reducing that over-determination, such terrorism only reinforced the will of the dominant powers to isolate, to make examples of, and to neutralize the conflicts.

The perspective of the revolutionary movement, in correspondence with real historical transformations, manifests itself altogether differently. How will the new subjective components be able to conquer supplementary spaces of life and liberty? How, by illuminating other types of force, intelligence, and sensibility, can the power of the enemy be deprived of its substance? These, more appropriately, are the questions of the revolutionary movement.

From all points of view, red terrorism was a disastrous interlude for the movement. But especially for the way it relaunched ideological and abstract centralist conceptions of organization. Its crazy search for central points of confrontation became redundant with an ossified leninism, which is disconnected from all historical materiality, reduced entirely to a statist interpretation, a sort of paranoid point of reference which it sought to impose on the recomposition of the movement. Nothing is more urgent than to have done with this false alternative. Access to the movement must be denied to these absurd messengers of the past. Red terrorism has only one end: that of failure and despair. It has only one function: to stem the immense liberatory potential which has revealed itself at the heart of this heavy period of reaction through which we are going. In as much as it complied with the rhythms of history and with the programmings of the opponent, red terrorism has revealed itself for what it is: a paradoxical form of conservatism.

But haven't the capitalist formations of power on the same occasion taken the measure of the autonomous movements and secreted "antibodies" capable of robbing them of power? It is precisely this question which confronts the militants of prior generations who "re-emerge," as from a fog, from the great reactionary disaster.

The terrorist interlude of proletarian origin in the '70s has become exceedingly, mortally dangerous for the progress of those revolutionary processes which had begun to detotalize, to deterritorialize the stratifications of power, at all levels. Clearly, the ideologies that nurtured it should be forcefully avoided as so many biases which can only adulterate the struggles of the real movement and lead them to defeat. Given this, it is necessary to recognize that this terrorist wave posed a real problem through radically false premises and responses: how can the resistance to reaction be linked to a new type of organization? The correct response to this question, and the strategic line which follows from it, are already in the movement, at those points where it constitutes itself through an institutional mode without going astray on the paths of statist legitimation. It has to do with constructing a new society, a new politics, a new womens' movement, an other workers' movement, other youth movements. "Other," "different," "new" — always the same feeble words to index the vectors of happiness and imagination which are capable of overthrowing the sclerotic world where politics is nothing but frustration and paranoia, where society is nothing but the triumph of conformism, where the workers' movement gets bogged down in corporatism, the womens' movement in the introjection of subordination, the youth movement in all sorts of drugs, and where, finally, the limit between the demand for power and terrorism continues to be confining.

It is equally possible that the external cesura was the symptom of an internal illness. It would be absurd to deny that the processes of recomposition also carry dogmatic and sectarian elements, "viruses" from old stratifications which threaten them from inside. It is thus the articulation between immediacy and mediation, tactics and strategy — which can only be established by way of multilateral and practical relations — which risks running headlong into chaos, maniacal agitation, and provocation. And if it has been so, then the only possible way to heal this kind of paranoia is to be found by the revelation and exaltation of its symptoms, the exploration of its etiology, the disengaging of the desires of which it is the expression and their radical liberation from all overcodings by the capitalist death drives.

The problem of the recourse to force has not for all this disappeared from our horizon. But we consider it to be all the more politically efficacious if the forces in question are diversified, multiplied by a thousand links to thought and the imagination. Force is the body — and we want to reconstruct the movement outside the dead body which tradition has left us; we want to reinvent a living, real body, to live and to experience a physiology of collective liberation. It is on the basis of this hypothesis of an other type of expression of power [*puissance*] that the movements of the '70s reaffirmed the urgency of liberation. There is no anarchism in this. Because the movement remains none the less collective and challenges individualist implosion. We distrust spontaneist myths for such as they devalue the dimensions of everydayness and of patient reformulation of the problems with which we are confronted. Neither is it idealism. Because here the body is, all at once, material expression of the subject and content, end and goal. Promoting it has the consequence of relativizing the formalism of the representation of contract and of law, to the benefit of the alliance and of the common project of the productive forces. The elimination of the concept of the practice of terrorism is thus correlative at once to the negation of out-dated political points of reference — even if spontaneist — and the affirmation of a radical materialism. This as well we have learned during the '70s, with their awful terrorist interlude.

III. A NEW REVOLUTIONARY POLITICS

The recomposition of the movement is undergoing a reorganization of its fronts of struggle as a process of self-valorization and auto-production at the highest level of subjectivation.

The rediscovery of politics, that is, the foundation of an other politics, calls for the deployment of social forces on fields of application which are indefinitely open. These forces depend, of course, on the intensity of the needs revealed by the immediate struggles and thus on the struggle against the obstacle, but also on the positivity of the world which we wish to construct, on the values which we wish to promote. This is not a dialectic. In any event, not a dialectic like that glorious and painful one which presides over the sociological class struggle — a rhetoric arising more out of confusion than of science. In fact, the negative and the positive are anchored here in the materiality of possible options. And one could conceive neither a transition nor a "qualitative leap" which would permit a passage from war to peace, from death to life, from the destruction of being to the construction of the world. At this phase of the movement and of historical development, it seems to us that only a continuous and multidimensional revolution can constitute an alternative to the failed projects of archeo-socialism. This obviously does not entail holding to general considerations. Each singular component of the movement develops systems of value which should be considered in themselves, without requiring either "translation" or "interpretation."[6] These systems are permitted to evolve in their own appropriate directions and to exist at times in contradictory relationships with each other. They don't participate any the less in the same project of constructing a new type of social reality.

In the '70s, a first experiment at bringing together the revolutionary processes began on a positive terrain: that of the antinuclear and ecology movements. They were immediately linked and implicated in alternative programs for the recovery of productive energy. Thus, ecology was not trapped by nostalgia or by protest; it demonstrated that a new style of action was possible. Moreover, the anti-nuclear struggles opened specific horizons in terms of the exploitation and accumulation of the scientific labor force. The struggles of technical and scientific workers, which will be revealed as essential to the development of the communist program, are beginning to illuminate the complex dimensions of an alternative use of science. Moreover, it is at the point of articulation between this use and the collective force of production that the decisive mutation of the communist project will occur. It is on the same continuum of struggles against exploitation and for positive alternatives that, more and more, the capitalist and/or socialist exploitation of time will be put in question and that a new type of communitarian organization of the productive forces will begin. Struggles against the labor process and its overcoding of time; struggles for alternative housing arrangements and for another way of conceptualizing domestic sociality, neighborliness, and cooperation between segments of the socius.

This has to do with positively conjugating the critique of science and the struggle against exploitation, for example, to conjugate research on alternative energy sources and the practical reconstruction of the productive community. It is only at this price that we will succeed in grasping the coherence of the current proletarian projects through the multiplicity and diversity of the initiatives which actualize those projects and the wealth of their productive end. We take for granted the fact that the destruction of property, as the fundamental juridical form of capitalist accumulation, and the destruction of bureaucratic control, as the fundamental juridical form of socialist accumulation, in one indissociable intertwining in which they present themselves today for analysis, constitute the essential conditions for the liberation of science and the elaboration of an open and communitarian social life and for the development of diffuse and creative forms of organization of social work which correspond to the new proletarian subjectivities. What we are evoking here is not a utopia. It is the explication of a real movement, which innumerable traces and indices designate as a power in action.

The elaboration of the political economy of this transition has become an urgent problem; the communist program will broach a new level of consciousness only to the extent that it makes advances regarding these questions. In terms of this, it goes without saying that the specific programs of the different movements cannot help but become intertwined. It is the same regarding their passage to organizational form, by way of diverse attempts of a highly spontaneous character. A priority in this domain is the positivity of perspectives which forbid lapsing into jacobinism or leninism. We must insist again on the materiality of these passages, on the manner in which they succeed in demonstrating their force, even in the worst sectors of capitalist reaction, and how they succeed in planting in the very marrow of the bosses and the bureaucrats the thorn of their changing perspective.

We have already invoked a major illustration of this conjunction of radically heterogeneous vectors for overcoming the worst plans of the reactionary employers: that of the international monetary system. In the summer of 1982, the declaration of non-payment of debts and the threat of bankruptcy among the large Latin American countries struck a perhaps fatal blow against Reaganomics. The internal resistance of the working classes in the developed countries to unemployment and inflation thus found itself objectively associated with the suppression of the proletariats of the Third World, themselves undermined by poverty and famine. The objective character of this new de facto alliance, its considerable political incidences, does not indicate to us the historical limits of reaction: they confirm the potential for intervention in collective arrangements of subjectivity, when they succeed in joining their interventions along the fault line of the crisis. For twelve years after 1971, from Nixon to Reagan, big multinational capital succeeded in instituting a perfidious mechanism for augmenting productivity within the framework of a general immobilization of the relations of force and of the distribution of incomes — in 1982, it was the very bases of capitalist power which were put in question, as a result of the conjoined resistance of the diverse sectors of the international proletariat. One must admit that during this long period of "historical latency," the collective subjectivity had to continue to metabolize its needs and its desires. If not, how could such a crisis have been possible — the first in the present historical cycle of reaction, but of a striking conspicuousness. This is a clear example of what we mean when we speak of the "materiality of the passageways of the recomposition of subjectivity."

Parallel to a growing consciousness of the irreversible character of the crisis of the capitalist mode of production arises a fundamental problem: capitalism and/or socialism control the means of destroying the world; will they use these means to defend their domination? And to what point? Now, it is precisely around this threat that the recomposition of revolutionary subjectivities and the development of movements has partially reconstructed its highest profile. It is in the struggles for peace that the movement attains its richest and most complex expression. In a sinuous and continuous fashion, the struggles are carried out across the enemy territory, preventing him from attaining the maximum concentration of the destructive force that defines his project and, in a continuous way, from attaining his force of persuasion and concentration. One could almost say that this "guerrilla of peace," which is taking root in the spaces between individual consciousnesses, constructed on a communitarian basis, collectively synchronizing the dispositions and sequences of the domination which constitutes them in terms of resistance and struggle, all of this is already a force, a project, which makes us relinquish the defensive, which surpasses the war of position and which can inspire us to a war of movement. What other method is there for struggling for peace than to encircle, to empty the enemy strategies of their substance, to destructure them from inside? In this regard, is it necessary to distinguish the advancement of the pacifist struggle from that of recomposing the projects of revolutionary action? Not at all, because, we repeat, the struggle for peace carries within it the highest possible alternative potentialities.

We hope no one will think us so naive as to imagine that there are not as many scoundrels as honest people under the mantle of pacifism. In certain countries, the peace movement is instrumentalized and perverted by methods which recall to us those abject times of the "stalinist peace." Neither are we taken by a "peace" of social neutralization which would accommodate, for example, the muzzling of the Polish people. On the contrary, we conceive the struggle for peace as a loom on which the collective struggles for liberation can be woven. That is, for us, the struggle is not synonymous with the status quo. It has to do fundamentally, therefore, with lifting that hypothesis of the overdetermination of death which weighs down all the capitalist and/or socialist relations of production. The struggle for peace is a struggle for a democracy in which the liberty of individuals would be guaranteed and in which the question of the res publica and of the goals of economic development would find their legitimation in the community. Green is born neither from the red of the socialist regimes nor from the black of the capitalist regimes. It is born from refusing poverty and of oppression wherever it proliferates and from the urgent desire to be freed from the fear of capitalist control wherever it is imposed. Everyone tells us: "You should choose sides." Some tell the Afghans that they would be occupied by the Americans if the Russians left. But would that be worse? "If the

Americans occupy us," those involved respond, "we will all become Scythians." Others tell us we would be occupied by the Russians if we refuse the American umbrella. But would that be worse? If the Russians occupy our country we will all become Poles. We have had enough of all of this blackmail. We similarly reject the blackmail of the bomb as well as the supposed values of capitalism or socialism.

Peace is a pre-condition of revolution.

Within the tragedy which Capital imposes on life, a collective response is sketched: in the shadow of destruction, an ethical exigency of happiness and of life is affirmed. The mobilization for peace opens up infinite routes for liberation; the constructive forms in which liberty is today draped can alone dissolve the power of death behind which the capitalist classes are retrenching. Yes, the revolution continues: the reactionary wave of the '70s has not destroyed it. It has enriched itself by a sort of irreversible strategic interiorization which permits it to be intrinsically articulated with the immense ethical project for peace.

5
THE NEW ALLIANCE

I. A MOLECULAR METHOD OF AGGREGATION

The transformations which trouble a society require a new type of organization. Leninism or anarchism are no longer anything today but fantasms of defeat, voluntarism, and disenchantment, a forced faith or solitary rebellion, an antithetical form of repression or a simple abstract assertion of singularity. The organizational choices of the future movement should be rethought independently of the ideological and political references to the traditional workers' movement which led that movement to defeat. The collapse of the two extreme models — leninism and anarchism — leave altogether open the question of the machines of struggle which the movement must make use of in order to be capable of winning. Their multi-functional and uniquely characterized articulation of the singularities which constitute them imply that the form of these machines no longer repeats the centralist project and no longer retains the illusion of filtering democracy through centralist structures. One always finds in pseudo-democratic centralism a traced copy of statist models. In it, the repressive and bureaucratic characteristics of the State of Richelieu, Robespierre, and Rothschild are replayed and illusorily reversed. For too long, the revolutionary movement has, through passivity or refusal, been subject to this homology. How can the State be destroyed by an organism which puts up with hegemony, even on a formal level? But how can such a task be made a primary concern of an "other" movement, a different one which is founded on the self-valorization and the self-production of singularities?

Obviously, we have no model of organizational replacement, but at least we know what we no longer want. We refuse everything which repeats the constitutive models of representative alienation and the rupture between the levels where political will is formed and the levels of its execution and administration. As always happens, in the real course of a revolutionary process, the new organizational "proposals" correspond to the new essence of the social productive force. And they are its fluidity, the multivalence of its conceptual references, its permanent capacity of abstraction, its pragmatic efficiency, and its power to deterritorialize undermining every attempt to divide and stratify the forces inside the organizational process. The formation, execution and administration of political direction should no longer be separated, because that constitutes a repression of the collective labor force's new characteristics. The time of Montesquieu and the separation of powers is over. The alienated relationships developed by pseudo-democratic centralism on the executive and administrative levels, regardless of how it presents itself, are in the process of disappearing from the political horizon of the revolution (from which Rousseau and the notion of the alienation of individual wills shall also be removed).

But, up to this point, our attempt at redefinition has only progressed negatively: more positively, what signifies the organization of revolutionary subjectivity?

Let's advance a step at a time and try

to better answer the question.

The supposedly "definitive" argument of those who uphold the traditional models of organization consists in affirming that only one centralized form can prove sufficiently efficacious in constituting general fronts of struggle; that is all the more true in capitalism's current phase of development, and this would imply as well an excess of centralizing force in the organization of the oppressed.

All of this is rather stupid. It would only be true if society's current submission to capital was dependent on a rule relating accumulated value to the quantity of exploitation and if a specific form of command were necessarily associated with a particular kind of social production. But isn't this precisely the sort of measure and the type of relationship that we have left behind? The generalization of capitalist exploitation is visibly accompanied by a change in the nature of the repressive functions, such that every structural regulation tends to be eliminated. Properly speaking, there is no longer value to be reappropriated. If the law of value continued to function, at a level of abstract generality, one could perhaps once again conceive of leninist type organizational projects. But there is no such thing. Capitalist command is presently developing in direct and antagonistic engagement with the free and proliferating singularities. Whatever rigid and repressive nets it throws after this wild faun, it will not succeed in reaching or catching either its mode of temporalization or its essential riches and goals.

Given these conditions, the task of organizing new proletarian forms must be concerned with a plurality of relations within a multiplicity of singularities — a plurality focused on collective functions and objectives that escape bureaucratic control and overcoding, in the sense that the plurality develops towards optimizing the processes of involved singularities. What is at stake here then is a functional multicentrism capable, on the one hand, of articulating the different dimensions of social intellection, and on the other hand of actively neutralizing the destructive power of capitalist arrangements. This is the first positive characteristic of the new revolutionary subjectivity. Its cooperative, plural, anti-centralist, anti-corporatist, anti-racist, anti-sexist dimensions further the productive capacities of the singularities. Only qualified in this way will proletarian struggles be able to reconstitute coherent and effective fronts of struggle. These organizational processes should be conceived as being essentially dynamic: each singularity is given impetus by objectives which are not only local but which themselves expand more and more until they begin to define points of transsectoral contact nationally and internationally.

Global projects of society, based in closed ideologies, thus lose all relevance, all operative ability. It is no longer a matter of being founded in abstract syntheses, but in open processes of analysis, critique, verification, and concrete, singular realization. From a molecular point of view, each attempt at ideological unification is an absurd and indeed reactionary operation. Desire, on a social terrain, refuses to allow itself to be confined to zones of consensus, in the arenas of ideological legitimation. Why ask a feminist movement to come to a doctrinal or programmatic accord with ecological movement groups or with a communitarian experiment by people of color or with a workers' movement, etc...? Ideology shatters; it only unifies on the level of appearance. On the contrary, what is essential is that each movement shows itself to be capable of unleashing irreversible molecular revolutions and of linking itself to either limited or unlimited molar struggles (and only collective analysis and critique can decide which) on the political and syndical terrain of defending the general rights of the national and/or international community...

The invention and construction of these new organizational schemas imply the creation of permanent mechanisms for analyzing the internal goals of the social subjectivity's own processes of self-production. This is the sine qua non for guaranteeing a real questioning of the modes of collective functioning and for preventing the emergence of sectarian tendencies.

This seems to us to be the positive starting-point of a revolutionary method of organization adequate to the collective subjectivity bearing it: a scientific method in its mode of analysis, yet open to historical processes and capable of imagination. "Work in progress" in the chain links of singularities, all oriented toward their self-production and multiplication. A method, therefore, which is constitutive of an organization which continually remakes itself, a method thereby conjoined to the productive forces which have made the singularities and their development the basis of material and spiritual wealth.

II. MACHINES OF STRUGGLE

The analysis has progressed; experience has accumulated. The method has already been given some verification. Is it possible to rethink and begin to realize the organizational forms of this new revolutionary subjectivity? To pose this question already implies a confrontation with the difficulties, the material modalities, the obstacles, the enemies of the collective liberation project. How to conceive the composition and reconstruction of the movements? How to rebegin developing each of them in their extensive articulations? We find ourselves faced with numerous, heterogeneous topics and with fluctuating options — the different organized structures of the movement are not only jealous of their singularity, but they seem sometimes to open themselves only for defensive struggles, for the reinforcement and the permanent affirmation of that singularity. In addition, their logics are presented according to changing and multiple matrices; they're always rearticulating the rhizome of their different autonomous components in a different way. It goes without saying that the problem of ideological agreement or disagreement is no longer posed here in terms of the usual political logic — neither one belongs to the same ideological universe. On the contrary, the first problem to be resolved is arranging for the coexistence of multiple ideological dimensions and developing an analysis and a confrontation which, without trying to overcome specific differences, nevertheless tries to prevent them from degenerating into passive and mute divisions. We therefore imagine a process of recomposition which takes for granted conflictual variations within the dynamics of singularization, respecting each's wealth and responsibility for carrying human productivity.

That said, it is nonetheless necessary to construct machines of struggle, organizational devices which are open to these dynamics and to this functional multicentrism. These machines of struggle will be all the more effective in that their field of action will be limited and in that they will establish for themselves the fundamental goal of perfecting the singularization processes.

Such modes of organizational crystalization appeared in North America in the '60s, at the time of the different "campaigns" of the movement. The same thing in Germany in the '70s, where the development of the alternative movement revealed the existence of lines of differentiation going in the direction of both maximizing singularization and in materially recomposing the possibilities of struggle. An open method, therefore, that takes substance from its openness to engender an open organization.

It frequently happens — as much in Arab, Slavic, Latin American as in Anglo-Saxon countries — that this experimentation with new forms of organization develops from within a religious imaginary. Undoubtedly, one must distinguish between religious motivations which attach to an act of liberation and those which are reterritorialized around theological alienation.

It is a fact that in a world whose sole "burrs" can only be non-significant ruptures, the reconquest of the value of witness, of personal engagement, of singular resistance, and of basic solidarity has become an essential motor of transformation. In order to constitute a machine of struggle, the movements are obliged to assume, as completely as possible, a contradictory relation between singularity and capitalist society, between ethics and politics. And this is scarcely conceivable except on the condition that the forms of militancy are totally reinvented. We should lead the analysis and critique of militancy and of previous experiences, when they make us sad, when they become historically tarnished, because they constitute obstacles to a liberating praxis. But it strikes us as impossible that a new open method of organization could be founded without concretely redefining a new militancy — whatever the breadth of its motivations. That is, a certain social crystalization of desire and of generosity runs through all singularities.

One can expect from this way of conceiving things not only the birth of new organizations, changed machines of struggle, but equally a profound modification of their "propositional context," in particular a redefinition of the "Rights of Man" guaranteeing and encouraging communitarian constructions. Generally speaking, this entails a renewal of constitutional mechanisms and of their capacity to register the conflicts and social changes which will be posed.

Only that subjectivity engaged in the singular processes of production can break the codes and norms of the production of subjectivity of I.W.C. It is only on this path that democracy can be reestablished. Juridical innovation necessarily takes place via the institutionalization of the real movement. The only acceptable juridical norm — corresponding in other words to the "instances of justice" inscribed in groups of people themselves — is the image-movement of the real. Inversely, I.W.C. presents us with societies in which rights are overthrown and in which the legal codes and constitutions are either put aside, or function as simple umbrellas for illegal practices on the part of castes acting in their own interest.

Taking charge of these constitutional problematics should no longer be overlooked and abandoned, as was the case in the movement for a long time, but belongs properly to the revolutionary orchestrations of political will. It is the relation between political will and the constitution of the State which is inverted here. It will be for the first to condition the second, not the reverse, as conservative ideologues suggest and as reactionary practices impose. This reversal does not imply renouncing the existence of a coherent juridical tradition. On the contrary, it derives from the will to promote in that tradition a higher rationality, a greater care for truth and justice, by integrating within its mechanisms a capacity for reading the essential mutational processes. In sum, the "spirit of the laws" must acquire a sharp sensibility and intelligence regarding the profound progressive transformations of the social "market."

It is interesting to note that the recent apologists of the market and its miracle-working power are outraged opponents of any promotion of this kind of market.

The fact is that at the current level of the capitalist crisis and the relations of force between the classes, such political and institutional free market devices, by facilitating and inciting collective liberty's potential, would destroy, even annul the conditions of the liberal-bourgeois market of exploitation.

It is thus clear that, while we contest the State's pretensions to lord over social conflict in a contractual manner (a practice which is invariably a source of totalitarianism), we do not for all that speak for those falsely naive attempts to seize the processes of social singularization, only pretending to acknowledge them under the aegis of a corporate project (which they try then to integrate into what is pompously called the "social economy." The pseudo-Proudhonian ideology cloaking certain of these attempts has no other goal than to render them captive to an expanded capitalist market.) Corporatism, however it presents itself, should be overturned; it can only generate ersatz, false solutions to the problematics of new subjectivities. All statist manipulations, the ingratiating as well as the disgraceful, must be relentlessly combatted. Statism and corporatism are two faces of the same obstacle to the development of autonomies and of singularities. We repeat: the machines of struggle, carried by new proletarian subjectivities, tend to essentially deepen the singularity of the collective situation from which they emanate, without in any way damaging their oppositional, revolutionary relation with the State.

This is only a paradox if one misapprehends the movement's liberating goals and, especially, the interest of each of its components in the disappearance of techniques of power and group manipulations inherent in traditional systems of representation "in the name of," supposedly, the general will. We have had our account of Menenius Agrippa and his apologists! Thus the machines of struggle will develop their productive activities and political action in direct contact with, and the same texture as the distinct contexts within which they are formed. They will engage in production and reproduction simultaneously. Within production, in order to prepare society's capacity for autonomous and communist management of human activities, and in order to construct a new type of economy founded on collective arrangements which connect different modalities of semiotic and machinic practice. And, within the whole of society, in order to set up the reproduction and organization of the distribution and functions of work time, self-managed and as-free-as-possible. Thus, a promotion of the collective as much as of initiative, of creation and of individual responsibility. As we know, the neo-liberal sycophants love to return to the mythologies of the boss, as the sole guarantor of the rational ordering of complex productive processes, as the only possible agent of the "dynamization" of the force of labor, etc.... At the same time, they try to discredit self-management as being synonymous with "mediocracy," (impossible to apply on a large scale, etc.). All their reasoning proceeds from a total misapprehension of the means of collective semiotization which are now at work in all the significant arenas of science and technology. A certain conception of tree-like hierarchies and oppressive disciplines has undoubtedly become passé. It no longer has to do with a simple question of taste or of democratic "prejudice." The extensive arrangement, in rhizome, of machinic components, of informational components, and of decision-making components has become an absolute necessity, if production is to keep up, to further society, science, art, in sum, human life on this planet. After a few centuries of socialist and/or capitalist domination, production and society have become one and the same thing. There is no turning-back from this fact. Machines of revolutionary struggle are themselves obliged to become disposed for producing new social realities and new subjectivities.

We emphasize again that the definition, the general program of this multidimensional liberation does not belong to these machines of struggle; it belongs to the rhizomatic multiplicity of singularity processes, within each of their production sites, which they transform, remaking and, should the case arise, multiplying the power that this liberation authorizes.

From now on, organizing signifies first: work on oneself, in as much as one is a collective singularity; construct and in a permanent way re-construct this collectivity in a multivalent liberation project. Not in reference to a directing ideology, but within the articulations of the real. Perpetually recomposing subjectivity and praxis is only conceivable in the totally free movement of each of its components, and in absolute respect of their own times — time for comprehending or refusing to comprehend, time to be unified or to be autonomous, time of identification or of the most exacerbated differences.

Liberation, production, the constitution of new social arrangements, all arise from distinct levels — equally important — on the basis of which the machines of struggle develop. The experiences of community and solidarity seen by the second half of this century illuminate the original paradigms of those new organizations which we call machines of struggle. It's necessary now to deploy their free play and their power. It is clear that only the direct experience of struggle will determine their contour — to try to describe in advance what the machines of struggle of new proletarian subjectivities will be on a practical level (of desire and cognition) would run contrary to their essential mode, which depends on what one no longer dares to call "the masses."

III. TODAY, NEW LINES OF ALLIANCE

At the end of a period of defensive retrenchment — the result of the current repressive wave under the aegis of capitalist and/or socialist organization — , a special form of alliance can and must be realized between the constitutive categories of the new proletariat and the most dynamic sectors of productive society. Distinguishing this alliance is, first, that it can break the corporatist obstacles to restructuring, which have shown themselves to be particularly effective amongst the industrial working classes as well as in the tertiary service and scientific sectors of social production. The basic revolutionary sequence presently confronting us concerns the possibilities of making the working classes, the tertiary production sectors, and those innumerable components of the universe of the "non-guaranteed" connect and interact. The movement will have to take up this problematic of conjunction with all of their intelligence and energy. Not because the working class would remain the determining element of the revolutionary process. Neither that the tertiary, intellectual, marginal, etc. sectors would be the bearers of essential economic changes. There's nothing to gain from entertaining such historic misunderstandings. It is clear that the discourses on workers' centrality and hegemony are thoroughly defunct and that they cannot serve as a basis for the organization of new political and productive alliances, or even simply as a point of reference. Breaking with this sort of trap, the true question concerns the invention of a system, not of unification, but of multivalent engagement of all social forces which are not only in the process of articulating new subjective forces, but also of breaking the blocks of capitalist power — in particular their powers of mass-media suggestion on a considerable portion of the oppressed.

It would be fictive and artificial to expect to find these new affiliations only at ruptures in the structure, in areas of friction in the labor market and the corporatist reorganization of different segments of the working class. Such an attitude would still be part of the spirit of I.W.C., which is always more ready to apply repression than to consider attempts to liberate production. Now, we have seen that the question of recomposing the movement's conjunctive unity goes hand in hand with that of the self-production of emancipation — at once intrinsically singular and externally offensive in their tendency — by each of its components. Now self-production implies effective and unreserved recognition of everything that really participates in new types of cooperation and subjectivity, unalloyed with the dominant power formations. The new anti-capitalist alliance will destroy the corporatist chains of repression and help replace their viewpoint with those of a collective self-transformation.

Instead of new political alliances, we could say just as well: new productive cooperation.

One always returns to the same point, that of production — production of useful goods, production of communication and of social solidarity, production of aesthetic universes, production of freedom...

The fact is that the center of gravity of these productive processes has been displaced toward the molecular web of marginal and minority concerns. Nevertheless, it's not a matter of founding a new religion and creating point by point oppositions between the whole group of guaranteed workers and the non-guaranteed workers. On the contrary, it has to do with finishing with the latter representing themselves as a heterogeneous ensemble, excluded in essence from the "true realities" of production, as all the representational coordinates of capitalism and/or socialism beguile them into thinking... Yet such a transformation implies as well that numerous sectors of the working class and the privileged categories of the productive proletariats give themselves other "representations" than those which they possess today and which, for the most part, are part of the corporatist regime. The molecular revolutions, the new subjective arrangements, autonomies and processes of singularization are capable of restoring a revolutionary meaning to the struggles of the working class and indeed many sectors of the collective force of labor, which are now reduced to vegetating in their sociological stratifications. We believe that the "proletarian recomposition" can head off the I.W.C. strategy of "precarization" of the labor market, and of pitting against each other those social segments which find themselves confronting the same market. On a small or a large scale, the potentials for molecular revolution appear every time that processes of detotalization and of deterritorialization encroach on the stratification of corporatism.

Now, if it's true that the fundamental

question is the inversion of the corporatist tendency, it seems equally true that the motor of that diminution of "social entropy" resides in consistently making a decompartmentalization of productive society the revolutionary project. And not only as an ideal horizon, as a communist ethics, but above all as a strategic struggle capable of taking the movement out of its current "failure neurosis." The most demoralizing situations and the most negative comparisons of apparent strength can rapidly change as soon as the precariousness of the current forms of I.W.C. domination appears in an even more pronounced way. Even the most "conservative" segments of the working class are beginning to manifest their unrest, their impatience, and their disgust in regard to those who are supposed to represent them. The idea, for so long accepted in good faith, by virtue of which there existed only one political economy as a reference point — that of I.W.C. — has had its day. The dismantling of companies, of branches of industries, of entire regions, the social and ecological costs of the crisis can no longer be written off as a necessary reconversion of the system. In fact, it has been clear for some time that this is not an ordinary crisis, but a radical attempt to destroy more than half a century's worth of "acquired advantages" and social victories of the reformism which corresponded to the previous forms of capitalism.

Obviously this does not mean that capitalism is in the process of collapsing on its own and that we have come, almost despite ourselves, to the eve of the "Great Night." What is certain is that capitalism and/or socialism intend to install a regime of frenzied "disciplinarization" over the entire planet, in which each segment of the collective labor force, each people, each ethnic group will be forced to submit to permanent control. In this regard, the guaranteed workers will be placed under the same regime as the non-guaranteed, and everything will be nuances, minute non-empirical transitions. No longer will anyone be able to assume a true statutory guarantee.

The traditional working classes should resign themselves to this. But what could the meaning of their revolt be if they do not understand that they no longer represent a social majority — neither numerically, nor as an ideal value, not even as a produced economic value? They are obliged, if they want to legitimate their rebellion, to socially recompose themselves, in alliance with the immense mass of exploited people, of marginalized people, which includes the large majority of young, women, immigrants, the subproletariats of the Third World and minorities of every kind. The principle task has become the reunification of the traditional components of the class struggle against exploitation with the new liberation movements and communist projects.

It is on this terrain that the new lines of alliance will be drawn. We draw a line through the tradition of the Third International, a black line over its totalitarian and/or corporatist results. A new revolutionary movement is in search of itself. It is born both inside and outside the traditional workers' movement; it proliferates and potentially converges along a front intrinsically unified by exploitation. It will destroy the repressive norms of the work-day and of the capitalist appropriation of the totality of life-time. New domains of struggle become possible everywhere. But the privileged point, the hot point in the production of new machines of revolutionary struggle resides within the zones of marginalized subjectivity. And there as well, it goes without saying, not in and of themselves — but because they are inscribed in the meaning of creative production processes considered in their evolutionary position, that is, not arbitrarily isolated within the capitalist economic sphere.

The social imaginary can recompose itself only through radical changes. In this regard, one should take into account that marginal phenomena are part of a context which does not define them as being at the margin, but which, on the contrary, confers on them a central place in the capitalist strategy. The marginal subjectivities, in as much as they are the product and the best "analysers" of command tendencies, are also those which resist it the best. The physical, bodily, plastic and external aspects of the liberation experiences of marginal subjects become equally the material of a new form of expression and creation. Language and image here are never ideological but always incarnated. Here, more than anywhere else, one can find the symptoms of the appearance of a new right to transformation and communitarian life, under the impetus of subjects in revolt.

New alliances: as a project of the production of singularities and as the possibility of conferring on this project a subversive social meaning. The self-analytical method of the forms of social subjectivity becomes revolutionary substance in the sense that it permits the semiotic understanding and political amplification of the implosion points of corporatism and the upheaval of its own lines of alliance. The common consciousness has already perceived this process of conjunction; the revolutionary imagination has begun to apprehend it; what remains is to make it the basis of the constitution of the future movement.

6
THINK AND LIVE IN ANOTHER WAY

PROPOSITIONS

Resentment, empty repetition and sectarianism are the modalities by which we live the betrayed hopes of the traditional workers' movement. For all that we do not renounce the history of struggles; on the contrary, we celebrate it because it is an integral part of our mental coordinates and sensibility. If we are dwarves on the shoulders of giants, we assume the benefits as much as the deplorable aspects of their heritage. At any rate, we want to move forward. Reuniting with the human roots of communism, we want to return to the sources of hope, that is, to a "being-for," to a collective intentionality, turned toward doing rather than toward a "being against," secured to impotent catchphrases of resentment. It is in real history that we intend to explore and experience the many realms of possibility which we call forth from everywhere. Let a thousand flowers bloom on the terrains which attempt to undermine capitalist destruction. Let a thousand machines of life, art, solidarity, and action sweep away the stupid and sclerotic arrogance of the old organizations! What does it matter if the movement trips over its own immaturity, over its "spontaneism" — its power of expression will ultimately only be reinforced. Without even being aware of it, despite the cacophony of the molecular movements which sustain it, an organizational crystalization is opening, oriented in the direction of new collective subjectivities. "Let a thousand flowers blossom, a thousand machines of struggle and of life," is not an organizational slogan and even less an enlightened prediction, but an analytic key to the new revolutionary subjectivity, a given on the basis of which can be grasped the social characteristics and dimensions of the singularities of productive labor. It is through an analysis of the real that they will be recomposed and will multiply as a subversive and innovative presence. The enemy has been incarnated in current forms of social command, through the elimination of differences and the imposition of a reductive logic of domination. Bringing to light the hegemony of singularization processes on the horizon of social production constitutes today the specific hallmark of communist political struggle.

The development, defense and expression of changing productive subjectivities, of dissident singularities, and of new proletarian temperments has become, in some respects, the primary content and task of the movement. That can take the form of the struggle on the welfare front, for the establishment of a guaranteed egalitarian income, against poverty in all its forms, for the defense and enlargement of alternative rights, and against the mechanisms of corporatist division... If one wants, one will find there as well the tradition of struggles against rent, and this such that it is not only fundamental, real, and financial, but that it is essentially undergirded by the articulations of capitalist command; i.e. a political rent, a rent reflecting position in the hierarchy of corporatist strata. New subjective components of production and revolution will find their first intervention opportunity at this level, redefining it in a positive mode as a liberation struggle against corporatist slavery and reactionary structures of production and as affirming the processes of singularity as an essential spring of social production.

This recomposition of the revolutionary movement implies, of course, immense efforts of courage, patience, and above all, intelligence. But what progress has already been made compared to preceding periods of struggle — which were indefatigable and often despairing — by the first groups conscious of this problematic, who only rarely succeeded in opening breaches in the union ghetto or in the political monopoly of the supposed labor parties! Here as well, life time must be imposed on production time. At this crossroads the second task of the revolutionary communist movement will be posed: consciously organizing the collective labor force independently of the capitalist and/or socialist structures, that is, of everything which touches on the production and reproduction of the mode of life. One thing, an effect, is to reveal new social productive forces and another is to organize them outside and against capitalist and/or socialist structures.

The development of science and technology and their massive incorporation in this transformation program are necessary, but not sufficient, conditions. No transformation is conceivable unless the entire field of productive labor is confronted with large movements of collective experimentation which break those conceptions which relate to profit-centered capitalist accumulation.

It is in this direction that the expansion power of the collective labor force should be grasped. Thus a double movement will be established, like that of the human heart, between the diastole of the expansive force of social production and the systole of radical innovation and rearrangement of the work day. The movement of the social proletariat and new collective subjectivities must lay siege to the corporations, viz. the stakes regarding legislation governing the the length of the work day, and impose its redefinitions and its permanent experimentation. They must impose not only a productive renewal, but also new ways of imagining and of studying production.

Think, live, experiment, and struggle in another way: such will be the motto of a working class which can no longer perceive itself as "self-sufficient" and which has everything to win by renouncing its arrogant myths of social centrality. As soon as one has finished with this sort of mystification, which ultimately has only profited the capitalist and/or socialist power formations, one will discover the great significance of the new lines of alliance which tie together the multiform and multivalent social stages at the heart of of our era's productive forces. It is time that communism's imagination raise itself to the height of the changing waves which are in the process of submerging the old dominant "realities."

Now it is necessary to introduce certain considerations regarding a first "diagrammatic proposition" integrating the definitions of the perspectives just introduced. It's only too evident that every effort at taking control of the length of the work day, by the movement of the new subjectivities, will be illusory if it does not attack frontally the network of command put in place by I.W.C. To tackle this network means putting in question the East-West relation, to derail the mechanism integrating the two super-powers, which has overcoded, from the 70s until today, all international relations. Breaking the relation of domination laboriously established between capitalism and socialism, and radically reversing the alliances — especially the european ones — in the direction of the North-South axis, against the East-West axis, constitutes an essential foundation for recomposing the intellectual and working class proletariat in the advanced capitalist countries. A basis of social production which will win its independence against hierarchical oppression and the command of the great powers; a basis which only has meaning if it begins with a collective will to create alternative flows and structures to those of the East-West relation.

We are not fallbacks to "Third Worldism"; we do not pretend to transform it by way of a traditional "insurrectionism"; neither for all that do we believe in its independent capacity for development and "redemption" — at least in the current capitalist context. None of the successful revolutions in the developed countries has succeeded in transforming in a lasting way the structures of the State. It is not likely that those of the

Third World will do any better. No, it is rather toward revolutionary cooperation and aggregation of forces among the intellectual and working proletariat of the North with the great mass of the proletariat of the South that it is necessary to turn to fulfill this historic task. All of this may seem utopian, even extravagant, because today we, the workers and intellectuals of the countries of the North, are slaves of corporatist politics, of segmentary divisions, of the logic of profit, of blocking and extermination operations, of the fear of nuclear war, as they are imposed on us and with which we make ourselves accomplices. Our liberation requires creating a project and a practice which unifies, in the same revolutionary will, the intellectual forces and the proletariats of the North and of the South.

As the union of processes of singularity advances toward the project of reinventing communism, the problem of power will be posed with increasing acuity; it remains at the heart of the antagonism between proletarian components and the capitalist and/or socialist State. The traditional workers' movement wanted to respond to this question in a simple and radical way through the conquest of State power, then through the progressive disappearance of the State. Everything was supposed to follow from itself. One would oppose destruction with destruction and terror with terror. It would be useless today to provide an epilogue regarding the fictive and mystifying character of this dialectic or to underline the scandalous reference by holders of this doctrine to the heroic experience of the Paris Commune.

The first basic task of the revolutionary communist movement consists in having done with this sort of conception and in affirming the movement's radical separation not only from the State which it directly confronts but also, more fundamentally, from the very model of the capitalist State and all its successors, replacements, derived forms, and assorted functions in all the wheels of the socius, at all levels of subjectivity. Thus, to the struggles around welfare, against the organization of productive labor and of labor's social time, and to communitarian initiatives in this domain, should be added questioning the State as the determinant of different forms of oppression, the machine for overdetermining social relations, in order to reduce, block, and radically subjugate them, under the threat of its forces of death and destruction.

This question leads us to formulate a second diagrammatic proposition of communism and liberation: it concerns the urgency of reterritorializing political practice. Confronting the State today means fighting against this particular formation of the State, which is entirely integrated into I.W.C.

After Yalta, political relations were further emptied of their territorial legitimacy and drifted toward levels impossible to attain. Communism represents tendential destruction of those mechanisms which make of money and other abstract equivalents the only territories of man. This does not imply nostalgia for "native lands," the dream of a return to primitive civilizations or to the supposed communism of the "good savage." It is not a question of denying the levels of abstraction which the deterritorialized processes of production made man conquer.

What is contested by communism are all types of conservative, degrading, oppressive reterritorialization imposed by the capitalist and/or socialist State, with its administrative functions, institutional organs, its collective means of normalization and blockage, its media, etc.... The reterritorialization induced by communist practice is of an entirely different nature; it does not pretend to return to a natural or universal origin; it is not a circular revolution; rather it allows an "ungluing" of the dominant realities and significations, by creating conditions which permit people to "make their territory," to conquer their individual and collective destiny within the most deterritorialized flows.

(In this regard, one is led to distinguish very concretely: the movements of nationalist reterritorialization — Basque, Palestinian, Kurdish... — which assume, to a certain extent, the great deterritorialized flows of Third World struggles and immigrant proletariats, and the movements of reactionary nationalist reterritorialization.)

Our problem is to reconquer the communitarian spaces of liberty, dialog and desire. A certain number of them are starting to proliferate in different countries of Europe. But it is necessary to construct, against the pseudo-reterritorializations of I.W.C. (example: the "decentralization" of France, or of the Common Market), a great movement of reterritorializing bodies and minds: Europe must be reinvented as a reterritorialization of politics and as a foundation for reversing the alliances of the North-South axis.

The third task of the revolutionary communist movement is thus also to "disarticulate" and dismantle the repressive functions of the State and its specialized apparatuses. This is the sole terrain on which new collective subjects confront the initiatives of the State, and only in the sense that the latter dispatches its "teutonic cavaliers" over those areas liberated by the revolutionary arrangements. Forces of love and humor should be put to work here so that they are not abolished, as is usually the case, in the mortally abstract and symbolic lunar image of their capitalist adversary! Repression is first and foremost the eradication and perversion of the singular. It's necessary to combat it within real life relations of force; it's also necessary to get rid of it in the registers of intelligence, imagination, and of collective sensitivity and happiness. Everywhere it's necessary to extract, including from oneself, the powers of implosion and despair which empty reality and history of their substance.

The State, for its part, can live out its days in the isolation and encirclement reserved for it by a reconstructed civil society! But if it appears about to come out of its "retreat" and to reconquer our spaces of freedom, then we will respond by submerging it within a new kind of general mobilization, of multiform subversive alliances. Until it dies smothered in its own fury.

The fourth task: Here we are inevitably returning to the anti-nuclear struggle and to the struggle for peace. Only, now it is in relation to a paradigm which brings to light the catastrophic implications of science's position in relation to the State, a position which presupposes a dissociation between the "legitimacy" of power and the goal of peace. It is truly a sinister mockery that States accumulate thousands of nuclear warheads in the name of their responsibility to guarantee peace and international order although it is evident that such an accumulation can only guarantee destruction and death. But this ultimate "ethical" legitimation of the State, to which reaction attaches itself as to a rampart, is also in the process of collapsing, and not only on a theoretical level, but also in the consciousness of those who know or suspect that collective production, freedom, and peace are in their proper place fundamentally irreducible to power.

Prevent the catastrophe of which the State is the bearer while revealing the extent to which that catastrophe is essential to the State. It remains true that "capitalism carries war as clouds carry storms." But, in a manner different than in the past, through other means and on a horizon of horror which at this point escapes all possible imagination, this perspective of the final holocaust has, in effect, become the basis of a veritable world civil war conducted by capitalist power and constituted by a thousand permanently erupting, pulverizing wars against social emancipation struggles and molecular revolutions. Nevertheless, in this domain, as in no other, nothing is fated. Not all the victories and defeats of the movement's new lines of alliance are inscribed in a mechanistic causality or a supposed dialectic of history. Everything is to be redone, everything is constantly to be reconsidered. And it's good that it is so. The State is only a cold monster, a vampire in interminable agony which derives vitality only from those who abandon themselves to its simulacra.

In '68, no one could imagine that war would so quickly become such a close and encroaching horizon. Today, war is no longer a prospect: it has become the permanent frame of our lives.

The third great imperialist war has already begun. A war no doubt grows old after thirty years, like the Thirty Years War, and no one recognizes it any longer; even though it has become the daily bread of "certain" among the press. Yet such has resulted from capitalism's reorganization and its furious assaults against the world proletariats. The third diagrammatic proposition of communism and liberation consists in becoming aware of this situation and assuming the problematic of peace as fundamental to the process of reversing alliances along the North-South axis. Less than ever, peace is not an empty slogan; a formula of "good conscience"; a vague aspiration.

Peace is the alpha and omega of the revolutionary program. The anguish of war sticks to our skin, pollutes our days and nights. Many people take refuge in a neutralist politics. But even this unconsciousness generates anguish. Communism will tear men and women away from the stupidity programmed by I.W.C. and make them face the reality of this violence and death, which the human species can conquer if it succeeds in conjugating its singular potentials of love and of reason.

And finally, to these alliances of productive organization and liberated collective subjectivities should be added a fifth dimension — of which we have already spoken amply — that of organization itself. The time has come to move from sparse resistance to constituting determinate fronts and machines of struggle which, in order to be effective, will lose nothing of their richness, their complexity, of the multivalent desires that they bear. It belongs to us to work for this transition.

To sum up: five tasks await the movements of the future: the concrete redefinition of the work force; taking control over and liberating the time of the work day; a permanent struggle against the repressive functions of the State; constructing peace and organizing machines of struggle capable of assuming these tasks.

These five tasks are made "diagrammatic" by three propositions: contribute to reorienting the lines of proletarian alliance along a North-South axis; conquer and invent new territories of desire and of political action, radically separated from the State and from I.W.C.; fight against war and work at constructing the proletariat's revolutionary movement for peace.

We are still far from emerging from the storm; everything suggests that the end of the "leaden years" will still be marked by difficult tests; but it is with lucidity, and without any messianism, that we envisage the reconstruction of a movement of revolution and liberation, more effective, more intelligent, more human, more happy than it has ever been.✷

Rome, Rebibbia Prison / Paris
1983–84

POSTSCRIPT, 1990
Toni Negri

"Rome, Rebibbia Prison/Paris, 1983-1984": this chronological note which concludes our French text, published in 1985, has nothing contrived about it. The dialogue between the two authors did not come to a halt during the long years in which one of them was imprisoned. In fact in the last year of that imprisonment we had decided to collaborate on a work that would deal with the continuity of the communist political program, beyond the repression and in spite of its effects. When one of us left prison and went into exile, the possibility arose in 1984 to actually collaborate on such a project.

That is how this text was born. The continuity of the communist program, the memory of our struggles, and a political and ethical fidelity to the revolutionary option all contributed to renew our friendship and our discussions. It is scarcely necessary to recall how dreary that period was. In Italy, the so-called "years of lead" never seemed to end, and with them there had developed a leaden political and social climate; in France, the social democrats, having reached power with a program of profound social renewal, had by then transformed their politics and were carrying out the sinister business of restructuring which had been entrusted to them by capital; within the Atlantic alliance the reactionary adventures of Reagan and Thatcher had reached their apex; and in the USSR (as we only now can perceive) what were to be the very last — though still ferocious — remnants of Stalinism still held power.

Nothing seemed to threaten this horrible immobility — except for a bit of background noise, an occasional "limited" or "local" war, such as the "little" bloodbath between Iran and Iraq, the re-emergence of collective cannibalism in Southeast Asia, and the fascism and "apartheid" of Latin America and south Africa. We were living in a period of permanent counter-revolution. The new movements that would become important in the second half of the 1980s — movements based on mobility and organization, anti-racist movements, movements rich in non-material desires — all of these had not yet appeared on the horizon. Instead those movements that had persisted through the 1970s lingered on, pathetic, enfeebled, and desperate.

Exactly against this background we decided to write once more of revolution, renewing a discourse of hope.

Ours was a discourse of hope, and a breaking away in a positive sense. But no one, not even friends, seemed to understand — our position was strange, improvised, out of fashion. We were not concerned with these objections, however, because we were interested in only one thing: reconstituting a nucleus, however small, of militancy and of subjectivity-in-progress. This meant resisting the political defeat of the 1970s, especially where it had been followed, on the capitalist side, with the production of an ideology of repentance, betrayal and self-pity, seasoned with the new, "weak" values of ethical cynicism, political relativism, and monetary realism.

Playing the card of "naiveté," we wanted to affirm that it was still possible to live and to produce revolutionary subjectivity.

If this was our basic message, it was nevertheless not irrelevant how we went about expressing and objectifying our desire. Re-reading ourselves today we can recognize that the themes of the analysis and the program of action proposed were and still remain essentially sound. In other words, the way we described the lines of development of the mode of production, the system of domination, and the crisis in both — and, on the other side, the prospects we outlined for the development of an alternative organization, as well as our judgments on the processes of constituting a new subject, on that subject's productive qualities, and on the cultural system that would constitute the subject — all of these elements of our analysis had been articulated in a way that captured the real trends. If we had made mistakes, they were errors of incompleteness — we hadn't risked pursuing the tendencies far enough, and we hadn't risked making our imagination revolutionary enough.

In brief: while the greater part of our analysis has been confirmed by subsequent events, certain elements have been contradicted, not by the historical developments, but by the intensity — foreseen — which those developments assumed. Let us review some of these elements.

a. We recognized very clearly that work, as it became more and more abstract, mobile, and socially diffused, required new forms of recomposition. We began to follow the processes involved in producing the subjectivity which the new organization of capitalist production entailed. But we should have gone more deeply and realized that this newly produced subjectivity was locked in an insuperable contradiction, for social cooperation was more and more violently in opposition to the structures of capitalist control. The contradiction was especially apparent in the case of intellectual work, which is non-material and which, as it became the center of production, manifested its irreconcilable difference with the capitalist norm. We ought to have noted more clearly the central importance of the struggles within the schools, throughout the educational system, in the meanders of social mobility, in the places where the labor force is formed; and we also ought to have developed a wider analysis of the processes of organization and revolt which were just beginning to surface in those areas.

b. There was certainly no mistaking the new dimension assumed by communications, which functioned as an instrument and promoter of deterritorialization, directed toward intellectual usurpation and moral impoverishment. And it was no paradox if exactly here, in this area where capitalist domination was so strong, one could detect mechanisms for recomposing the subject and giving a new territorialization to desire. But while our work stopped at the point of identifying the possibility of such a rebellion, we should have persisted in our analysls, tracing out the new moments of reconstruction, of recomposition of the subject. This latter process needs to be seen not in the context of some home-made operation, or some unique experiment. We are not talking about some utopia to come, but about a real formative power, a material force for political and social reconstruction.

c. We should have better defined the scope of the ecological struggle, a movement which appeared consistent with the program of proletarian liberation. We ought to have acknowledged not only the necessity of defending nature against the menace of destruction and the imminent apocalypse that hangs over it, but also the urgency of constructing new systems and conditions for re-producing the human species, as well as defining the modes and timetables for revolutionary action in this direction. It is easy to see that our text was written before Chernobyl.

d. And now we must take up the point most deserving of criticism and self-censure. In defining Integrated World capitalism, we did not sufficiently measure the intensity of the process set in motion by the direct participation of the Soviet Union in that mechanism. Of course all through our pamphlet we had insisted on the identity of the exploitation taking place in capitalist countries and that taking place in socialist countries. Now the world market's definitive overcoming of the Stalinist pressure only confirms this observation. But the acceleration of the processes of integration taking place in the last five years and the effects thereof cannot be underestimated. Very acute contradictions are being created within each of the two blocs as well as in the relationship between East and West. The problem of peace can be put in much less utopian terms today than when we composed our pamphlet. But precisely for that reason, the achievement and the maintenance of peace become a positive force for reopening the processes of liberation, revolt, and radical transformation.

e. Certainly our book did not underestimate the question of North-South relations. But we were far too optimistic. We believed that in the face of the disastrous decline in the prospects of the Southern nations, some kind of new alliance with the North would inevitably be laid out. Nothing of the sort occurred, and indeed the situation has become much worse. Entire continents are adrift without a compass and there has not been a single political initiative worthy of the name which has been offered to combat the enormous problems posed by this disaster. Benefit concerts and acts of state-sponsored charity have multiplied — and at the same time the isolation and the lack of news from these poorest countries have become more ominous.

It is with desperation and anguished impotence that we look upon that massacre of innocents, that unending genocide... It is with anger that we contemplate these things.

We could continue analyzing the defects of our discourse, while still affirming its substantial validity. But to what end? The evidence that allows us to still believe today that communism has never been nearer to fruition derives not from our own words but from the radical change of direction taken by history in the last four or five years. What we once believed in as a utopia now seems common sense. The age of the Reagan counter-revolution and the very gloomy period of neo-liberal power now seem definitively superseded. We knew that they would not last long, and we never ceased laughing at their "new philosophers" and being nauseated by those who had "repented." Nevertheless, we are surprised to see how fragile such arrogance really was. The grand declarations about neo-liberalism, about a new social contract, about a new Enlightenment are today obviously charades — as they were in the past. In the past, however, it took courage to say so; nowadays this truth seems banal.

But we are not so much interested in talking as in being. Being, and thus organizing. Organizing, and hence having the possibility of overthrowing the sense of production which capital, for the sake of profit, enforces within our information-oriented social fabric. Overthrowing that sense, subverting it... For that we look to praxis. And praxis, today, is found in the East bloc.

Before speaking of praxis, a brief clarification of terminology is in order. People say that communism is dead. We think this affirmation is inexact, and that it is socialism which is moribund. How are these two terms distinguished? For the old-line militant, the distinction between socialism and communism was obvious: socialism was that political-economic order in which "to each was given according to his work "; whereas communism was that system in which "to each was given according to his needs." Socialism and communism represented two different stages of the revolutionary process, the first being characterized by the socialization of the means of production and by the political administration of this transition, the second characterized by the extinction of the state and by the spontaneous management of both the economy and power.

If this distinction was clear to the old-line communist militants, today, in the era of a collapse of "real socialism," it has been obliterated, and communism and socialism are easily confused. They are confused via a hostile, wholesale reduction performed by the adversaries of socialism, who have undertaken a brutal liquidation of all things socialist that were created in the world after 1917, whether in Eastern Europe or in the Third World. Of course these all too easy liquidations take sustenance from favorable conditions: in the socialist states of Eastern Europe during the last forty years the sole methods of legitimizing power have been the mystification of ideology, frauds perpetrated by the bureaucracy, and cynicism in dealing with theory — all of which, predictably enough, have produced symptoms of radical refusal and disgust. How could the "radiant future" promised by communism have avoided being discredited in societies that were socialist in name only, societies that were in fact bureaucratic organizations, in which utopia was achieved by hiding realities?

Having said this, let us return to the concepts themselves and their history, noting that, in all probability, they are not reducible to the guises in which they appear in present-day polemics, nor subject to the current wholesale dismissals. Indeed for about a century and a half, that is, from the foundation of the "League of Communists" which looked to Marx for leadership in the middle of the last century, communism has been the central political ideology for the modern age. In opposition to the old utopias, it is based on a real, forward-looking analysis of the mechanism of development of capitalism from the worker's point of view. Taking a scientific look at the social-economic dynamics of the capitalist system as it lives and grows solely by exploiting the labor force, the party of the working class can define the strategies and tactics for the communist future, setting as its objectives the destruction of the mechanism of capitalist accumulation and the conquest of political power. Marx brings us up to this point, offering a formidable scientific apparatus for dealing with this project.

The subsequent transfer of Marx's theoretical analysis to the problem of revolutionary mobilization within the new context of European capitalism at the beginning of a century marked by a radical instability in the various political and social systems, is the task which Lenin takes up and which leads him to formulate the organizational principles of a new kind of party, the "Bolshevik Communist Party." This party is the vanguard of the working class which, having broken with the mere economic demands of the unions, the mere opportunistic spontaneity of the anarchists, and the legalistic version of the class struggle practiced by the parties of the Second International, has shaped itself into a disciplined, flexible instrument specifically adapted for seizing power and installing the dictatorship of the proletariat. The objective of this dictatorship is the institution of socialism, or the nationalization of the means of production and a centralization of planning. But all of this was supposed to take place within a radical process of democratic participation, within a transitional period that would create conditions of economic growth for everyone and at the same time would dissolve the central power of the state and the law, bestowing both wealth and freedom on the citizens. What an illusion, and what disappointments!

The Leninist conceptions of the party and the revolutionary transition were contested within the left wing of the workers' movement by Rosa Luxemburg, both at the time of the 1905 uprising and after the 1917 revolution. For her, organization meant the permanent refusal, exactly in the workplace, of any mediation of workers' self-expression or the class struggle through the agency of the unions or the reformist party; her idea of organization coincided with the rising levels of worker spontaneity and with the specific political institutions generated by such spontaneity, including the "soviets" in Russia in 1905 and 1917, and the "workers' councils" in Germany in 1918-1919. Lenin, on the other hand, held that the workers' own self-directed organization for struggle could not prefigure the party, since a revolutionary political directorate, standing outside the individual struggles, would have to supervise all the various expressions of spontaneity in order to assure the fundamental goal of a dictatorship of the proletariat.

Is it this contradiction between Luxemburg and Lenin — between an idea of communism as a democracy constituted by masses in struggle, or, on the other hand, as a dictatorship of the proletariat — that gives rise to the crisis in the management of socialist power once the insurrection has been victorious and power has been seized? Many communists (and there are still many of them in the world) think so, and it is very probable that as the subversive movement revives in the coming decades (for it is evident that it will revive) It will have to reconsider these issues.

But other problems can also become central in the discussions motivated by the present crisis of communism and the collapse of "real socialism." In particular, it is interesting to follow developments in Russia in the wake of the dilemma that surfaced after Lenin's death. At that point the Soviet political debate centered on the two alternatives of a "permanent revolution," or, on the other hand, "socialism in a single country." These alternatives were discussed in terms of their relationship to Leninism and to the October revolution. Leon Trotsky, an ardent defender of the first thesis as a means of inoculating the revolution against the bureaucratization of the state and the party, was defeated by those who, embracing the second alternative, believed that the unequal development of capitalist countries and the exceptional nature of a proletarian victory at the weak link in the imperialist chain had rendered the construction of socialism in a single country an obligatory course of action. Among the advocates of the second thesis Stalin soon emerged as the merciless executor of an extreme centralization of the party and an enormous concentration of power in the administrative-repressive apparatus. Thus the distance between Marx's theory of a class struggle against the capitalist system and the actual practice in the construction of socialism widened vertiginously. Paradoxically, communism — defined by Marx as "the real movement which abolishes the present state of affairs" — became the productive activity which created at whatever cost the material bases of an industrial society that was locked in a competition with the rhythm of its own development and with that of the capitalist countries.

Socialism did not commit itself to overcoming the capitalist system and the system of wage labor, but instead became a social-economic alternative of capitalism.

Can we thus claim that the present crisis of "real socialism" amounts to nothing more than the crisis in the socialist management of capital? That the present situation has nothing to do with any ultimate crisis of communism? We can indeed make such claims if, having accepted the lessons of a century and a half of history, we re-assert with the greatest possible emphasis the distinction between socialism and communism. For the first is nothing more than one of the forms in which capital can be organized and administered — and that is why most of the advanced capitalist countries today have economic systems in which the socialist component is extremely strong. But communism is the form in which society can be organized after the destruction of both the capitalist system, that is, after the destruction of the class system and the system of exploitation, when the organizing role of the state, as opposed to that of society, has been cancelled. We must further insist that it is absolutely untrue that socialism is a phase of, or an instrument of transition toward, communism. Historically speaking, the exact contrary has been true, for the most ferocious forms of political and economic oppression have occurred within "real socialism," whose so-called "new socialist man" was nothing other than a perfected form of the beast of burden. As Marx teaches us, communism is born directly from class antagonism, from the refusal of both work and the organization of work, whether in the bourgeois form or the socialist form. The new modes of this antagonism and this refusal can be seen in Western Europe, but are even more apparent today in the East bloc's crisis of "real socialism." That is why the revolt in the eastern European nations constitutes a strong incentive for a renewed discussion and a renewed militancy within communism. The need to distinguish between "socialism" and "communism" has once again become obvious: but this time not because of the blurred boundaries between them, but because they are so opposed. Socialism is nothing other than one of the forms taken by capitalist management of the economy and of power, whereas communism is an absolutely radical political economic democracy and an aspiration to freedom.

What do the events in Eastern Europe reveal to us? First of all — and we have already recognized this — they mark the end of the illusion that there might be shortcuts to communism. Whatever might have been the beliefs of our predecessors, whether workers by profession or intellectuals in the vanguard, we must acknowledge that there can be no progress, no transition from capitalism to communism via socialism. Communism, thus, is the minimum essential program. It can and must be constructed starting from the conditions of socialist and/or capitalist society — within these conditions. There are not two or three or four or *n* phases or stages of development: there is only one, and that is the re-taking of freedom into one's own hands and the construction of collective means for controlling cooperation in production. This single stage of development allows us to discover to what extent capitalism and/or socialism have rendered production social, abstract and shared, and it also permits us to reorganize this cooperation outside and against the capitalist system of command, outside and against the daily theft of power and wealth which is perpetrated by the few at the expense of the whole society.

Communism is already alive within the capitalist and/or socialist societies of today, in the form of a secret order dedicated to cooperation in production: an order covered up by the capitalist system of command and/or bureaucracy, crushed between the opposing forces of those who command and those who follow commands, a new order which strains to become manifest but cannot. In the East bloc we saw mass protest explode in the form of a pure negation of the past.

But we also saw the expression of a potential that was unknown to us in the West: in the Eastern European nations we saw a fully alive civil society come to the surface, one that had not been homogenized, one capable of expressing a collective political will in a way no longer found in the West — a drive for power founded on the social base rather than on the forms of the state. I am certain that in the West as well all of this will take place, and quite soon — for what has happened in the East was not born from the special experience of those countries.

What took place in the East is the beginning of a revolt against a capitalism which had reached the apex of its tyranny. There are always those imbeciles who identify capitalist development with the number of computers sold: of course in that case one would have to believe that there was no capitalism in the East and that its revolution will quickly be calmed by selling computers. And there are those who will attempt this strategy. But that is not really how things stand: the level of capitalist development is defined by the degree of social cooperation in production. From this point of view, the Eastern bloc is in no way behind the West.

It is against this background that we read the revolution which has exploded; and we further suggest that, as with all revolutions that are truly such, this one will spread — from the East to the West, a new '68, moving in the opposite direction.

What else do the events in the East reveal? Another element, less visible to the majority of the public, but nonetheless extraodinarily important: the birth of a new model of democracy. In our civilization we are accustomed to thinking that there is only one model of democracy, the Western one, and that it need only be applied generally.

History has come to an end, there is nothing more to invent, and Western democracy and the "American way of life" represent the absolutely final product of the human spirit! All of this is an arrogant illusion. What has happened in the East demonstrates just the opposite, for (despite what Hegel says) not only has the world Spirit not finished its travels, but in fact it gives signs of having reversed its course, returning from across the Atlantic and heading east, toward the Russian steppes. That is where it has been reborn, and that is where the debate about democracy is taking place. Democracy cannot be simply political emancipation, but must include social and economic liberation. No democracy is possible unless the problems of work and of command are solved. Every form of democratic government must also be a form of liberation from the slavery of work, must yield a new, free organization of cooperation in production. It is not a question of putting factories and the organization of social work in the hands of new bosses, entrusting them to the hypocritical freedom of the marketplace, handing them back to the exploitative desires of capitalists and bureaucrats. Rather, it is a question of understanding what might be the rules for the democratic management of economic entrepreneurship. An impossible utopia? Fewer and fewer people think so. Not only in the East but even in the West, more and more people are asking themselves how to achieve a democracy that includes the democratic management of production. And their stupefaction is directed not at communism, but at the present form of production — their amazement (and their grief) derive from the fact that every day we are compelled to witness the persistence of figures as obsolete and useless as the capitalist and bureaucratic bosses. In the East, within the revolution, people are experiencing a new form of democracy: the democracy of work, a communist democracy.

A third lesson has reached us from the East bloc. Who has revolted? The working class? In part yes, but often not. The middle classes, then? To a fair degree, but only when they were not linked to the bureaucracy. What about the students, scientists, workers linked to advanced technologies, intellectuals, and in short, all those who deal with abstract and intellectual work? Certainly this represents the nucleus of the rebellion. Those who rebelled, in brief, were the new kind of producers. A social producer, manager of his own means of production and capable of supplying both work and intellectual planning, both innovative activity and a cooperative socialization. From this point of view as well, what has happened in the East is not foreign to us: indeed we might say, "de te fabula narratur." For in the countries where capitalism reigns idiotic and triumphant, corrupt and incapable of self-criticism, arrogant and confused, here as well the subject who constantly proposes to revolt is the same: the new productive subject, intellectual and abstract, students, scientists, workers linked to advanced technologies, university workers, etc. It is because of this subject with whom we identify that the events of the East pertain to us. Whether Gorbachev remains in power or is removed by Ligachev, whether perestroika succeeds in the present form or in a second wave that will inevitably follow, whether the Russian empire endures or not — these are all problems that concern only the Soviets.

We have our Cossacks to defeat, and there are many of them, and we are very late in joining the battle. Nonetheless we are grateful to the Soviets for having initiated, for the second time in this century, a profound process in the renewal of the spirit. It is a process that we believe to be irreversible, not only in Russia, but also in the life of humankind.

Toni Negri, Paris
Christmas 1989

Translated by Jared Becker

Translator's Notes

1. Since the '60s in French philosophy, the dialectic has come to be associated with the imposition of power and the neutralization of radical, alternative energies. The mediation of conflicting opposites and their resolution into a higher order of unity now is linked with a politics that neutralizes conflict in the name of Party or State order.

2. Both Guattari and Negri have studied Spinoza, the first modern materialist philosopher. The term "potential" refers to the creative possibility inherent in material reality.

3. A term from the French Revolution for "putschist" or leninist style revolutionary movements which attempt to seize power using a small conspiratorial band rather

than relying on self-initiated mass mobilization, democratic processes, or self-government by the people.

4. Guaranteed workers are subsidized with unemployment insurance by the state. Non-guaranteed workers are more marginal and are not covered by insurance.

5. A term from French psychoanalysis which refers to the system of self-delusion that is inherent in the ego. It has come to have the broader more sociological meaning of the shared delusions of social groups.

6. This refers to the leninist idea that the economic aspirations of the proletariat need to be "translated" into political form by a vanguard party.

SEMIOTEXT(E) USA

JIM FLEMING & PETER LAMBORN WILSON, EDITORS

DESIGNED BY SUE ANN HARKEY

A huge compendium of works in American psychotopography. Anarchists, unidentifed flying leftists, neo-pagans, secessionists, the lunatic fringe of survivalism, cults, foreign agents, mad bombers, ban-the-bombers, nudists, monarchists, chidren's liberationsists, zero-workers, tax resisters, mimeo poets, vampires, xerox pirates, pataphysicians, witches, unrepentant faggots, hardcore youth, poetic terrorists... The best of current American *samizdat.*

Now available — $12 postpaid

SEMIOTEXT(E)'S FIRST DIRTY DOZEN

JIM FLEMING & SYLVÈRE LOTRINGER, EDITORS

The mammoth anthology reprinting selections from all of the earliest twelve issues of the journal, including writing by more than fifty contributors to issues like *Polysexuality, Anti-Oedipus, Ego Traps, Oasis, Schizo-Culture, Nietzsche's Return, The German Issue,* and more.

Winter, 1990 — $12 postpaid

Additional Semiotext(e) / Autonomedia Titles

XEROX PIRATES

"HIGH" TECH & THE NEW COLLAGE UNDERGROUND

AUTONOMEDIA COLLECTIVE, EDITORS

Art and politics meet in heady ways in this amazing and incendiary collection of work in the "high" tech medium of photocopy collage. Post-surrealist traditions of oneiric reverie meet the radical hard-edge of "détourned" advertisements and other recuperations of the mass-mediated image. Works by many well-known marginal artists like Winston Smith, James Koehnline, Dadata, Freddie Baer, Anti-Authoritarians Anonymnous, Sue Ann Harkey.

Spring, 1991 — $14 postpaid

FILM & POLITICS IN THE THIRD WORLD

JOHN DOWNING, EDITOR

The only anthology of its kind in English, with critical articles — most of them written by Third World writers — on leading figures and national cinemas, including analyses of important single films, political/aesthetic manifestoes, and interviews with directors from Africa, China, India, Turkey, Iran, the Arab World, the Philippines, Cuba, Latin America, and more.

Now Available — $12 postpaid

Additional Semiotext(e) / Autonomedia Titles

FATAL STRATEGIES

JEAN BAUDRILLARD

A major work by the controversial author of *Simulations, In the Shadow of the Silent Majorities, Forget Foucault, The Ecstasy of Communication, The Critique of the Political Economy of the Sign, The Mirror of Production,* and *America,* offering "fatal alternatives" to the failure of radical responses to postmodernity. Topics range from modes of political representation and strategies of refusal to aesthetic theory and commodification, situationist theory, seduction, gambling and obesity.

Now Available — $12 postpaid

AESTHETICS OF DISAPPEARANCE

PAUL VIRILIO

From infantile narcolepsy to the illusion of movement in speed, the author of *Pure War* , *Speed and Politics, The Lost Dimension,* and other works examines the "aesthetic" of disappearance: in film,
in politics, in war, in the philosophy of subjectivity, and elsewhere.

Now Available — $10 postpaid

Additional Semiotext(e) / Autonomedia Titles

A DAY IN THE LIFE

TALES FROM THE LOWER EAST SIDE

ALAN MOORE AND JOSH GOSCIAK, EDITORS

This provocative anthology of voices old and new from New York's East Village will offend those who like their literature quaint, pretty, and much too tidy to touch. Stories reflecting the turbulent mosaic of artists, ethnics, poets, junkies, barflies, radicals, mystics, street people, con men, flower children, losers, screwballs and professional eccentrics that inhabit the city's edgiest neighborhood. Allen Ginsberg, Ted Berrigan, Herbert Huncke, Lynne Tillman, Ed Sanders, Miguel Piñero, Emily XYZ, Zoe Anglesley, Jorge Cabalquinto, Cookie Mueller, Ron Kolm, and many more, with art by Seth Tobacman, Keiko Bonk, Martin Wong, and others. An Evil Eye Book.
Now Available — $10 postpaid

THE LOST DIMENSION

PAUL VIRILIO

The French urban planner and cultural theorist examines aspects of post-modern society ranging from space travel to time and the physical sciences.
Fall, 1990 — $12 postpaid

POPULAR REALITY

IRREVEREND DAVID CROWBAR, EDITOR

The oversized anthology of selections from the controversial — and now autodissolute— marginal magazine, the "Vital Organ of the Shimo Undeground." Graphics and text, détourned advertisements and more from Bob Black, Blaster Al Ackerman, the Irreverend Crowbar, Bob McGlynn, Hakim Bey, Celeste Oatmeal, Yael Dragwyla, tENTATIVELY a cONVENIENCE, the Wretched Dervish, and many more.

Fall, 1990 — $12 postpaid

CASSETTE MYTHOS

MAKING MUSIC AT THE MARGINS

ROBIN JAMES, EDITOR

Essays, reports, stories, and manifestoes from the real musical underground, where the medium of the tape cassette has made it possible for individuals and groups to produce and distribute their own music in their own style and for their own purposes, free of the censuring, perception-clogging nets of cash and commerce.

Fall, 1990 — $12 postpaid

NEW ENCLOSURES
MIDNIGHT NOTES COLLECTIVE

Eleven essays assessing the the development of the new "common denominator of proletarian experience across the globe," the "secret and corrosive New Enclosures," which the Midnight Notes Collective examines from China, Nigeria and Zurich to Maine, Massachusetts, and New York's Lower East Side, covering issues like homelessness, union struggles, debt crises, racism, self-reproducing automata, and "jubilee."

Now Available — $6 postpaid

LUSITANIA
KULTURA CONTROL
MARTIM AVILLEZ, EDITOR

A collection of essays on the theme of cultural control — control by, of and through culture — as conducted by multi-national corporations, industrial capital, mass media conglomerates, artistic elites, dominant cultural ideologies, and the like. Profusely illustrated, and a bi-lingual edition, with all material in Portuguese as well as English.

Now Available — $9 postpaid

Additional Semiotext(e) / Autonomedia Titles

GOD & PLASTIC SURGERY
MARX, NIETZSCHE, FREUD & THE OBVIOUS
JEREMY BARRIS

An unusual and intensive examination of the work of the intellectual progenitors of contemporary Western thought, with a battery of insights into how to and how *not* to think, act, feel, eat, dress, dance, take tea, or make love. A text written with an eye on the concept of justice, intended to provoke, upset, and transfigure modern culture.

Now Available — $12 postpaid

ON AN(ARCHY) AND SCHIZOANALYSIS
ROLANDO PEREZ

Using the "anti-oedipal" insights of Gilles Deleuze and Félix Guattari's *Capitalism and Schizophrenia,* Perez argues for "anti-fascist strategies in everyday life," and reads philosophy, literature, films and popular culture to critique deep political sympathies and antagonisms. Treats writers from Kafka to D. M. Thomas, filmmakers like David Lynch, punk and post-punk music, Nietzsche and radical philosophy, feminism.

Now Available — $10 postpaid

Gallery Books
Editor: Peter Fallon

COLLECTED POEMS

Derek Mahon

COLLECTED POEMS

Gallery Books

Collected Poems
was first published
simultaneously in paperback
and in a clothbound edition
on 30 November 1999.
Reprinted 2001 and 2004.

The Gallery Press
Loughcrew
Oldcastle
County Meath
Ireland

ISBN 1 85235 255 8

A CIP catalogue record for this book
is available from the British Library.

Contents

for Rory and Katie

Spring in Belfast

Walking among my own this windy morning
In a tide of sunlight between shower and shower,
I resume my old conspiracy with the wet
Stone and the unwieldy images of the squinting heart.
Once more, as before, I remember not to forget.

There is a perverse pride in being on the side
Of the fallen angels and refusing to get up.
We could *all* be saved by keeping an eye on the hill
At the top of every street, for there it is,
Eternally, if irrelevantly, visible —

But yield instead to the humorous formulae,
The spurious mystery in the knowing nod;
Or we keep sullen silence in light and shade,
Rehearsing our astute salvations under
The cold gaze of a sanctimonious God.

One part of my mind must learn to know its place.
The things that happen in the kitchen houses
And echoing back streets of this desperate city
Should engage more than my casual interest,
Exact more interest than my casual pity.

Glengormley

Wonders are many and none is more wonderful than man
Who has tamed the terrier, trimmed the hedge
And grasped the principle of the watering can.
Clothes-pegs litter the window-ledge
And the long ships lie in clover; washing lines
Shake out white linen over the chalk thanes.

Now we are safe from monsters, and the giants
Who tore up sods twelve miles by six
And hurled them out to sea to become islands
Can worry us no more. The sticks
And stones that once broke bones will not now harm
A generation of such sense and charm.

Only words hurt us now. No saint or hero,
Landing at night from the conspiring seas,
Brings dangerous tokens to the new era —
Their sad names linger in the histories.
The unreconciled, in their metaphysical pain,
Dangle from lamp-posts in the dawn rain;

And much dies with them. I should rather praise
A worldly time under this worldly sky —
The terrier-taming, garden-watering days
Those heroes pictured as they struggled through
The quick noose of their finite being. By
Necessity, if not choice, I live here too.

Grandfather

They brought him in on a stretcher from the world,
Wounded but humorous; and he soon recovered.
Boiler-rooms, row upon row of gantries rolled
Away to reveal the landscape of a childhood
Only he can recapture. Even on cold
Mornings he is up at six with a block of wood
Or a box of nails, discreetly up to no good
Or banging round the house like a four-year-old —

Never there when you call. But after dark
You hear his great boots thumping in the hall
And in he comes, as cute as they come. Each night
His shrewd eyes bolt the door and set the clock
Against the future, then his light goes out.
Nothing escapes him; he escapes us all.

September in Gt. Yarmouth

The woodwind whistles down the shore
Piping the stragglers home; the gulls
Snaffle and bolt their final mouthfuls.
Only the youngsters call for more.

Chimneys breathe and beaches empty,
Everyone queues for the inland cold —
Middle-aged parents growing old
And teenage kids becoming twenty.

Now the first few spots of rain
Spatter the sports page in the gutter.
Council workmen stab the litter.
You have sown and reaped; now sow again.

The band packs in, the banners drop,
The ice-cream stiffens in its cone.
The boatman lifts his megaphone:
'Come in, fifteen, your time is up.'

In Carrowdore Churchyard

(*at the grave of Louis MacNeice*)

Your ashes will not stir, even on this high ground,
However the wind tugs, the headstones shake.
This plot is consecrated, for your sake,
To what lies in the future tense. You lie
Past tension now, and spring is coming round
Igniting flowers on the peninsula.

Your ashes will not fly, however the rough winds burst
Through the wild brambles and the reticent trees.
All we may ask of you we have; the rest
Is not for publication, will not be heard.
Maguire, I believe, suggested a blackbird
And over your grave a phrase from Euripides.

Which suits you down to the ground, like this churchyard
With its play of shadow, its humane perspective.
Locked in the winter's fist, these hills are hard
As nails, yet soft and feminine in their turn
When fingers open and the hedges burn.
This, you implied, is how we ought to live —

The ironical, loving crush of roses against snow,
Each fragile, solving ambiguity. So
From the pneumonia of the ditch, from the ague
Of the blind poet and the bombed-out town you bring
The all-clear to the empty holes of spring,
Rinsing the choked mud, keeping the colours new.

First Love

This is a circling of itself and you —
A form of words, compact and compromise,
Prepared in the false dawn of the half-true
Beyond which the shapes of truth materialize.
This is a blind with sunlight filtering through.

This is a stirring in the silent hours,
As lovers do with thoughts they cannot frame
Or leave, but bring to darkness like night-flowers,
Words never choosing but the words choose them —
Birds crowing, wind whistling off pale stars.

This is a night-cry, neither here nor there,
A ghostly echo from the clamorous dead
Who cried aloud in anger and despair
Outlasting stone and bronze, but took instead
Their lost grins underground with them for ever.

This is at one remove, a substitute
For final answers; but the wise man knows
To cleave to the one living absolute
Beyond paraphrase, and shun a shrewd repose.
The words are aching in their own pursuit

To say 'I love you' out of indolence
As one might speak at sea without forethought,
Drifting inconsequently among islands.
This is a way of airing my distraught
Love of your silence; you are the soul of silence.

Bird Sanctuary

(for Jill Schlesinger)

Towards sleep I came
Upon the place again,
Its muted sea and tame
Eddying wind. The mist and rain
Come only after dark, and then
Steam out to sea at dawn.

I have erected
A bird sanctuary to hold
The loaded world in check.
This is where all my birds collect —
Gannet, puffin and kittiwake
All duly enrolled.

I live elsewhere —
In a city down the coast
Composed of earth and fire.
At night I walk beside the river
So that the elements of air
And water are not lost.

I expect great things
Of these angels of wind,
Females, males and fledglings.
The sudden whirring of their wings
Disturbs the noon, and midnight rings
With echoes from their island.

Will come a time
When they sit on the housetops
Shouting, thousands of them,
This is their own, their favourite dream
Beyond reason, beyond rhyme,
So that the heart stops.

De Quincey in Later Life

Tonight the blessèd state, that long repose
Where time is measured
Not by the clock but by the hours
Of the wind; his seventh heaven when it snows
The valley under, and the frosty stars
Sing to his literary leisure.

Hearth rugs, a teapot and a quart
Decanter of laudanum —
Perihelion of paradise! No sort
Or condition of men but is the less human
For want of this; *mens sana*
In corpore sano.

Excellent as an antidote for toothache
And the busy streets. Wood crackles better
In a head removed, and fresh water
Springs wiselier in a heart that isn't sick.
And then the dreams came, and his children
Woke him every day at noon —

Until he cried out, 'I will sleep no more!',
And quit the hot sheets and the enormous
Apparitions dying on the floor.
He left the house,
Walked out to the sunlight on the hill
And heard, in the whispering-gallery of his soul,

His own small, urgent discord echoing back
From dark roads taken at random
And the restless thunder of London —
Where he had gone in his eighteenth year
And walked the embankments after dark
With Anne, looking for some such panacea.

Breton Walks

1. *Morning*
No doubt the creation was something like this —
A cold day breaking on silent stones,
Slower than time, spectacular only in size.
First there is darkness, then somehow light;
We call this day, and the other night,
And watch in vain for the second of sunrise.

Suddenly, near at hand, the click of a wooden shoe —
An old woman among the primeval shapes
Abroad in the field of light, sombrely dressed.
She calls good-day, since there are bad days too,
And her eyes go down. She has seen perhaps
Ten thousand dawns like this, and is not impressed.

2. *Man and Bird*
All fly away at my approach,
As they have done time out of mind,
And hide in the thicker leaves to watch
The shadowy ingress of mankind.

My whistle-talk fails to disarm
Presuppositions of ill-will;
Although they rarely come to harm
The ancient fear is in them still.

Which irritates my *amour-propre*
As an enlightened alien
And renders yet more wide the gap
From their world to the world of men.

So perhaps they have something after all —
Either we shoot them out of hand
Or parody them with a bird-call
Neither of us can understand.

3. *After Midnight*
They are all round me in the dark
With claw-knives for my sleepy anarch —

Beasts of the field, birds of the air,
Their slit-eyes glittering everywhere.

I am man self-made, self-made man,
No small-talk now for those who ran

In and out of my muddy childhood.
We have grown up as best we could.

4. *Exit Molloy*
Now at the end I smell the smells of spring
Where in a dark ditch I lie wintering,
And the little town only a mile away
Happy and fatuous in the light of day.
A bell tolls gently; I should start to cry
But my eyes are closed and my face dry —
I am not important and I have to die.
Strictly speaking I am already dead
But still I can hear the birds sing on over my head.

A Portrait of the Artist

(*for Colin Middleton*)

Shivering in the darkness
Of pits, slag-heaps, beetroot fields,
I gasp for light and life
Like a caged bird in springtime
Banging the bright bars.

Like a glow-worm I move among
The caged Belgian miners,
And the light on my forehead
Is the dying light of faith.
God gutters down to metaphor —

A subterranean tapping, light
Refracted in a glass of beer
As if through a church window,
Or a basin ringed with coal-dust
After the ritual evening bath.

Theo, I am discharged for being
Over-zealous, they call it,
And not dressing the part.
In time I shall go south
And paint what I have seen —

A meteor of golden light
On chairs, faces and old boots,
Setting fierce fire to the eyes
Of sunflowers and fishing boats,
Each one a miner in disguise.

The Forger

When I sold my fake Vermeers to Goering
Nobody knew, nobody guessed
The agony, the fanaticism
Of working beyond criticism
And better than the best.

When they hauled me before the war-crimes tribunal
No one suspected, nobody knew
The agony of regrets
With which I told my secrets.
They missed the point, of course —
To hell with the national heritage,
I sold my *soul* for potage.

The experts were good value, though,
When they went to work on my studio.
Not I, but *they* were the frauds;
I revolutionized their methods.

Now, nothing but claptrap
About 'mere technique' and 'true vision',
As if there were a distinction —
Their way of playing it down.
But my genius will live on;
For even at one remove
The thing I meant was love.

And I too have wandered
In the dark streets of Holland
With hunger at my belly
When the mists rolled in from the sea;
And I too have suffered
Obscurity and derision,
And sheltered in my heart of hearts
A light to transform the world.

Day Trip to Donegal

We reached the sea in early afternoon,
Climbed stiffly out; there were things to be done,
Clothes to be picked up, friends to be seen.
As ever, the nearby hills were a deeper green
Than anywhere in the world, and the grave
Grey of the sea the grimmer in that enclave.

Down at the pier the boats gave up their catch,
A writhing glimmer of fish; they fetch
Ten times as much in the city as here,
And still the fish come in year after year —
Herring and mackerel, flopping about the deck
In attitudes of agony and heartbreak.

We left at eight, drove back the way we came,
The sea receding down each muddy lane.
Around midnight we changed-down into suburbs
Sunk in a sleep no gale-force wind disturbs.
The time of year had left its mark
On frosty pavements glistening in the dark.

Give me a ring, goodnight, and so to bed . . .
That night the slow sea washed against my head,
Performing its immeasurable erosions —
Spilling into the skull, marbling the stones
That spine the very harbour wall,
Muttering its threat to villages of landfall.

At dawn I was alone far out at sea
Without skill or reassurance — nobody
To show me how, no promise of rescue —
Cursing my constant failure to take due
Forethought for this; contriving vain
Overtures to the vindictive wind and rain.

An Unborn Child

(for Michael and Edna Longley)

I have already come to the verge of
Departure; a month or so and
I shall be vacating this familiar room.
Its fabric fits me almost like a glove
While leaving latitude for a free hand.
I begin to put on the manners of the world
Sensing the splitting light above
My head, where in the silence I lie curled.

Certain mysteries are relayed to me
Through the dark network of my mother's body
While she sits sewing the white shrouds
Of my apotheosis. I know the twisted
Kitten that lies there sunning itself
Under the bare bulb, the clouds
Of goldfish mooning around upon the shelf.
In me these data are already vested;

I know them in my bones — bones which embrace
Nothing, for I am completely egocentric.
The pandemonium of encumbrances
Which will absorb me, mind and senses,
Intricacies of the maze and the rat-race,
I imagine only. Though they linger and,
Like fingers, stretch until the knuckles crack,
They cannot dwarf the dimensions of my hand.

I must compose myself at the nerve centre
Of this metropolis, and not fidget —
Although sometimes at night, when the city
Has gone to sleep, I keep in touch with it,
Listening to the warm red water
Racing in the sewers of my mother's body;
Or the moths, soft as eyelids, or the rain
Wiping its wet wings on the window-pane.

And sometimes too, in the small hours of the morning
When the dead filament has ceased to ring,
After the goldfish are dissolved in darkness
And the kitten has gathered itself up into a ball
Between the groceries and the sewing,
I slip the trappings of my harness
To range these hollows in discreet rehearsal
And, battering at the concavity of my caul,

Produce in my mouth the words, 'I want to live!' —
This my first protest, and shall be my last.
As I am innocent, everything I do
Or say is couched in the affirmative.
I want to see, hear, touch and taste
These things with which I am to be encumbered.
Perhaps I needn't worry; give
Or take a day or two, my days are numbered.

Canadian Pacific

From famine, pestilence and persecution
Those gaunt forefathers shipped abroad to find
Rough stone of heaven beyond the western ocean
And staked their claim, and pinned their faith.
Tonight their children whistle through the dark.
Frost chokes the windows; they will not have heard
The wild geese flying south over the lakes
While the lakes harden beyond grief and anger —
The eyes fanatical, rigid the soft necks,
The great wings sighing with a nameless hunger.

Thinking of Inis Oírr in Cambridge, Mass.

(*for Eamon Grennan*)

A dream of limestone in sea-light
Where gulls have placed their perfect prints.
Reflection in that final sky
Shames vision into simple sight;
Into pure sense, experience.
Atlantic leagues away tonight,
Conceived beyond such innocence,
I clutch the memory still, and I
Have measured everything with it since.

After the Titanic

They said I got away in a boat
And humbled me at the inquiry. I tell you
I sank as far that night as any
Hero. As I sat shivering on the dark water
I turned to ice to hear my costly
Life go thundering down in a pandemonium of
Prams, pianos, sideboards, winches,
Boilers bursting and shredded ragtime. Now I hide
In a lonely house behind the sea
Where the tide leaves broken toys and hatboxes
Silently at my door. The showers of
April, flowers of May mean nothing to me, nor the
Late light of June, when my gardener
Describes to strangers how the old man stays in bed
On seaward mornings after nights of
Wind, takes his cocaine and will see no one. Then it is
I drown again with all those dim
Lost faces I never understood, my poor soul
Screams out in the starlight, heart
Breaks loose and rolls down like a stone.
Include me in your lamentations.

Jail Journal

For several days I have been under
House arrest. My table has become
A sundial to its empty bottle.
With wise abandon
Lover and friend have gone.

In the window opposite
An old lady sits each afternoon
Talking to no one. I shout.
Either she is deaf or
She has reason.

I have books, provisions, running water
And a little stove. It wouldn't matter
If cars moved silently at night
And no light or laughter
Came from the houses down the street.

It's taking longer than almost anything —
But I know, when it's over
And back come friend and lover,
I shall forget it like a childhood illness
Or a sleepless night-crossing.

No Rest for the Wicked

No rest for the wicked —
Curled up in armchairs
Or flat out on the floors
Of well-furnished apartments
Belonging to friends of friends,
We lie where we fell.

One more shiftless habit,
It joins the buttered books,
Stale loaves and wandering dishes,
The shirts in the oven
And the volcanic ashtray.
Forgive us, this is our way,

We were born to this —
Deckchairs, train corridors,
American bus depots,
Park benches, open boats
And wind-worried terraces
Of 19th-century Paris.

Forgive us, we mean well
To your wives' well-wrought ankles,
Their anthropomorphic shoes.
We love your dying embers,
Your happy moonstruck bottles,
And we lie where we fell.

Back home at mid-morning
We wash, we change and drink
Coffee, perhaps we sing;
Then off we go once more,
Smiling our secret smile and only
Slightly the worse for wear.

Homecoming

Has bath and shave,
clean shirt etc.,
full of potatoes,
rested, yet
badly distraught
by six-hour flight
(Boston to Dublin)
drunk all night
with crashing bore
from Houston, Tex.,
who spoke at length
of guns and sex.
Bus into town
and, sad to say,
no change from when
he went away
two years ago.
Goes into bar,
affixes gaze
on evening star.
Skies change but not
souls change; behold
this is the way
the world grows old.
Scientists, birds,
we cannot start
at this late date
with a pure heart,
or having seen
the pictures plain
be ever innocent again.

A Dying Art

'That day would skin a fairy —
A dying art,' she said.
Not many left of the old trade.
Redundant and remote, they age
Gracefully in dark corners
With lamplighters, sailmakers
And native Manx speakers.

And the bone-handled knives with which
They earned their bread? My granny grinds
Her plug tobacco with one to this day.

Ecclesiastes

God, you could grow to love it, God-fearing, God-
   chosen purist little puritan that,
for all your wiles and smiles, you are (the
   dank churches, the empty streets,
the shipyard silence, the tied-up swings) and
   shelter your cold heart from the heat
of the world, from woman-inquisition, from the
   bright eyes of children. Yes, you could
wear black, drink water, nourish a fierce zeal
   with locusts and wild honey, and not
feel called upon to understand and forgive
   but only to speak with a bleak
afflatus, and love the January rains when they
   darken the dark doors and sink hard
into the Antrim hills, the bog meadows, the heaped
   graves of your fathers. Bury that red
bandana and stick, that banjo; this is your
   country, close one eye and be king.
Your people await you, their heavy washing
   flaps for you in the housing estates —
a credulous people. God, you could do it, God
   help you, stand on a corner stiff
with rhetoric, promising nothing under the sun.

The Studio

You would think with so much going on outside
The deal table would make for the window,
The ranged crockery freak and wail
Remembering its dark origins, the frail
Oil-cloth, in a fury of recognitions,
Disperse in a thousand directions
And the simple bulb in the ceiling, honed
By death to a worm of pain, to a hair
Of heat, to a light snowflake laid
On a dark river at night — and wearied
Above all by the life-price of time
And the failure by only a few tenths
Of an inch but completely and for ever
Of the ends of a carefully drawn equator
To meet, sing and be one — abruptly
Roar into the floor.
                                        But it
Never happens like that. Instead
There is this quivering silence
In which, day by day, the play
Of light and shadow (shadow mostly)
Repeats itself, though never exactly.

This is the all-purpose bed-, work- and bedroom.
Its mourning faces are cracked porcelain only quicker,
Its knuckles doorknobs only lighter,
Its occasional cries of despair
A function of the furniture.

Aran

(for Tom and Peggy Mac Intyre)

He is earthed to his girl, one hand fastened
In hers, and with his free hand listens,
An earphone, to his own rendition
Singing the darkness into the light.
I close the pub door gently and step out
Into the yard and the song goes out
And a gull creaks off from the tin roof
Of an outhouse, planing over the ocean,
Circling now with a hoarse inchoate
Screaming the boned fields of its vision.
God, that was the way to do it,
Hand-clasping, echo-prolonging poet!

Scorched with a fearful admiration,
Walking over the nacreous sand,
I dream myself to that tradition
Generations off the land —
One hand to an ear for the vibration,
The far wires, the reverberation
Down light-years of the imagination
And a loved hand in the other hand.

The long glow springs from the dark soil, however —
No marsh-light holds a candle to this;
Unearthly still in its white weather
A crack-voiced rock-marauder, scavenger, fierce
Friend to no slant fields or the sea either,
Folds back over the forming waters.

A Tolerable Wisdom

You keep the cold from the body, the cold from the mind.
Heartscloth, soulswool, without you there would be
Short shrift for the pale beast in a winter's wind,
Too swift exposure by too harsh a sea.
Cold I have known, its sports pages adrift
Past frozen dodgems in the amusement park,
One crumpled Gauloise thumbing a late lift
Where Paris flamed on the defining dark.

You've heard the gravel at the window, seen
A lost figure unmanned by closing time.
More honour to you that you took him in,
Fed buns and cocoa, sweetness, the sought dream
Of warmth and light against your listening skin
And rocked him to a tolerable wisdom.

Two Songs for Doreen

1. *His Song*
Months on, you hold me still;
at dawn, bright-rising, like a hill-
horizon, gentle, kind with rain
and the primroses of April.
I shall never know them again
but still your bright shadow
puts out its shadow, daylight, on
the shadows I lie with now.

2. *Her Song*
A hundred men imagine
love when I drink wine;
and then I begin to think
of your words and mine.
The mountain is silent now
where the snow lies fresh,
and my love like the sloe-
blossom on a blackthorn bush.

An Image from Beckett

In that instant
There was a sea, far off,
As bright as lettuce,

A northern landscape
And a huddle
Of houses along the shore.

Also, I think, a white
Flicker of gulls
And washing hung to dry —

The poignancy of those
Back yards — and the gravedigger
Putting aside his forceps.

Then the hard boards
And darkness once again.
But in that instant

I was struck by the
Sweetness and light,
The sweetness and light,

Imagining what grave
Cities, what lasting monuments,
Given the time.

They will have buried
Our great-grandchildren, and theirs,
Beside us by now

With a subliminal batsqueak
Of reflex lamentation.
Our knuckle bones

Litter the rich earth
Changing, second by second,
To civilizations.

It was good while it lasted,
And if it only lasted
The Biblical span

Required to drop six feet
Through a glitter of wintry light,
There is No One to blame.

Still, I am haunted
By that landscape,
The soft rush of its winds,

The uprightness of its
Utilities and schoolchildren —
To whom in my will,

This, I have left my will.
I hope they have time,
And light enough, to read it.

A Stone Age Figure Far Below

(*for Bill McCormack*)

Through heaving heather, fallen stones
From the wrecked piles of burial cairns
As they fly in over the moors —
Racing about in cloud shadow,
A stone age figure far below
Wildly gesticulating as if
He sees, at last, a sign of life
Or damns them to hell-fires.

When they come with poles, binoculars, whistles,
Blankets and flasks, they will find him dead —
Unkempt, authentic, furnace-eyed
And dead, and his heavy flint hearth-stones
Littered with dung and animal bones;

Or a local resident out for a walk
In tweeds and a hunting hat. 'You must be
Mad,' he will say, 'to suppose this rock
Could accommodate life indefinitely.
Nobody comes here now but me.'

J. P. Donleavy's Dublin

'When you stop to consider
The days spent dreaming of a future
And say then, that was my life.'

For the days are long —
From the first milk van
To the last shout in the night,
An eternity. But the weeks go by
Like birds; and the years, the years
Fly past anti-clockwise
Like clock hands in a bar mirror.

Lives

(for Seamus Heaney)

First time out
I was a torc of gold
And wept tears of the sun.

That was fun
But they buried me
In the earth two thousand years

Till a labourer
Turned me up with a pick
In eighteen fifty-four

And sold me
For tea and sugar
In Newmarket-on-Fergus.

Once I was an oar
But stuck in the shore
To mark the place of a grave

When the lost ship
Sailed away. I thought
Of Ithaca, but soon decayed.

The time that I liked
Best was when
I was a bump of clay

In a Navaho rug,
Put there to mitigate
The too god-like

Perfection of that
Merely human artifact.
I served my maker well —

He lived long
To be struck down in
Denver by an electric shock

The night the lights
Went out in Europe
Never to shine again.

So many lives,
So many things to remember!
I was a stone in Tibet,

A tongue of bark
At the heart of Africa
Growing darker and darker . . .

It all seems
A little unreal now,
Now that I am

An anthropologist
With my own
Credit card, dictaphone,

Army-surplus boots
And a whole boatload
Of photographic equipment.

I know too much
To be anything any more;
And if in the distant

Future someone
Thinks he has once been me
As I am today,

Let him revise
His insolent ontology
Or teach himself to pray.

Rage for Order

Somewhere beyond
The scorched gable end
And the burnt-out
Buses there is a poet indulging his
Wretched rage for order —

Or not as the case
May be, for his
Is a dying art,
An eddy of semantic scruple
In an unstructurable sea.

He is far
From his people,
And the fitful glare
Of his high window is as
Nothing to our scattered glass.

His posture is
Grandiloquent and
Deprecating, like this,
His diet ashes,
His talk of justice and his mother

The rhetorical
Device of a Claudian emperor —
Nero if you prefer,
No mother there;
And this in the face of love, death and the wages of the poor.

If he is silent
It is the silence
Of enforced humility,
If anxious to be heard
It is the anxiety of a last word

When the drums start —
For his is a dying art.
Now watch me
As I make history,
Watch as I tear down

To build up
With a desperate love,
Knowing it cannot be
Long now till I have need of his
Terminal ironies.

As It Should Be

We hunted the mad bastard
Through bog, moorland, rock, to the starlit west
And gunned him down in a blind yard
Between ten sleeping lorries
And an electricity generator.

Let us hear no idle talk
Of the moon in the Yellow River;
The air blows softer since his departure.

Since his tide-burial during school hours
Our children have known no bad dreams.
Their cries echo lightly along the coast.

This is as it should be.
They will thank us for it when they grow up
To a world with method in it.

Consolations of Philosophy

When we start breaking up in the wet darkness
And the rotten boards fall from us, and the ribs
Crack under the constriction of tree-roots
And the seasons slip from the fields unknown to us,

Oh, then there will be the querulous complaining
From citizens who had never dreamt of this —
Who, shaken to the bone in their stout boxes
By the latest bright cars, will not inspect them

And, kept awake by the tremors of new building,
Will not be there to comment. When the broken
Wreath bowls are speckled with rainwater
And the grass grows wild for want of a caretaker,

There will be time to live through in the mind
The lives we might have lived, and get them right;
To lie in silence listening to the wind
Mourn for the living through the livelong night.

I Am Raftery

I am Raftery, hesitant and confused among the
loud-voiced graduate students and inter-
changeable instructors; were it not for the
nice wives who do the talking I would have
run out of hope some time ago, and of love.
I have traded-in my 'simplistic maunderings'
for slick imagery and a wry dissimulation.
Death is near, I have come of age, I doubt if
I shall survive another New England winter.
Jameson, plenty of water. Is it empty
pockets I play to? Not on your life;
they ring with a bright imperious music —
two seminars a week and my own place reserved
in the record library, look at me now,
my back to the wall, taking my cue from
a grinning disc-jockey between commercials.

Beyond Howth Head

(*for Jeremy Lewis*)

The wind that blows these words to you
bangs nightly off the black-and-blue
Atlantic, hammering in its haste
dark doors of the declining west
whose rock-built houses year by year
collapse, whose children disappear
(no homespun cottage industries'
embroidered cloths will patch up these

lost townlands on the crumbling shores
of Europe); shivers the dim stars
in rainwater, and spins a single
garage sign behind the shingle.
Fresh from Long Island or Cape Cod
night music finds the lightning rod
of young girls coming from a dance
(you thumbs a lift and takes your chance)

and shakes the radio sets that play
from Carraroe to Dublin Bay
where, bored to tears by Telefís,
vox populi vox Dei, we reach
with twinkling importunity
for good news on the BBC,
our heliotropic Birnam Wood
reflecting an old gratitude.

What can the elders say to this?
The young must kiss and then must kiss
and so by this declension fall
to write the writing on the wall.
A little learning in a parked
Volkswagen torches down the dark
and soon disperses tired belief
with an empiric *joie de vivre*.

The pros outweigh the cons that glow
from Beckett's bleak reductio —
and who would trade self-knowledge for
a prelapsarian metaphor,
love-play of the ironic conscience
for a prescriptive innocence?
'Lewde libertie', whose midnight work
disturbed the peace of Co. Cork

and fired Kilcolman's windows when
the flower of Ireland looked to Spain,
come and inspire us once again!
But take a form that sheds for love
that prim conventual disdain
the world beyond knows nothing of;
and flash, an *aisling*, through the dawn
where Yeats's hill-men still break stone.

The writing on the wall, we know,
elsewhere was written long ago.
We fumble with the matches while
the hebona behind the smile
of grammar gets its brisk forensic
smack in the *realpolitik*
and the old fiery instincts dim
in the cool courts of academe —

leaving us, Jeremy, to flick
blank pages of an empty book
where exponential futures lie
wide to the runways and the sky;
to spin celestial globes of words
over a foaming pint in Ward's,
victims of our own linear thought
(though 'booze is bourgeois, pot is not')

rehearsing for the *fin de siècle*
gruff Jeremiads to redirect
lost youth into the knacker's yard
of humanistic self-regard;
to praise what will be taken from us,
the memory of Dylan Thomas,
and sign off with a pompous pen
from Seaford or from Cushendun.

I woke this morning (March) to hear
church bells of Monkstown through the roar
of waves round the Martello tower
and thought of the lost swans of Lir
when Kemoc rang the Christian bell
to crack a fourth-dimensional
world picture, never known again,
and changed them back to girls and men.

It calls as oddly through the wild
eviscerations of the troubled
waters between us and North Wales
where Lycid's ghost for ever sails
(unbosomings of seaweed, wrack,
industrial bile, a boot from Blackpool,
contraceptives deftly tied
with best regards from Merseyside)

and tinkles with as blithe a sense
of man's cosmic significance
who wrote his world from broken stone,
installed his word-God on the throne
and placed, in Co. Clare, a sign:
'Stop here and see the sun go down'.
Meanwhile, for a word's sake, the plastic
bombs go off around Belfast;

from the unquiet Cyclades
a Greek poet consults the skies
where sleepless, cold, computed stars
in random sequence light the bars;
and everywhere the ground is thick
with the dead sparrows rhetoric
demands as fictive sacrifice
to prove its substance in our eyes.

Roaring, its ten-lane highways pitch
their naked bodies in the ditch
where once Molloy, uncycled, heard
thin cries of a surviving bird;
and Washington, its grisly aim
to render the whole earth the same,
sends the B-52's to make it
safe for Chase and the stock market.

Spring lights the country; from a thousand
dusty corners, house by house,
from under beds and vacuum cleaners,
empty Calor Gas containers,
bread bins, car seats, crates of stout,
the first flies cry to be let out,
to cruise a kitchen, find a door
and die clean in the open air

whose smokeless clarity distils
a chisel's echo in the hills
as if some Noah, weather-wise,
could read a deluge in clear skies.
But nothing ruffles the wind's breath —
this peace is the great peace of death
or *l'outre-tombe*; make no noise,
the foxes have quit Clonmacnoise.

I too, uncycled, might exchange,
since 'we are changed by what we change',
my forkful of the general mess
for hazelnuts and watercress
like one of those old hermits who,
less virtuous than some, withdrew
from the world-circles lovers make
to a small island in a lake.

Chomēi at Tōyama, his blanket
hemp, his character a rank
not-to-be-trusted river mist,
events in Kyōto all grist
to the mill of a harsh irony,
since we are seen by what we see;
Thoreau like ice among the trees
and Spenser, 'farre from enemies',

might serve as models for a while
but to return in greater style.
Centripetal, the hot world draws
its children in with loving paws
from rock and heather, rain and sleet
with only Calor Gas for heat
and spins them at the centre where
they have no time to know despair

but, without final purpose, must
'accept the universe' on trust
and offer to a phantom future
blood and bones in forfeiture —
each one, his poor loaf on the sea,
monstrous before posterity,
our afterlives a coming true
of perfect worlds we never knew.

The light that left you streaks the walls
of Georgian houses, pubs, cathedrals,
coasters moored below Butt Bridge
and old men at the water's edge
where Anna Livia, breathing free,
weeps silently into the sea,
her tiny sorrows mingling with
the wandering waters of the earth.

And here I close; for look, across
dark waves where bell-buoys dimly toss
the Baily winks beyond Howth Head
and sleep calls from the silent bed;
while the moon drags her kindred stones
among the rocks and the strict bones
of the drowned, and I put out the light
on shadows of the encroaching night.

Afterlives

(for James Simmons)

1.
I wake in a dark flat
To the soft roar of the world.
Pigeons neck on the white
Roofs as I draw the curtains
And look out over London
Rain-fresh in the morning light.

This is our element, the bright
Reason on which we rely
For the long-term solutions.
The orators yap, and guns
Go off in a back street;
But the faith does not die

That in our time these things
Will amaze the literate children
In their non-sectarian schools
And the dark places be
Ablaze with love and poetry
When the power of good prevails.

What middle-class shits we are
To imagine for one second
That our privileged ideals
Are divine wisdom, and the dim
Forms that kneel at noon
In the city not ourselves.

2.

I am going home by sea
For the first time in years.
Somebody thumbs a guitar
On the dark deck, while a gull
Dreams at the masthead,
The moon-splashed waves exult.

At dawn the ship trembles, turns
In a wide arc to back
Shuddering up the grey lough
Past lightship and buoy,
Slipway and dry dock
Where a naked bulb burns;

And I step ashore in a fine rain
To a city so changed
By five years of war
I scarcely recognize
The places I grew up in,
The faces that try to explain.

But the hills are still the same
Grey-blue above Belfast.
Perhaps if I'd stayed behind
And lived it bomb by bomb
I might have grown up at last
And learnt what is meant by home.

Leaves

The prisoners of infinite choice
Have built their house
In a field below the wood
And are at peace.

It is autumn, and dead leaves
On their way to the river
Scratch like birds at the windows
Or tick on the road.

Somewhere there is an afterlife
Of dead leaves,
A stadium filled with an infinite
Rustling and sighing.

Somewhere in the heaven
Of lost futures
The lives we might have led
Have found their own fulfilment.

Homage to Malcolm Lowry

For gear your typewriter and an old rugby boot,
The voyage started, clearly, when you were born
That danced those empty bottles; when you set out
On a round-the-cosmos trip with the furious Muse
Or lay sweating on a hotel bed in Vera Cruz,
Did you not think you had left that pool astern
Where a soul might bathe and be clean or slake its drought?
In any case, your deportment in those seas
Was faultless. Lightning-blind, you, tempest-torn
At the poles of our condition, did not confuse
The Gates of Ivory with the Gates of Horn.

A Curious Ghost

While your widow clatters water into a kettle
You lie at peace in your southern grave —
A sea captain who died at sea, almost.
Lost voyager, what would you think of me,
Husband of your fair daughter but impractical?
You stare from the mantelpiece, a curious ghost
In your peaked cap, as we sit down to tea.
The bungalows still signal to the sea,
Rain wanders the golf-course as in your day,
The river still flows past the distillery
And a watery sun shines on Portballintrae.

I think we would have had a lot in common —
Alcohol and the love of one woman
Certainly; but I failed the eyesight test
When I tried for the Merchant Navy,
And lapsed into this lyric lunacy.
When you lost your balance like Li Po
They found unfinished poems in your sea-chest.

The Snow Party

(for Louis Asekoff)

Bashō, coming
To the city of Nagoya,
Is asked to a snow party.

There is a tinkling of china
And tea into china;
There are introductions.

Then everyone
Crowds to the window
To watch the falling snow.

Snow is falling on Nagoya
And farther south
On the tiles of Kyōto;

Eastward, beyond Irago,
It is falling
Like leaves on the cold sea.

Elsewhere they are burning
Witches and heretics
In the boiling squares,

Thousands have died since dawn
In the service
Of barbarous kings;

But there is silence
In the houses of Nagoya
And the hills of Ise.

The Last of the Fire Kings

I want to be
Like the man who descends
At two milk churns

With a bulging
String bag and vanishes
Where the lane turns,

Or the man
Who drops at night
From a moving train

And strikes out over the fields
Where fireflies glow,
Not knowing a word of the language.

Either way, I am
Through with history —
Who lives by the sword

Dies by the sword.
Last of the fire kings, I shall
Break with tradition and

Die by my own hand
Rather than perpetuate
The barbarous cycle.

Five years I have reigned
During which time
I have lain awake each night

And prowled by day
In the sacred grove
For fear of the usurper,

Perfecting my cold dream
Of a place out of time,
A palace of porcelain

Where the frugivorous
Inheritors recline
In their rich fabrics
Far from the sea.

But the fire-loving
People, rightly perhaps,
Will not countenance this,

Demanding that I inhabit,
Like them, a world of
Sirens, bin-lids
And bricked-up windows —

Not to release them
From the ancient curse
But to die their creature and be thankful.

The Antigone Riddle

Elocution, logic, political science,
Antibiotics, do-it-yourself,
And a plover flops in his oil slick.

Shy minerals contract at the sound of his voice,
Cod point in silence when his bombers pass,
And the windfall waits
In silence for his departure
Before it drops in
Silence to the long grass.

Gipsies

I have watched the dark police
rocking your caravans
to wreck the crockery
and wry thoughts of peace
you keep there on waste
ground beside motorways
where the snow lies late
(all this on television)
and am ashamed; fed,
clothed, housed and ashamed.
You might be interested
to hear, though, that on
stormy nights our strong
double glazing groans with
foreknowledge of death,
the fridge with a great wound,
and not surprised to know
the fate you have so long
endured is ours also.
The cars are piling up.
I listen to the wind
and file receipts; the heap
of scrap metal in my
garden grows daily.

The Mayo Tao

I have abandoned the dream kitchens for a low fire
and a prescriptive literature of the spirit;
a storm snores on the desolate sea.
The nearest shop is four miles away —
when I walk there through the shambles
of the morning for tea and firelighters
the mountain paces me in a snow-lit silence.
My days are spent in conversation
with deer and blackbirds;
at night fox and badger gather at my door.
I have stood for hours
watching a salmon doze in the tea-gold dark,
for months listening to the sob story
of a stone in the road, the best,
most monotonous sob story I have ever heard.

I am an expert on frost crystals
and the silence of crickets, a confidant
of the stinking shore, the stars in the mud —
there is an immanence in these things
which drives me, despite my scepticism,
almost to the point of speech,
like sunlight cleaving the lake mist at morning
or when tepid water
runs cold at last from the tap.

I have been working for years
on a four-line poem
about the life of a leaf;
I think it might come out right this winter.

The Apotheosis of Tins

Having spent the night in a sewer of precognition
consoled by moon-glow, air-chuckle
and the retarded pathos of mackerel,
we wake among shoelaces and white wood
to a raw wind and the cries of gulls.
Deprived of use, we are safe now
from the historical nightmare
and may give our attention at last
to things of the spirit,
noticing for example the consanguinity
of sand and stone, how they are thicker than water.

This is the terminal democracy of hatbox and crab,
of wine and Windolene; it is always rush-hour.
If we have learnt one thing from our desertion
by the sour smudge on the horizon,
from the erosion of labels,
it is the value of self-definition.
No one, not even the pensioner
whose shadow strains above us after
dawn and before dusk, will have our trust;
we resist your patronage, your reflective leisure.

Promoted artifacts by the dereliction of our creator
and greater now than the sum of his skills,
we shall be with you while there are beaches.
Imperishable by-products of the perishable will,
we shall lie like skulls in the hands
of soliloquists; the longest queues
in the science museum will form at our last homes
saying think now, what saintly devotion
to the notion
of permanence in the flux of sensation
and crisis, perhaps we can learn from them.

Light Music

1. *Architecture*
Twinkletoes in the ballroom,
light music in space.

2. *History*
The blinking puddles
reflected day-long
twilights of misery.

Smoke rose in silence
to the low sky.

3. *Negatives*
Gulls in a rain-dark cornfield,
crows on a sunlit sea.

4. *North Sea*
The terminal light of beaches,
pebbles speckled with oil;
old tins at the tide-line
where a gull blinks on a pole.

5. *Please*
I built my house
in a forest far
from the venal roar.

Somebody please
beat a path
to my door.

6. *Rory*
He leads me into
a grainy twilight
of old photographs.

The sun is behind us,
his shadow in mine.

7. *Spring*
Dawn light pearling the branches,
petals freckling the mould,
and the stereo birds.

It is time for the nymphs,
a glimpse of skin in the woods.

8. *Twilight*
A stone at the roadside
watches snow fall
on the silent gate-lodge.

Later the gate shuts
with a clanging of bars;
the stone is one with the stars.

9. *Mozart*
The Clarinet Concerto
in A, K.622,
the second movement.

Turn it up
so they can hear
on the other planets!

10. *Morphology*
Beans and foetuses,
brains and cauliflowers;
in a shaft of sunlight
a dust of stars.

11. *Enter*
The steel regrets the lock,
a word will open the rock,
the wood awaits your knock.

12. *Dawn Moon*
A slip of soap in the sky,
I do my faint shining
in the golden dawn
of an alien dispensation.

13. *Elpenor*
Edacity in the palace
and in the sandy timber
of my crumbling monument,
its lengthening shadow
pointing towards home.

14. *East Strand*
Tedium of sand and sea —
then at the white rocks
a little girl fleetingly,
blazer and ankle-socks.

Sand drifts from a rock
like driven snow, and one
gull attentive to my walk
obscures the winter sun.

15. *Absence*
I wake at night
in a house white
with moonlight.

Somewhere my son,
his vigour, his laughter;
somewhere my daughter.

16. *Waterfront*
I cover the waterfront,
its fish and chips,
while better men
go down to the sea in ships.

17. *Outside*
The sculpted bird-bath and the pine,
the post-box and the telephone line.

18. *Donegal*
The vast clouds migrate
above turf-stacks
and a dangling gate.

A tiny bike squeaks
into the wind.

19. *Smoke*
Vertical, horizontal,
the smoke of last resorts.

20. *Rogue Leaf*
Believe it or not
I hung on all winter
outfacing wind and snow.

Now that spring
comes and the birds sing
I am letting go.

21. *Revelation*
A colour the fish know
we do not know so
long have we been ashore.

When that colour
shines in the rainbow
there will be no more sea.

22. *Flying*
A wand of sunlight
touches the rush-hour
like the finger of heaven.

A land of cumulus
seen from above
is the life to come.

Nostalgias

The chair squeaks in a high wind,
Rain falls from its branches;
The kettle yearns for the mountain,
The soap for the sea.
In a tiny stone church
On a desolate headland
A lost tribe is singing 'Abide with Me'.

Ford Manor

Even on the quietest days the distant
growl of cars remains persistent,
reaching us in this airy box
we share with the fieldmouse and the fox;
but she drifts in maternity blouses
among crack-paned greenhouses —
a smiling Muse come back to life,
part child, part mother, and part wife.

Even on the calmest nights the fitful
prowl of planes is seldom still
where Gatwick tilts to guide them home
from Tokyo, New York or Rome;
yet even today the earth disposes
bluebells, roses and primroses,
the dawn throat-whistle of a thrush
deep in the dripping lilac bush.

Penshurst Place

The bright drop quivering on a thorn
in the rich silence after rain,
lute music in the orchard aisles,
the paths ablaze with daffodils,
intrigue and venery in the air
à l'ombre des jeunes filles en fleurs,
the iron hand and the velvet glove —
come live with me and be my love.

A pearl face, numinously bright,
shining in silence of the night,
a muffled crash of smouldering logs,
bad dreams of courtiers and of dogs,
the Spanish ships around Kinsale,
the screech-owl and the nightingale,
the falcon and the turtle dove —
come live with me and be my love.

How to Live

(Horace, *Odes* I, ii)
Don't waste your time, Leuconoë, living in fear and hope
of the imprevisible future; forget the horoscope.
Accept whatever happens. Whether the gods allow
us fifty winters more or drop us at this one now
which flings the high Tyrrhenian waves on the stone piers,
decant your wine; the days are more fun than the years
which pass us by while we discuss them. Act with zest
one day at a time, and never mind the rest.

Ovid in Love

1. (*Amores* I, v)
The day being humid and my head
heavy, I stretched out on a bed.
The open window to the right
reflected woodland-watery light,
a keyed-up silence as of dawn
or dusk, the vibrant and uncertain
hour when a brave girl might undress
and caper naked on the grass.
You entered in a muslin gown,
bare-footed, your fine braids undone,
a fabled goddess with an air
as if in heat yet debonair.
Aroused, I grabbed and roughly tore
until your gown squirmed on the floor.
At first you resisted, but like one
who knows resistance is in vain;
and, when you stood revealed, my eyes
feasted on shoulders, breasts and thighs.
I held you hard and down you slid
beside me, as we knew you would.
Oh, come to me again as then you did!

2. (*Amores* II, xi)
This strange sea-going craze began
with Jason; pine from Pelion,
weathered and shaped, was first to brave
the whirlpool and the whistling wave.
I wish the *Argo* had gone down
and seafaring remained unknown;
for now Corinna, scornful of
her safety and my vigilant love,
intends to tempt the winds and go
cruising among the treacherous blue

waters where no shade-giving ilex,
temple or marble pavement breaks
with its enlightened artistry
the harsh monotony of the sea.
Walk on the beach where you can hear
the whorled conch whisper in your ear;
dance in the foam, but never trust
the water higher than your waist.
I'm serious. Listen to those with real
experience of life under sail —
believe their frightening anecdotes
of rocks and gales and splintered boats.
You won't be able to change your mind
when once your ship is far from land
and the most sanguine seamen cease
their banter as the waves increase.
How pale you'd grow if Triton made
the waters crash around your head —
so much more comfortable ashore
reading, or practising the lyre!
Still, if you're quite determined, God
preserve you from a watery bed:
Nereus' nymphs would be disgraced
if my Corinna should be lost.
Think of me when your shrinking craft
is a poignant pinpoint in the afternoon, and again when homeward bound
with canvas straining in the wind.
I'll be the first one at the dock
to meet the ship that brings you back;
I'll carry you ashore and burn
thank-offerings for your safe return.
Right there we'll make a bed of sand,
a table of a sand-dune, and
over the wine you'll give a vivid
sketch of the perils you survived —

how, faced with a tempestuous sea,
you hung on tight and thought of me!
Make it up if you like, as I
invent this pleasant fantasy . . .

The Mute Phenomena

(after Nerval)

Your great mistake is to disregard the satire
Bandied among the mute phenomena.
Be strong if you must, your brisk hegemony
Means fuck-all to the somnolent sunflower
Or the extinct volcano. What do you know
Of the revolutionary theories advanced
By turnips, or the sex-life of cutlery?
Everything is susceptible, Pythagoras said so.

An ordinary common-or-garden brick wall, the kind
For talking to or banging your head on,
Resents your politics and bad draughtsmanship.
God is alive and lives under a stone;
Already in a lost hub-cap is conceived
The ideal society which will replace our own.

from *The Drunken Barge*

(*after Rimbaud*)

Hearing the thunder of the intransitive weirs
I felt my guiding tow-ropes slacken; crazed
Apaches, yelping, nailed my gondoliers
Naked to stakes where fiery feathers blazed.

Not that I cared. Relieved of the dull weight
Of cautious crew and inventoried cargo —
Phlegmatic flax, quotidian grain — I let
The current carry me where I chose to go.

Deaf to the furious whisperings of the sand,
My heart rose to a tidal detonation;
Peninsulas, ripped screaming from the land,
Crashed in a stinging mist of exultation.

Storms smiled on my salt sea-morning sleep.
I danced, light as a cork, nine nights or more
Upon the intractable, man-trundling deep,
Contemptuous of the blinking lights ashore.

Juice of the oceans, tart as unripe fruit,
Burst on my spruce boards in tongues of brine
That tore the spinning binnacle from its root,
Rinsing the curdled puke and the blue wine;

And then I was submerged in a sea-poem
Infused with milky stars, gulped the profound
Viridian where, disconsolate and calm,
Rapt faces drifted past of the long drowned.

I saw skies split by lightning, granite waves
Shaking the earth, ambrosial dusks and dawns,
Day risen aloft, a multitude of doves —
And, with the naked eye, vouchsafed visions;

Watched horizontal orbs, like spotlights trained
On some barbaric tragedy of old,
Direct their peacock rays along the sun-blind
Waters, and heard their clattering slats unfold.

I dreamed the emerald snow of dazzling chasms,
Kisses ascending to the eyes of the sea,
The circulation of mysterious plasms
And mornings loud with phosphorous harmony.

Trembling, I heard volcanic eructations,
A thrash of behemoths; but now, my ears
Weary of this crescendo of sensations,
I thought of Europe and her ancient towers.

Delirious capes! Strewn archipelagoes!
Do you nurse there in your galactic foam
The glistening bodies of obscure flamingoes
Tranced in a prescience of the life to come?

Europe of cloud canals, I would ask of you
Only the pond where, on a quiet evening,
An only child launches a toy canoe
As frail and pitiful as a moth in spring.

The Banished Gods

Paros, far-shining star of dark-blue earth,
   Reverts to the sea its mother.
      The tiny particles,
   Rose, quartz and amethyst,
Panic into the warm brine together.

Near the headwaters of the longest river
   There is a forest clearing,
      A dank, misty place
   Where light stands in columns
And birds sing with a noise like paper tearing.

Far from land, far from the trade routes,
   In an unbroken dream-time
      Of penguin and whale
   The seas sigh to themselves
Reliving the days before the days of sail.

Down a dark lane at the back of beyond
   A farm dog lies by a dead fire
      Dreaming of nothing
   While a window goes slowly grey
Brightening a laid table and hung clothing.

Where the wires end the moor seethes in silence,
   Scattered with scree, primroses,
      Feathers and faeces;
   It shelters the hawk and hears
In dreams the forlorn cries of lost species.

It is here that the banished gods are in hiding,
   Here they sit out the centuries
      In stone, water
   And the hearts of trees,
Lost in a reverie of their own natures —

Of zero-growth economics and seasonal change
In a world without cars, computers
Or nuclear skies,
Where thought is a fondling of stones
And wisdom a five-minute silence at moonrise.

A Refusal to Mourn

He lived in a small farmhouse
At the edge of a new estate.
The trim gardens crept
To his door, and car engines
Woke him before dawn
On dark winter mornings.

All day there was silence
In the bright house. The clock
Ticked on the kitchen shelf,
Cinders moved in the grate,
And a warm briar gurgled
When the old man talked to himself;

But the doorbell seldom rang
After the milkman went,
And if a shirt-hanger
Knocked in an open wardrobe
That was a strange event
To be pondered on for hours

While the wind thrashed about
In the back garden, raking
The roof of the henhouse,
And swept clouds and gulls
Eastwards over the lough
With its flap of tiny sails.

Once a week he would visit
An old shipyard crony,
Inching down to the road
And the blue country bus
To sit and watch sun-dappled
Branches whacking the windows

While the long evening shed
Weak light in his empty house,
On the photographs of his dead
Wife and their six children
And the Missions to Seamen angel
In flight above the bed.

'I'm not long for this world,'
Said he on our last evening,
'I'll not last the winter,'
And grinned, straining to hear
Whatever reply I made;
And died the following year.

In time the astringent rain
Of those parts will clean
The words from his gravestone
In the crowded cemetery
That overlooks the sea
And his name be mud once again

And his boilers lie like tombs
In the mud of the sea bed
Till the next Ice Age comes
And the earth he inherited
Is gone like Neanderthal Man
And no records remain.

But the secret bred in the bone
On the dawn strand survives
In other times and lives,
Persisting for the unborn
Like a claw-print in concrete
After the bird has flown.

A Disused Shed in Co. Wexford

Let them not forget us, the weak souls among the asphodels.
— Seferis, *Mythistorema*

(*for J. G. Farrell*)

Even now there are places where a thought might grow —
Peruvian mines, worked out and abandoned
To a slow clock of condensation,
An echo trapped for ever, and a flutter
Of wild flowers in the lift-shaft,
Indian compounds where the wind dances
And a door bangs with diminished confidence,
Lime crevices behind rippling rain-barrels,
Dog corners for bone burials;
And in a disused shed in Co. Wexford,

Deep in the grounds of a burnt-out hotel,
Among the bathtubs and the washbasins
A thousand mushrooms crowd to a keyhole.
This is the one star in their firmament
Or frames a star within a star.
What should they do there but desire?
So many days beyond the rhododendrons
With the world waltzing in its bowl of cloud,
They have learnt patience and silence
Listening to the rooks querulous in the high wood.

They have been waiting for us in a foetor
Of vegetable sweat since civil war days,
Since the gravel-crunching, interminable departure
Of the expropriated mycologist.
He never came back, and light since then
Is a keyhole rusting gently after rain.
Spiders have spun, flies dusted to mildew
And once a day, perhaps, they have heard something —
A trickle of masonry, a shout from the blue
Or a lorry changing gear at the end of the lane.

There have been deaths, the pale flesh flaking
Into the earth that nourished it;
And nightmares, born of these and the grim
Dominion of stale air and rank moisture.
Those nearest the door grow strong —
'Elbow room! Elbow room!'
The rest, dim in a twilight of crumbling
Utensils and broken pitchers, groaning
For their deliverance, have been so long
Expectant that there is left only the posture.

A half century, without visitors, in the dark —
Poor preparation for the cracking lock
And creak of hinges; magi, moonmen,
Powdery prisoners of the old regime,
Web-throated, stalked like triffids, racked by drought
And insomnia, only the ghost of a scream
At the flash-bulb firing-squad we wake them with
Shows there is life yet in their feverish forms.
Grown beyond nature now, soft food for worms,
They lift frail heads in gravity and good faith.

They are begging us, you see, in their wordless way,
To do something, to speak on their behalf
Or at least not to close the door again.
Lost people of Treblinka and Pompeii!
'Save us, save us,' they seem to say,
'Let the god not abandon us
Who have come so far in darkness and in pain.
We too had our lives to live.
You with your light meter and relaxed itinerary,
Let not our naive labours have been in vain!'

Autobiographies

(*for Maurice Leitch*)

1. *The Home Front*
While the frozen armies trembled
At the gates of Leningrad
They took me home in a taxi
And laid me in my cot,
And there I slept again
With siren and black-out;

And slept under the stairs
Beside the light meter
When bombs fell on the city;
So I never saw the sky
Ablaze with a fiery glow,
Searchlights roaming the stars.

But I do remember one time
(I must have been four then)
Being held up to the window
For a victory parade —
Soldiers, sailors and airmen
Lining the Antrim Road;

And, later, hide-and-seek
Among the air-raid shelters,
The last ration coupons,
Oranges and bananas,
Forage caps and badges
And packets of Lucky Strike.

Gracie Fields on the radio!
Americans in the art-deco
Milk bars! The released Jews
Blinking in shocked sunlight . . .
A male child in a garden
Clutching the *Empire News*.

2. *The Lost Girls*

'In ancient shadows and twilights
Where childhood had strayed'
I ran round in the playground
Of Skegoneil Primary School
During the lunch break,
Pretending to be a plane.

For months I would dawdle home
At a respectful distance
Behind the teacher's daughter,
Eileen Boyd, who lived
In a house whose back garden
Was visible from my window.

I watched her on summer evenings,
A white dress picking flowers,
Her light, graceful figure
Luminous and remote.
We never exchanged greetings;
Her house was bigger than ours.

She married an older man
And went to live in Kenya.
Perhaps she is there still
Complaining about the 'natives'.
It would be nice to know;
But who can re-live their lives?

Eileen Boyd, Hazel and Heather
Thompson, Patricia King —
The lost girls in a ring
On a shadowy school playground
Like the nymphs dancing together
In the *Allegory of Spring*.

3. *The Last Resort*
Salad-and-sand sandwiches
And dead gulls on the beach;
Ice-cream in the Arcadia,
Rain lashing the windows;
Dull days in the harbour,
Sunday mornings in church.

One hot July fortnight
In the Strandmore Hotel
I watched the maid climb
The stairs, and went to my room
Quivering with excitement,
Aroused for the first time.

Years later, the same dim
Resort has grown dimmer
As if some centrifugal
Force, summer by summer,
Has moved it ever farther
From an imagined centre.

The guest-houses are crazy
For custom; but the risen
People are playing football
On the sands of Tenerife,
Far from the unrelaxing
Scenes of sectarian strife.

Yet the place really existed
And still can crack a smile
Should a sunbeam pick out
Your grimy plastic cup
And consecrate your vile
Bun with its parting light.

4. *The Bicycle*

There was a bicycle, a fine
Raleigh with five gears
And racing handlebars.
It stood at the front door
Begging to be mounted;
The frame shone in the sun.

I became like a character
In *The Third Policeman*, half
Human, half bike, my life
A series of dips and ridges,
Happiness a free-wheeling
Past fragrant hawthorn hedges.

Cape and sou'wester streamed
With rain as I rode to school
Side-tracking the bus routes.
Night after night I dreamed
Of valves, pumps, sprockets,
Reflectors and repair kits.

Soon there were long rides
In the country, wet weekends
Playing cards in the kitchens
Of mountain youth hostels,
Day-runs to Monaghan,
Rough and exotic roads.

It went with me to Dublin
Where I sold it the same winter;
But its wheels still sing
In the memory, stars that turn
About an eternal centre,
The bright spokes glittering.

Going Home

(for John Hewitt)

I am saying goodbye to the trees,
The beech, the cedar, the elm,
The mild woods of these parts
Misted with car exhaust
And sawdust, and the last
Gasps of the poisoned nymphs.

I have watched girls walking
And children playing under
Lilac and rhododendron,
And me flicking my ash
Into the rose bushes
As if I owned the place;

As if the trees responded
To my ignorant admiration
Before dawn when the branches
Glitter at first light,
Or later on when the finches
Disappear for the night;

And often thought if I lived
Long enough in this house
I would turn into a tree
Like somebody in Ovid
— A small tree certainly
But a tree nevertheless —

Perhaps befriend the oak,
The chestnut and the yew,
Become a home for birds,
A shelter for the nymphs,
And gaze out over the downs
As if I belonged here too.

But where I am going the trees
Are few and far between.
No richly forested slopes,
Not for a long time,
And few winking woodlands.
There are no nymphs to be seen.

Out there you would look in vain
For a rose-bush; but find,
Rooted in stony ground,
A last stubborn growth
Battered by constant rain
And twisted by the sea-wind

With nothing to recommend it
But its harsh tenacity
Between the blinding windows
And the forests of the sea,
As if its very existence
Were a reason to continue.

Crone, crow, scarecrow,
Its worn fingers scrabbling
At a torn sky, it stands
On the edge of everything
Like a burnt-out angel
Raising petitionary hands.

Grotesque by day, at twilight
An almost tragic figure
Of anguish and despair,
It merges into the funeral
Cloud-continent of night
As if it belongs there.

The Chinese Restaurant in Portrush

Before the first visitor comes the spring
Softening the sharp air of the coast
In time for the first seasonal 'invasion'.
Today the place is as it might have been,
Gentle and almost hospitable. A girl
Strides past the Northern Counties Hotel,
Light-footed, swinging a book-bag,
And the doors that were shut all winter
Against the north wind and the sea-mist
Lie open to the street, where one
By one the gulls go window-shopping
And an old wolfhound dozes in the sun.

While I sit with my paper and prawn chow mein
Under a framed photograph of Hong Kong
The proprietor of the Chinese restaurant
Stands at the door as if the world were young,
Watching the first yacht hoist a sail
— An ideogram on sea-cloud — and the light
Of heaven upon the hills of Donegal;
And whistles a little tune, dreaming of home.

Old Roscoff

(after Corbière)

Bolt-hole of brigandage, old keep
Of piracy, the ocean booms
On membranes of your granite sleep
And thunders in your brackish dreams.
Snore the sea and snore the sky,
Snore the foghorn in your ears;
Sleep with your one watchful eye
On England these three hundred years.

Sleep, old hulk for ever anchored
Where the wild goose and cormorant,
Your elegists, cry to the barred
And salt-laced shutters on the front.
Sleep, old whore of the homing seamen
Heady with wind and wine; no more
Will the hot gold subdue your women
As a spring tide engulfs your shore.

Sleep in the dunes beneath the grey
Gunmetal sky; the flags are gone.
No grape-shot now will ricochet
From spire and belfry. Pungent dawn
Will find your children dream-ensnared
By the great days when giants shook
The timbered piers and cynosured
The streets and market-place; but look —

Your cannon, swept by wintry rain,
Lie prostrate on their beds of mud.
Their mouths will never speak again;
They sleep the long sleep of the dead,
Their only roar the adenoidal
Echoes of equinoctial snores
From the cold muzzles pointing still
At England, trailing a few wild flowers.

Camus in Ulster

Deprived though we were of your climatic privileges
And raised in a northern land of rain and haze
We too knew the cherished foe, the blaze
Of headlights on a coast road, the cicadas
Chattering like watches in our sodden hedges;
Yet never imagined the plague to come,
So long had it slept there in the mind —
The police charge and the stricken home,
An old blues number playing to the plague wind.

North Wind: Portrush

I shall never forget the wind
On this benighted coast.
It works itself into the mind
Like the high keen of a lost
Lear-spirit in agony
Condemned for eternity

To wander cliff and cove
Without comfort, without love.
It whistles off the stars
And the existential, stark
Face of the cosmic dark.
We crouch to roaring fires.

Yet there are mornings when,
Even in midwinter, sunlight
Flares, and a rare stillness
Lies upon roof and garden —
Each object eldritch-bright,
The sea scarred but at peace.

Then, from the ship we say
Is the lit town where we live
(Our whiskey-and-forecast world),
A smaller ship that sheltered
All night in the restless bay
Will weigh anchor and leave.

What did they think of us
During their brief sojourn?
A string of lights on the prom
Dancing mad in the storm —
Who lives in such a place?
And will they ever return?

But the shops open at nine
As they have always done,
The wrapped-up bourgeoisie
Hardened by wind and sea.
The newspapers are late
But the milk shines in its crate.

Everything swept so clean
By tempest, wind and rain!
Elated, you might believe
That this was the first day —
A false sense of reprieve,
For the climate is here to stay.

So best prepare for the worst
That chaos and old night
Can do to us; were we not
Raised on such expectations,
Our hearts starred with frost
Through countless generations?

Elsewhere the olive grove,
Naked lunch in the grass,
Poppies and parasols,
Blue skies and mythic love.
Here only the stricken souls
No springtime can release.

Prospero and his people never
Came to these stormy parts;
Few do who have the choice.
Yet, blasting the subtler arts,
That weird, plaintive voice
Sings now and for ever.

Greta

The old motorbike she was
The first woman in those
Parts to ride — a noble
Norton — disintegrates
With rusty iron gates
In some abandoned stable;

But lives in sepia shades
Where an emancipated
Country schoolteacher
Of nineteen thirty-eight
Grins from her frame before
Broaching the mountain roads.

Forty years later she
Shakes slack on the fire
To douse it while she goes
Into Bushmills to buy
Groceries and newspaper
And exchange courtesies.

Then back to a pot of tea
And the early-evening news
(Some fresh atrocity);
Washes up to the sound
Of a chat-show, one phrase
Of Bach going round and round

In her head as she stares
Out at the wintry moon
And thinks of her daughters
So very far away —
Although the telephone
Makes nonsense of that today.

Out there beyond the edge
Of the golf-course tosses
The ghost of the *Girona*,
Flagship of the Armada —
History; does the knowledge
Alter the world she sees?

Or do her thoughts travel
By preference among
Memories of her naval
Husband, thirty years
Drowned, the watercolours
And instruments unstrung?

A tentatively romantic
Figure once, she became
Merely an old lady like
Many another, with
Her favourite programme
And her sustaining faith.

She sits now and watches
Incredulously as some mad
Whippersnapper howls
His love-song and the gulls
Snuggle down on the beaches,
The rooks in the churchyard.

'Songs of Praise'

Tonight, their simple church grown glamorous,
The proud parishioners of the outlying parts
Lift up their hymn-books and their hearts
To please the outside-broadcast cameras.
The darkness deepens; day draws to a close;
A well-bred sixth-former yawns with her nose.

Outside, the hymn dies among rocks and dunes.
Conflicting rhythms of the incurious sea,
Not even contemptuous of these tiny tunes,
Take over where our thin ascriptions fail.
Down there the silence of the laboratory,
Trombone dispatches of the beleaguered whale.

Courtyards in Delft

— Pieter de Hooch, 1659

(*for Gordon Woods*)

Oblique light on the trite, on brick and tile —
Immaculate masonry, and everywhere that
Water tap, that broom and wooden pail
To keep it so. House-proud, the wives
Of artisans pursue their thrifty lives
Among scrubbed yards, modest but adequate.
Foliage is sparse, and clings; no breeze
Ruffles the trim composure of those trees.

No spinet-playing emblematic of
The harmonies and disharmonies of love,
No lewd fish, no fruit, no wide-eyed bird
About to fly its cage while a virgin
Listens to her seducer, mars the chaste
Perfection of the thing and the thing made.
Nothing is random, nothing goes to waste.
We miss the dirty dog, the fiery gin.

That girl with her back to us who waits
For her man to come home for his tea
Will wait till the paint disintegrates
And ruined dikes admit the esurient sea;
Yet this is life too, and the cracked
Outhouse door a verifiable fact
As vividly mnemonic as the sunlit
Railings that front the houses opposite.

I lived there as a boy and know the coal
Glittering in its shed, late-afternoon
Lambency informing the deal table,
The ceiling cradled in a radiant spoon.

I must be lying low in a room there,
A strange child with a taste for verse,
While my hard-nosed companions dream of fire
And sword upon parched veldt and fields of rain-swept gorse.

Rathlin

A long time since the last scream cut short —
Then an unnatural silence; and then
A natural silence, slowly broken
By the shearwater, by the sporadic
Conversation of crickets, the bleak
Reminder of a metaphysical wind.
Ages of this, till the report
Of an outboard motor at the pier
Shatters the dream-time and we land
As if we were the first visitors here.

The whole island a sanctuary where amazed
Oneiric species whistle and chatter,
Evacuating rock-face and cliff-top.
Cerulean distance, an oceanic haze —
Nothing but sea-smoke to the ice-cap
And the odd somnolent freighter.
Bombs doze in the housing estates
But here they are through with history —
Custodians of a lone light which repeats
One simple statement to the turbulent sea.

A long time since the unspeakable violence —
Since Somhairle Buí, powerless on the mainland,
Heard the screams of the Rathlin women
Borne to him, seconds later, upon the wind.
Only the cry of the shearwater
And the roar of the outboard motor
Disturb the singular peace. Spray-blind,
We leave here the infancy of the race,
Unsure among the pitching surfaces
Whether the future lies before us or behind.

Derry Morning

The mist clears and the cavities
Glow black in the rubbled city's
Broken mouth. An early crone,
Muse of a fitful revolution
Wasted by the fray, she sees
Her *aisling* falter in the breeze,
Her oak-grove vision hesitate
By empty wharf and city gate.

Here it began, and here at last
It fades into the finite past
Or seems to: clattering shadows whop
Mechanically over pub and shop.
A strangely pastoral silence rules
The shining roofs and murmuring schools;
For this is how the centuries work —
Two steps forward, one step back.

Hard to believe this tranquil place,
Its desolation almost peace,
Was recently a boom-town wild
With expectation, each unscheduled
Incident a measurable
Tremor on the Richter Scale
Of world events, each vibrant scene
Translated to the drizzling screen.

What of the change envisioned here,
The quantum leap from fear to fire?
Smoke from a thousand chimneys strains
One way beneath the returning rains
That shroud the bomb-sites, while the fog
Of time receives the ideologue.
A Russian freighter bound for home
Mourns to the city in its gloom.

Rock Music

The ocean glittered quietly in the moonlight
While heavy metal rocked the discotheques;
Space-age Hondas gurgled half the night,
Fired by the prospect of fortuitous sex.
I sat late at the window, blind with rage,
And listened to the tumult down below,
Trying to concentrate on the printed page
As if such obsolete bumph could save us now.

(Frank Ifield, Clodagh Rodgers, where are you now?
Every night by the window here I sit.
Sandie and Bobby, I still remember you —
As for the Arcadia, though I remember it,
It no longer remembers the uncouth Coke-heads
Who trembled here in nineteen fifty-six
In ice-cream parlours and amusement arcades;
Oddities all, we knew none of the tricks.

Cinema organ, easy listening, swing, doowop, bebop,
Sedate me with your subliminal sublime
And give me that old trashy '50s pop,
Suburban burblings of an earlier time;
The boogie bins bouncing in rotary light,
Give me my toxic shame, mean woman blues,
That old self-pity where, lonesome tonight,
I sit here snarling in my blue suede shoes.)

Next morning, wandering on the strand, I heard
Left-over echoes of the night before
Dwindle to echoes, and a single bird
Drown with a whistle that residual roar.
Rock music started up on every side —
Whisper of algae, click of stone on stone,
A thousand limpets left by the ebb-tide
Unanimous in their silent inquisition.

The Blackbird

One morning in the month of June
I was coming out of this door
And found myself in a garden,
A sanctuary of light and air
Transplanted from the Hesperides,
No sound of machinery anywhere,
When from a bramble bush a hidden
Blackbird suddenly gave tongue,
Its diffident, resilient song
Breaking the silence of the seas.

The Attic

(for John and Evelyn Montague)

Under the night window
  A dockyard fluorescence,
Muse-light on the city,
  A world of heightened sense.

At work in your attic
  Up here under the roof —
Listen, can you hear me
  Turning over a new leaf?

Silent by ticking lamplight
  I stare at the blank spaces,
Reflecting the composure
  Of patient surfaces —

I who know nothing
  Scribbling on the off-chance,
Darkening the white page,
  Cultivating my ignorance.

The Old Snaps

I keep your old snaps in the bottom drawer —
The icons of a more than personal love.
Look, three sisters out of Chekhov
('When will we ever go to Moscow?')
Ranged on the steps of the schoolhouse
Where their mother is head teacher,
Out on the rocks, or holding down their hair
In a high wind on a North Antrim shore.

Later, yourself alone among sand-hills
Striking a slightly fictional pose,
Life-ready and impervious to harm
In your wind-blown school uniform,
While the salt sea air fills
Your young body with ozone
And fine sand trickles into your shoes.
I think I must have known you even then.

We 'went to Moscow', and we will again.
Meanwhile we walk on the strand
And smile as if for the first time
While the children play in the sand.
We have never known a worse winter
But the old snaps are always there,
Framed for ever in your heart and mine
Where no malicious hands can twist or tear.

Everything Is Going To Be All Right

How should I not be glad to contemplate
the clouds clearing beyond the dormer window
and a high tide reflected on the ceiling?
There will be dying, there will be dying,
but there is no need to go into that.
The lines flow from the hand unbidden
and the hidden source is the watchful heart.
The sun rises in spite of everything
and the far cities are beautiful and bright.
I lie here in a riot of sunlight
watching the day break and the clouds flying.
Everything is going to be all right.

Heraclitus on Rivers

Nobody steps into the same river twice.
The same river is never the same
Because that is the nature of water.
Similarly your changing metabolism
Means that you are no longer you.
The cells die, and the precise
Configuration of the heavenly bodies
When she told you she loved you
Will not come again in this lifetime.

You will tell me that you have executed
A monument more lasting than bronze;
But even bronze is perishable.
Your best poem, you know the one I mean,
The very language in which the poem
Was written, and the idea of language,
All these things will pass away in time.

The Sea in Winter

(*for Desmond O'Grady*)

Desmond, what of the blue nights,
the ultramarines and violets
of your white island in the south,
'far-shining star of dark-blue earth',
and the boat-lights in the tiny port
where we drank so much retsina?
Up here where the air is thinner
in a draughty bungalow in Portstewart

beside my 'distant northern sea',
I imagine a moon of Asia Minor
bright on your nightly industry.
Sometimes, rounding the cliff top
at dusk, under the convent wall,
and finding the little town lit up
as if for some island festival,
I pretend not to be here at all;

that the shopfronts along the prom,
whose fluorescence blinds the foam
and shingle, are the dancing lights
of Náousa — those calescent nights! —
that these frosty pavements are
the pavements of that distant star;
that the cold, glistening sea-mist
eclipses Naxos to the east.

But morning scatters down the strand
relics of last night's gale-force wind;
far out, the Atlantic faintly breaks,
seaweed exhales among the rocks
and fretfully the spent winds fan
the cenotaph and the lifeboat mine;
from door to door the Ormo van
delivers, while the stars decline.

Portstewart, Portrush, Portballintrae —
un beau pays mal habité,
policed by rednecks in dark cloth
and roving gangs of tartan youth.
No place for a gentleman like you.
The good, the beautiful and the true
have a tough time of it; and yet
there *is* that Hebridean sunset,

and a strange poetry of decay
charms the condemned hotels by day,
while in the dark hours the rattle
of a cat knocking over a milk-bottle
on a distant doorstep by moonlight
can set you thinking half the night.
The moon of Nineveh and Tyre
shines still on the Harbour Bar.

You too have known the curious sense
of working on the circumference —
the midnight oil, familiar sea,
elusive dawn epiphany,
faith that the trivia doodled here
will bear their fruit sometime, somewhere;
that the long winter months may bring
gifts to the goddess in the spring.

The sea in winter, where she walks,
vents its displeasure on the rocks;
the something rotten in the state
infects the innocent; the spite
mankind has brought to this infernal
backwater destroys the soul;
it sneaks into the daily life,
sunders the husband from the wife.

But let me never forget the weird
facticity of this strange seaboard,
the heroism and cowardice
of living on the edge of space,
or ever again contemptuously
refuse its plight; for history
ignores those who ignore it, not
the ignorant whom it begot.

To start from scratch, to make it new,
forsake the grey skies for the blue,
to find the narrow road to the deep
north the road to Damascus, leap
before we look! The ideal future
shines out of our better nature,
dimly visible from afar:
'The sun is but a morning star.'

One day, the day each one conceives —
the day the Dying Gaul revives,
the day the girl among the trees
strides through our wrecked technologies,
the stones speak out, the rainbow ends,
the wine goes round among the friends,
the lost are found, the parted lovers
lie at peace beneath the covers.

Meanwhile the given life goes on;
there is nothing new under the sun.
The dogs bark and the caravan
glides mildly by; and if the dawn
that wakes us now should also find us
cured of our ancient colour-blindness . . .
I who know nothing go to teach
while a new day crawls up the beach.

Hunger

(*for Paul Durcan*)

While a late thaw began in the boarded eaves
I left, exhausted, that city nobody leaves
Without being marked by it; signed on
For Newcastle-upon-Tyne and so to Spain,
Renouncing the tightly corseted lives,
The many windows flashing in the sun.
Dream on, dream homes, until I come again!

Later the wives and the hard-earned estate,
The admiration of the acknowledged great;
But who could hope wholly to sublimate
The bad years, the imperious gratitude
Working like hunger at the very bone?
And so, my larder dim with surplus food,
My polished windows blazing in the sun,

Waking these days I sometimes think myself
Back in that attic with its empty shelf.
Strangely enough, it was enormous fun
Glaring, a madman, into the bap faces
Of outraged butchers and policemen
And acting the idiot in public places.
The conquering soul betrayed a manic grin.

Born of the earth, I made terms with the earth,
This being the only thing of lasting worth.
Beside my bed the dog-eared gods of art
Made way for fragrant works on crop rotation,
The agriculture where all cultures start.
The typewriter fell silent; rod and gun
Went out with me to prowl the watchful dawn.

Yes, I shook hands with Hitler; knew disgrace.
But time heals everything; I rose again.
Now I can look my butcher in the face.
Besides, did I not once, as a young man,
Cure myself of incipient tuberculosis
Inhaling four sub-zero nights and days
Perched on the screaming roof of a freight train?

One fortunate in both would have us choose
'Perfection of the life or of the work'.
Nonsense, you work best on a full stomach
As everybody over thirty knows —
For who, unbreakfasted, will love the lark?
Prepare your protein-fed epiphanies,
Your heavenly mansions blazing in the dark.

Tractatus

(*for Aidan and Alannah*)

'The world is everything that is the case'
From the fly giving up in the coal-shed
To the Winged Victory of Samothrace.
Give blame, praise, to the fumbling God
Who hides, shame-facèdly, His agèd face;
Whose light retires behind its veil of cloud.

The world, though, is also so much more —
Everything that is the case imaginatively.
Tacitus believed mariners could *hear*
The sun sinking into the western sea;
And who would question that titanic roar,
The steam rising wherever the edge may be?

Katie at the Pool

My four-year-old daughter
points up at the low
ceiling with a cry:
'Look at the shadow
of the water on the sky!'

The Andean Flute

He dances to that music in the wood
As if history were no more than a dream.
Who said the banished gods were gone for good?

The furious rhythm creates a manic mood,
Piercing the twilight like a mountain stream.
He dances to that music in the wood.

We might have put on Bach or Buxtehude,
But a chance impulse chose the primal scream.
Who said the banished gods were gone for good?

An Inca frenzy fires his northern blood.
His child-heart picking up the tribal beam,
He dances to that music in the wood.

A puff of snow bursts where the birches brood;
Along the lane the earliest snowdrops gleam.
Who said the banished gods were gone for good?

It is the ancient cry for warmth and food
That moves him. Acting out an ancient theme,
He dances to that music in the wood.
Who said the banished gods were gone for good?

The Dawn Chorus

It is not sleep itself but dreams we miss,
Say the psychologists; and the poets too.
We yearn for that reality in this.

There is another world resides in this,
Said Eluard — not original, but true.
It is not sleep itself but dreams we miss.

If we could once achieve a synthesis
Of the archaic and the entirely new . . .
We yearn for that reality in this.

But, wide awake, clear-eyed with cowardice,
The flaming seraphim we find untrue.
It is not sleep itself but dreams we miss.

Listening heartbroken to the dawn chorus,
Clutching the certainty that once we flew,
We yearn for that reality in this.

Awaiting still our metamorphosis,
We hoard the fragments of what once we knew.
It is not sleep itself but dreams we miss.
We yearn for that reality in this.

Morning Radio

(for John Scotney)

The silence of the ether . . .
What can be going on
In the art-deco liner?

Ah, now the measured pips,
A stealth of strings
Tickling the fretwork throat,

Woodwinds entering
Delicately, the clarinet
Ascending to a lark-like note.

Seven o'clock —
News-time, and the merciful
Voice of Tom Crowe

Explains with sorrow
That the world we know
Is coming to an end.

Even as he speaks
We can hear furniture
Creak and slide on the decks.

But first a brief recital
Of resonant names —
Mozart, Schubert, Brahms.

The sun shines,
And a new day begins
To the strains of a horn concerto.

The Drawing Board

You think I am your servant but you are wrong —
The service lies with you. During your long
Labours at me, I am the indulgent wood,
Tolerant of your painstaking ineptitude.
Your poems were torn from me by violence;
I am here to receive your homage in dark silence.

Remembering the chainsaw surgery and the seaward groan,
Like a bound and goaded exodus from Babylon,
I pray for a wood-spirit to make me dance,
To scare your pants off and upset your balance,
Destroy the sedate poise with which you pour
Forth your ephemeral stream of literature.

When I was a pine and lived in a cold climate
I listened to leaf-rumours about our fate;
But I have come a long way since then
To watch the sun glint on your reflective pen.
The hurt I do resent, and my consolation
Will be the unspoilt paper when you have gone.

And yet I love you, even in your ignorance,
Perhaps because at last you are making sense —
Talking to me, not through me, recognizing
That it is I alone who let you sing
Wood music; hitherto shadowy and dumb,
I speak to you now as your indispensable medium.

Sunday Morning

We wake and watch the sun make bright
The corners of our London flat —
No sound but the sporadic, surly
Snarl of a car making an early
Dash for the country or the coast.
This is the time I like the most
When, for an hour or two, the strife
And strain of the late bourgeois life

Let up, we lie and grin to hear
The children bickering next door —
Hilarious formulations based
On a weird logic we have lost.
Oil crises and vociferous crowds
Seem as far off as tiny clouds;
The long-range forecast prophesies
Mean temperatures and azure skies.

Out in the park where Celia's father
Died, the Sunday people gather —
Residents towed by Afghan hounds,
Rastafarians trailing 'sounds',
Provincial tourists, Japanese
Economists, Saudi families,
Fresh-faced American college kids
Making out in the green shades.

A chiliastic prig, I prowl
Among the dog-lovers and growl,
Among the kite-fliers and fly
The private kite of poetry —
A sort of winged sandwich board
El-Grecoed to receive the word;
An airborne, tremulous brochure
Proclaiming that the end is near.

Black diplomats with gorgeous wives,
Promenading, notice the natives
Dozing beside the palace gates —
Old ladies under wide straw-hats
Who can remember *Chu Chin Chow*
And Kitchener. Exhausted now
By decades of retrenchment, they
Wait for the rain at close of play.

Asia now for a thousand years —
A flower that blooms and disappears
In a sand-storm; every artifact
A pure, self-referential act,
That the intolerant soul may be
Retrieved from triviality
And the locked heart, so long in pawn
To steel, redeemed by wood and stone.

One of These Nights

(*for Fleur Fitzgerald*)

A pregnant moon of August
Composes the roof-tops'
Unventilated slopes;
Dispenses to the dust
Its milky balm. A blue
Buzzard blinks in the zoo.

Cashel and Ank'hor Vat
Are not more ghostly than
London now, its squares
Bone-pale in the moonlight,
Its quiet thoroughfares
A map of desolation.

The grime of an ephemeral
Culture is swept clean
By that celestial hoover,
The refuse of an era
Consumed like polythene
In its impartial glare.

A train trembles deep
In the earth; vagrants sleep
Beside the revolving doors
Of vast department stores
Past whose alarm systems
The moonlight blandly streams.

A breeze-ruffled news-stand
Headlines the dole queues,
The bleak no-longer-news
Of racism and inflation —
Straws in the rising wind
That heralds the cyclone.

It all happened before —
The road to Wigan Pier,
The long road from Jarrow
To the tea room at the Ritz;
Munich, the Phony War,
The convoys and the Blitz.

One of these nights quiescent
Sirens will start to go
— A dog-howl reminiscent
Of forty years ago —
And sleepy people file
Down to the shelters while

Radiant warplanes come
Droning up the Thames from
Gravesend to Blackfriars,
Westminster and Mayfair,
Their incandescent flowers
Unfolding everywhere.

Enchanted foliage, bright
Water as in an old film
In sumptuous black and white
— This is the true realm,
The real earth before
Business and empire;
And life begins tonight.

A Garage in Co. Cork

Surely you paused at this roadside oasis
In your nomadic youth, and saw the mound
Of never-used cement, the curious faces,
The soft-drink ads and the uneven ground
Rainbowed with oily puddles, where a snail
Had scrawled its slimy, phosphorescent trail.

Like a frontier store-front in an old western
It might have nothing behind it but thin air,
Building materials, fruit boxes, scrap iron,
Dust-laden shrubs and coils of rusty wire,
A cabbage-white fluttering in the sodden
Silence of an untended kitchen garden —

Nirvana! But the cracked panes reveal a dark
Interior echoing with the cries of children.
Here in this quiet corner of Co. Cork
A family ate, slept, and watched the rain
Dance clean and cobalt the exhausted grit
So that the mind shrank from the glare of it.

Where did they go? South Boston? Cricklewood?
Somebody somewhere thinks of this as home,
Remembering the old pumps where they stood,
Antique now, squirting juice into a cream
Lagonda or a dung-caked tractor while
A cloud swam on a cloud-reflecting tile.

Surely a whitewashed sun-trap at the back
Gave way to hens, wild thyme, and the first few
Shadowy yards of an overgrown cart track,
Tyres in the branches such as Noah knew —
Beyond, a swoop of mountain where you heard,
Disconsolate in the haze, a single blackbird.

Left to itself, the functional will cast
A death-bed glow of picturesque abandon.
The intact antiquities of the recent past,
Dropped from the retail catalogues, return
To the materials that gave rise to them
And shine with a late sacramental gleam.

A god who spent the night here once rewarded
Natural courtesy with eternal life —
Changing to petrol pumps, that they be spared
For ever there, an old man and his wife.
The virgin who escaped his dark design
Sanctions the townland from her prickly shrine.

We might be anywhere but are in one place only,
One of the milestones of earth-residence
Unique in each particular, the thinly
Peopled hinterland serenely tense —
Not in the hope of a resplendent future
But with a sure sense of its intrinsic nature.

The Woods

Two years we spent
down there, in a quaint
outbuilding bright with recent paint.

A green retreat,
secluded and sedate,
part of a once great estate,

it watched our old
banger as it growled
with guests and groceries through heat and cold,

and heard you tocsin
meal-times with a spoon
while I sat working in the sun.

Above the yard
an old clock had expired
the night Lenin arrived in Petrograd.

Hapsburgs and Romanovs
had removed their gloves
in the drawing-rooms and alcoves

of the manor house;
but these illustrious
ghosts never imposed on us.

Enough that the pond
steamed, the apples ripened,
the chestnuts on the gravel opened.

Ragwort and hemlock,
cinquefoil and ladysmock
throve in the shadows at the back;

beneath the trees
foxgloves and wood-anemones
looked up with tearful metamorphic eyes.

We woke the rooks
on narrow, winding walks
familiar from the story-books,

or visited
a disused garden shed
where gas-masks from the war decayed;

and we knew peace
splintering the thin ice
on the bathtub drinking-trough for cows.

But how could we
survive indefinitely
so far from the city and the sea?

Finding, at last,
too creamy for our taste
the fat profusion of that feast,

we carried on
to chaos and confusion,
our birthright and our proper portion.

Another light
than ours convenes the mute
attention of those woods tonight —

while we, released
from that pale paradise,
confront the darkness in another place.

Craigvara House

That was the year
of the black nights and clear
mornings, a mild elation touched with fear;

a watchful anomie,
heart silence, day-long reverie
while the wind made harpstrings on the sea

and the first
rain of winter burst
earthwards as if quenching a great thirst.

A mist of spray
hung over the shore all day
while I slumped there re-reading *La Nausée*

or watched a cup
turn mantra on a tabletop
like Scott Fitzgerald after the crack-up;

or knocked a coal,
releasing squeaky gas until
it broke and tumbled into its hot hole.

Night fell on a rough
sea, on a moonlit basalt cliff,
huts with commandments painted on the roof,

and rain wept down
the raw slates of the town,
cackling maniacally in pipe and drain.

I slowly came
to treasure my ashram
(a flat with a sea view, the living-room

furnished with frayed
chintz, cane chairs and faded
watercolours of Slemish and Fair Head —

no phone, no television,
nothing to break my concentration,
the new-won knowledge of my situation);

and it was there,
choosing my words with care,
I sat down and began to write once more.

When snowflakes
wandered on to the rocks
I thought, home is where the heart breaks —

the lost domain
of weekends in the rain,
the Sunday sundae and the sexual pain.

I stared each night
at a glow of yellow light
over the water where the interned sat tight

(I in my own prison
envying their fierce reason,
their solidarity and extroversion)

and during storms
imagined the clenched farms
with dreadful faces throng'd and fiery arms.

Sometime before
spring I found in there
the frequency I had been looking for

and crossed by night
a dark channel, my eyesight
focused upon a flickering pier-light.

I slept then and,
waking early, listened
entranced to the pea-whistle sound

of a first thrush
practising on a thorn bush
a new air picked up in Marrakesh.

And then your car
parked with a known roar
and you stood smiling at the door —

as if we might
consider a bad night
as over and step out into the sunlight.

The Terminal Bar

(*for Philip Haas*)

The television set hung
in its wire-net cage,
protected from the flung
bottles of casual rage,
is fetish and icon
providing all we want
of magic and redemption,
routine and sentiment.
The year-old tinsels hang
where an unclaimed no-hoper
trembles; fly-corpses cling
to the grimy flypaper.
Manhattan snows swarm
on constellated waters,
steam trails from warm
subway ventilators . . .
Welcome to the planet,
its fluorescent beers
buzzing in the desolate
silence of the spheres.
Slam the door and knock
the snow from your shoe,
admit that the vast dark
at last defeated you.
Nobody found the Grail
or conquered outer space;
join the clientele
watching itself increase.

After Pasternak

1. *White Night*
In the distant past I can see
A house on a Moscow quay,
Your first flat, where you,
A daughter of the steppe,
Had come from Kursk to be
A student and fall in love.

One white night we sat late
At your window, gazing out
At the city stretching away
Beyond the oil-dark Volga,
Gas-flames flickering
Like moths in the streetlamps.

That spring-white night we spoke
Tentatively, constrained
By mysteries while, far off
In the countryside, nightingales
Thronged the thick forests
With the thunder of their song.

The singing went on and on,
The birds' tiny voices
Echoing like a choir
Deep in enchanted woods;
And there the dawn wind bore
The sound of our own words.

Orchards were in flower
As far as the eye could reach,
And ghostly birches crowded
Into the roads as though
To wave goodbye to the white
Night which had seen so much.

2. *The Earth*

Spring bursts in the houses
Of Moscow; a moth quits
Its hiding place and flits
Into the light of day
To gasp on cotton blouses;
Fur coats are locked away.

The cactus shakes itself
And stretches in its pot;
Attic and dusty shelf
Inhale the open air.
This is the time for twilit
Trysts beside the river,

Time for the injudicious
Out-in-the-open voices
And gossip like thaw-water
Dripping from the eaves;
Sob stories and laughter
Dance in the woken leaves.

Outside and in, the same
Mixture of fire and fear,
The same delirium
Of apple-blossom at
Window and garden gate,
Tram stop and factory door.

So why does the dim horizon
Weep, and the dark mould
Resist? It is my chosen
Task, surely, to nurse
The distances from cold,
The earth from loneliness.

Which is why, in the spring,
Our friends come together
And the vodka and talking
Are ceremonies, that the river
Of suffering may release
The heart-constraining ice.

The Globe in Carolina

There are no religions, no revelations;
there are women.
— Voznesensky, *Antiworlds*

The earth spins to my fingertips and
Pauses beneath my outstretched hand;
White water seethes against the green
Capes where the continents begin.
Warm breezes move the pines and stir
The hot dust of the piedmont where
Night glides inland from town to town.
I love to see that sun go down.

It sets in a coniferous haze
Beyond Georgia while the anglepoise
Rears like a moon to shed its savage
Radiance on the desolate page,
On Dvořàk sleeves and Audubon
Bird-prints; an electronic brain
Records the concrete music of
Our hardware in the heavens above.

From Hatteras to the Blue Ridge
Night spreads like ink on the unhedged
Tobacco fields and clucking lakes,
Bringing the lights on in the rocks
And swamps, the farms and motor courts,
Substantial cities, kitsch resorts —
Until, to the mild theoptic eye,
America is its own night-sky.

Out in the void and staring hard
At the dim stone where we were reared,
Great mother, now the gods have gone
We place our faith in you alone,

Inverting the procedures which
Knelt us to things beyond our reach.
Drop of the ocean, may your salt
Astringency redeem our fault!

Veined marble, if we only knew,
In practice as in theory, true
Redemption lies not in the thrust
Of action only, but the trust
We place in our peripheral
Night garden in the glory-hole
Of space, a home from home, and what
Devotion we can bring to it!

. . . You lie, an ocean to the east,
Your limbs composed, your mind at rest,
Asleep in a sunrise which will be
Your midday when it reaches me;
And what misgivings I might have
About the true importance of
The 'merely human' pale before
The mere fact of your being there.

Five miles away a southbound freight
Sings its euphoria to the state
And passes on; unfinished work
Awaits me in the scented dark.
The halved globe, slowly turning, hugs
Its silence, while the lightning bugs
Are quiet beneath the open window,
Listening to that lonesome whistle blow . . .

A Kensington Notebook

I

South Lodge is blue-
Plaqued where Ford set out
His toy soldiers on the
Razed table of art.

There was a great good place
Of clean-limbed young men
And high-minded virgins,
Cowslip and celandine;

Henry James to be visited,
Lawrence to be prized,
Conrad to be instructed,
Yeats to be lionized.

Sussex chirped in the sun.
A man could stand up
Then, and a woman too,
Before the thunderclap.

(Intrigue at German spas,
Bombast on golf-courses,
Perfidy in the ministries,
Generals in country houses . . .)

What price the dewy-eyed
Pelagianism of home
To a lost generation
Dumbfounded on the Somme?

An old cod in a land
Unfit for heroes,
He consecrates his new life to
Mnemosyne and Eros.

'The last of England'
Crumbles in the rain
As he embarks for
Paris and Michigan.

II

The operantics of
Provence and Languedoc
Shook the Gaudier marbles
At No. 10 Church Walk

Where 'Ezra Pound, M.A.,
Author of *Personae*',
Sniffed out the image with
Whiskery antennae;

Rihaku, nursed Osiris'
Torn limbs; came to know
Holland St. stone by stone
As he knew San Zeno;

And watched in disbelief,
An innocent abroad,
Dirigibles like buzzards
Above the Brompton Rd.

Meanwhile his Sunday mornings
Are scrambled by the din
Of bells from St. Mary
Abbots down the lane.

(Not Dowland, not Purcell
'The age demanded',
But the banalities
Of the *Evening Standard*.)

The Spirit of Romance
Flowered briefly there
Among jade animals;
And years later where,

Confucius of the dooryard,
Prophet of *to kalòn*
He drawls 'treason' into
A Roman microphone.

III
Asquith was not amused
When the editor of *Blast*,
Dining with the Prince of Wales
At Lady Drogheda's, placed

A pearl-handled revolver
On the white tablecloth —
Anarchy masquerading
As art, dangerous both.

Aesthetic bombardiering
Prefigured the real thing,
The *monstre gai* in a vortex
Of 'stone laughing' —

A moonscape, trees like gibbets,
Shrapnel, wire, the thud
Of howitzers, spike-helmeted
Skeletons in the mud.

War artist, he depicts
The death-throes of an era
While Orpen glorifies
Haig, Gough etc.;

Holed up in Holland Park,
Practises an implacable
Ordnance of the body
And casts out the soul.

Vitriol versus cocoa,
Adam versus the Broad
Church of received opinion,
He goads the Apes of God.

Nietzschean politics,
Urbane rejection, debt,
Six years of Canadian
Exile, psychic defeat.

IV

No more parades . . .
Ghostly bugles sound
The 'Last Post'; the last fox
Has gone to ground

Beneath the shadow of
A nuclear power plant,
Its whirling radar dishes
Anxious and vehement.

Empire is fugitive
And the creative thrust.
Only the chimps remain;
The rest is dust.

Tragic? No, 'available
Reality' was increased,
The sacred flame kept alive,
The Muse not displeased;

And if one or two
Were short on *agapè*
What was that to the evil
Done in their day?

Ford dies abroad,
A marginal figure still;
And Lewis, self-condemned,
Eyeless in Notting Hill.

Pound, released, reads
To his grandchildren; 'helps'
With the garden; dozes off in a high
Silence of the Alps —

Un rameur, finally,
Sur le fleuve des morts,
Poling his profile toward
What farther shore?

Squince

The eyes are clouded where
   He lies in a veined dish.
Is this the salmon of knowledge
   Or merely a dead fish?

A forest of symbols here —
   Swan, heron, goat,
Druidic stone circle, fuchsia-
   Buried hillfort;

And the village is of clear-cut
   Resonant artifacts:
A pink-washed grocery shop,
   A yellow *telefón* box.

We live now in a future
   Prehistory, the ancient
Mystery surviving in
   The power to enchant

Of the sun going down
   In a thicket of hazel trees
While ferns at the window
   Nod in the everbreeze.

Mt. Gabriel

As if planted there by giant golfers in the skies,
White in the gloaming, last before New Brunswick,
The geodesic domes have left their caves
To sit out in the summer sunset; angels
Beamed at Namancos and Bayona, sick
With exile, they yearn homeward now, their eyes
Tuned to the ultramarine, first-star-pierced dark
Reflected on the dark, incoming waves —
Who, aliens, burnt-out meteorites, time capsules,
Are here for ever now as intermediaries
Between the big bang and our scattered souls.

The Hunt by Night

— Uccello, 1465

Flickering shades,
Stick figures, lithe game,
Swift flights of bison in a cave
Where man the maker killed to live;
But neolithic bush became
The midnight woods

Of nursery walls,
The ancient fears mutated
To play, horses to rocking-horses
Tamed and framed to courtly uses,
Crazed no more by foetid
Bestial howls

But rampant to
The pageantry they share
And echoes of the hunting horn
At once peremptory and forlorn.
The mild herbaceous air
Is lemon-blue,

The glade aglow
With pleasant mysteries,
Diuretic depots, pungent prey;
And midnight hints at break of day
Where, among sombre trees,
The slim dogs go

Wild with suspense
Leaping to left and right,
Their cries receding to a point
Masked by obscurities of paint
As if our hunt by night,
So very tense,

So long pursued,
In what dark cave begun
And not yet done, were not the great
Adventure we suppose but some elaborate
Spectacle put on for fun
And not for food.

Girls on the Bridge

— Munch, 1900

Audible trout,
Notional midges. Beds,
Lamplight and crisp linen wait
In the house there for the sedate
Limbs and averted heads
Of the girls out

Late on the bridge.
The dusty road that slopes
Past is perhaps the high road south,
A symbol of world-wondering youth,
Of adolescent hopes
And privileges;

But stops to find
The girls content to gaze
At the unplumbed, reflective lake,
Their plangent conversational quack
Expressive of calm days
And peace of mind.

Grave daughters
Of time, you lightly toss
Your hair as the long shadows grow
And night begins to fall. Although
Your laughter calls across
The dark waters,

A ghastly sun
Watches in pale dismay.
Oh, you may laugh, being as you are
Fair sisters of the evening star,
But wait — if not today
A day will dawn

When the bad dreams
You scarcely know will scatter
The punctual increment of your lives.
The road resumes, and where it curves,
A mile from where you chatter,
Somebody screams.

Brighton Beach

(*for Paul Smyth*)

1.
Remember those awful parties
In dreary Belfast flats,
The rough sectarian banter
In Lavery's back bar,
The boisterous takeaways
And moonlight on wet slates?

Remember the place you rented
At the end of a muddy lane
Somewhere near Muckamore?
No light, so in midwinter
You slept in the afternoon
And lay there until dawn.

Remember the time we drove
To Donegal and you talked
For hours to fishermen
You had worked with while I,
Out of my depths in those
Waters, loafed on the quays?

Now, pushing forty, we roam
At ease along the prom,
Life-buffeted to be sure
But grown sober and wise.
The sea shuffles ashore
Beneath pale mackerel skies.

2.

From the far end of the pier
I imagine the sun-gleam
On a thousand *deux-chevaux*.
Over there they explore
Balbec and sip Pernod
In a Monet-monoxide dream.

Europe thrives, but the offshore
Islanders year by year
Decline, the spirit of empire
Fugitive as always.
Now, in this rancorous peace,
Should come the spirit of place.

Too late though, for already
Places as such are dead
Or nearly; the loved sea
Reflects banality.
Not so in the old days
The retired sailor says.

But the faded Georgian bricks
Towering over the shore
Remain, like the upright
Old men with walking-sticks
Out for a last stroll before
Turning in for the night.

Achill

I lie and imagine a first light gleam in the bay
   After one more night of erosion and nearer the grave,
Then stand and gaze from the window at break of day
   As a shearwater skims the ridge of an incoming wave;
And I think of my son a dolphin in the Aegean,
   A sprite among sails knife-bright in a seasonal wind,
And wish he were here where currachs walk on the ocean
   To ease with his talk the solitude locked in my mind.

I sit on a stone after noon and consider the glow
   Of the sun through mist, a pearl bulb containèdly fierce;
A rain-shower darkens the schist for a minute or so,
   Then it drifts away and the sloe-black patches disperse.
Croagh Patrick towers like Naxos over the water
   And I think of my daughter at work on her difficult art
And wish she were with me now between thrush and plover,
   Wild thyme and sea-thrift, to lift the weight from my heart.

The young sit smoking and laughing on the bridge at evening
   Like birds on a telephone pole or notes on a score.
A tin whistle squeals in the parlour, once more it is raining,
   Turfsmoke inclines and a wind whines under the door;
And I lie and imagine the lights going on in the harbour
   Of white-housed Náousa, your clear definition at night,
And wish you were here to upstage my disconsolate labour
   As I glance through a few thin pages and switch off the light.

Ovid in Tomis

What coarse god
Was the gearbox in the rain
Beside the road?

What nereid the unsinkable
Coca-Cola
Knocking the icy rocks?

They stare me out
With the chaste gravity
And feral pride

Of noble savages
Set down
On an alien shore.

It is so long
Since my own transformation
Into a stone,

I often forget
That there was a time
Before my name

Was mud in the mouths
Of the Danube,
A dirty word in Rome.

Imagine Byron banished
To Botany Bay
Or Wilde to Dawson City

And you have some idea
How it is for me
On the shores of the Black Sea.

I who once strode
Head-high in the forum,
A living legend,

Fasten my sheepskin
By greasy waters
In a Scythian wind.

My wife and friends
Do what they can
On my behalf;

Though from Tiberius,
Whom God preserve,
I expect nothing.

But I don't want
To die here
In the back of beyond

Among these morose
Dice-throwing Getes
And the dust of Thrace.

No doubt, in time
To come, this huddle of
Mud huts will be

A handsome city,
An important port,
A popular resort

With an oil pipeline,
Martini terraces
And even a dignified

Statue of Ovid
Gazing out to sea
From the promenade;

But for the moment
It is merely a place
Where I have to be.

Six years now
Since my relegation
To this town

By the late Augustus.
The *Halieutica*,
However desultory,

Gives me a sense
Of purpose,
However factitious;

But I think it's the birds
That please me most,
The cranes and pelicans.

I often sit in the dunes
Listening hard
To the uninhibited

Virtuosity of a lark
Serenading the sun
And meditate upon

The transience
Of earthly dominion,
The perfidy of princes.

Mediocrity, they say,
Consoles itself
With the reflection

That genius so often
Comes to a bad end.
The things adversity

Teaches us
About human nature
As the aphorisms strike home!

I know the simple life
Would be right for me
If I were a simple man.

I have a real sense
Of the dumb spirit
In boulder and tree;

Skimming stones, I wince
With vicarious pain
As a slim quoit goes in.

And the six-foot reeds
Of the delta,
The pathos there!

Whenever they bend
And sigh in the wind
It is not merely Syrinx

Remembering Syrinx
But Syrinx keening
Her naked terror

Of the certain future,
She and her kind
Being bulk-destined

For pulping machines
And the cording
Of motor-car tyres.

Pan is dead, and already
I feel an ancient
Unity leave the earth,

The bowl avoid my eye
As if ashamed
Of my failure to keep faith.

(It knows that I
Have exchanged belief
For documentation.)

The Muse is somewhere
Else, not here
By this frozen lake —

Or, if here, then I am
Not poet enough
To make the connection.

Are we truly alone
With our physics and myths,
The stars no more

Than glittering dust,
With no one there
To hear our choral odes?

If so, we can start
To ignore the silence
Of the infinite spaces

And concentrate instead
On the infinity
Under our very noses —

The cry at the heart
Of the artichoke,
The gaiety of atoms.

Better to contemplate
The blank page
And leave it blank

Than modify
Its substance by
So much as a pen-stroke.

Woven of wood-nymphs,
It speaks volumes
No one will ever write.

I incline my head
To its candour
And weep for our exile.

October in Hyde Park

The whitewashed monastery where we sat
listening to the Aegean and watched
a space capsule among the stars
will be closed now for the winter;
and the harbour bars,
cleared of the yacht crowd,
will be serving dawn ouzos to the crews
of the *Aghios Ioannis* and *Nikolaos*
where they play dominoes
by the light of a paraffin lamp
and the bouzouki music of Mikis Theodorakis.

Europe, after the first rain of winter,
glitters with sex and opinion.
A cold wind scours the condemned
playground; leaves swarm like souls
down bleak avenues as if they led
to the kingdom of the dead,
computer systems down with flu,
our death not from darkness but from cold.

Like the leaves we are coming within
sight of the final river,
its *son et lumière*
and breath of the night sea.
As if ghosts already,
we search our pockets for the Stygian fare.

Dejection Ode

Bone-idle, I lie listening to the rain,
Not tragic now nor yet to frenzy bold.
Must I stand out in thunderstorms again
Who have twice come in from the cold?

Night Drive

— St. Petersburg, 1900

(*after Rilke*)

Not drawn but flown by glistening mares
past silent, tomb-lit porticoes
and lamp-posts hung like chandeliers,
past granite palaces where a first
dawn-glow lightened the roofs, we burst
on to the windy Neva quays,
rumbling there in an anxious, thin
half-light neither of earth nor heaven,
leaving behind the unwoken, dark
woods of the Czar's private park
protected from the risen breeze,
its statues fading, every gesture frozen for ever in the past.
St. Petersburg ceased to exist,
disclosed that it had never been;
asked only peace now, as if one
long mad should find the knot untied
and watch, recovered and clear-eyed,
a fixed idea in its Byzantine,
varnished and adamantine shrine
spin off from the whirling mind
and vanish, leaving not a trace behind.

Antarctica

(*for Richard Ryan*)

'I am just going outside and may be some time.'
The others nod, pretending not to know.
At the heart of the ridiculous, the sublime.

He leaves them reading and begins to climb,
Goading his ghost into the howling snow;
He is just going outside and may be some time.

The tent recedes beneath its crust of rime
And frostbite is replaced by vertigo:
At the heart of the ridiculous, the sublime.

Need we consider it some sort of crime,
This numb self-sacrifice of the weakest? No,
He is just going outside and may be some time —

In fact, for ever. Solitary enzyme,
Though the night yield no glimmer there will glow,
At the heart of the ridiculous, the sublime.

He takes leave of the earthly pantomime
Quietly, knowing it is time to go.
'I am just going outside and may be some time.'
At the heart of the ridiculous, the sublime.

Kinsale

The kind of rain we knew is a thing of the past —
deep-delving, dark, deliberate you would say,
browsing on spire and bogland; but today
our sky-blue slates are steaming in the sun,
our yachts tinkling and dancing in the bay
like racehorses. We contemplate at last
shining windows, a future forbidden to no one.

Birdlife

The gulls are out at the Old Head
where the *Lusitania* went down
so we make do with rooks instead
among the tiered roofs of the town.
The gulls are down among the fish,
raiding the trawlers at the quay;
crows pace among our spilt rubbish
staring ferociously at the sea.

Dawn at St. Patrick's

There is an old
statue in the courtyard
that weeps, like Niobe, its sorrow in stone.
The griefs of the ages she has made her own.
Her eyes are rain-washed but not hard,
her body is covered in mould,
the garden overgrown.

One by one
the first lights come on,
those that haven't been on all night.
Christmas, the harshly festive, has come and gone.
No snow, but the rain pours down
in the first hour before dawn,
before daylight.

Swift's home
for 'fools and mad' has become
the administrative block. Much there
has remained unchanged for many a long year —
stairs, chairs, Georgian windows shafting light and dust,
radiantly white the marble bust
of the satirist;

but the real
hospital is a cheerful
modern extension at the back
hung with restful reproductions of Dufy, Klee and Braque.
Television, Russian fiction, snooker with the staff,
a snifter of Lucozade, a paragraph
of *Newsweek* or the *Daily Mail*

are my daily routine
during the festive season.
They don't lock the razors here
as in Bowditch Hall. We have remained upright —
though, to be frank, the Christmas dinner scene,
with grown men in their festive gear,
was a sobering sight.

I watch the last
planes of the year go past,
silently climbing a cloud-lit sky.
Earth-bound, soon I'll be taking a train to Cork
and trying to get back to work
at my sea-lit, fort-view desk
in the turf-smoky dusk.

Meanwhile,
next door, a visiting priest
intones to a faithful dormitory.
I sit on my Protestant bed, a make-believe existentialist,
and stare at the clouds of unknowing. We style,
as best we may, our private destiny;
or so it seems to me

as I chew my thumb
and try to figure out
what brought me to my present state —
an 'educated man', a man of consequence, no bum
but one who has hardly grasped what life is about,
if anything. My children, far away,
don't know where I am today,

in a Dublin asylum
with a paper whistle and a mince pie,
my bits and pieces making a home from home.
I pray to the rain-clouds that they never come
where their lost father lies; that their mother thrives;
   and that I
may measure up to them
before I die.

Soon a new year
will be here demanding, as before,
modest proposals, resolute resolutions, a new leaf,
new leaves. This is the story of my life,
the story of all lives everywhere,
mad fools wherever we are,
in here or out there.

Light and sane
I shall walk down to the train,
into that world whose sanity we know,
like Swift, to be a fiction and a show.
The clouds part, the rain ceases, the sun
casts now upon everyone
its ancient shadow.

An Orphan at the Door

(from the Irish of Nuala Ní Dhomhnaill)

As fragile as a shell
cast up on a rocky shore,
I stand outside your door
in the afternoon. The bell
rings deep in your house,
echoing in the long, empty rooms.

The kitchen radio howls
rock music and, for a moment,
I feel a surge of hope before
I realize it's only on
to deter thieves, and a long
wait lies before me
with no sound of your step.

I ring again and the echo rises
among high ceilings, wooden stairs.
Peering through the letter-box
I recognize in the Georgian proportions
an intricate crystal structure
that bodies forth and hides a god.

A red rose stands in a vase
on the hall table; a sweater
hangs from the banister;
unopened letters lie about
carelessly on the floor;
but nowhere is there a sign
of you to be seen.

Over the drawing-room fireplace
a postcard from your lover
boasts that hers is the first

mail in your new house. It shows
a simple tourist view
of the tumulus at Newgrange.

There is a reference — not lost
on you, of course —
to the *hieros gamos*, the marriage
made in heaven. Outside
the warm conspiracy of your love
I stand, a nobody,
an orphan at the door.

An icy wind blows through the cold porches
of the farthest pavilions
in the depths of my soul;
the rivers of emotion are frozen solid;
my heart beats wildly
like strange and treacherous seas.

Damn my wooden head, my feather brain,
why am I waiting here
at your closed door?
When the bell peals inside
like the Angelus, do I really
expect the sky to open and a dove
to descend upon me from above?

It's only in the soul
that the miracles take place
of love, forgiveness and grace;
it's only in dream-truth
that the sun and moon shine
together in a bright sky
while day dawns on them both.

The Race

(from the Irish of Nuala Ní Dhomhnaill)

Like a mad lion, like a wild bull, like one
of the crazy pigs in the Fenian cycle
or the hero leaping upon the giant
with his fringe of whistling silk,
I drive at high speed through
the small midland towns of Ireland,
catching up with the wind ahead
while the wind behind me whirls and dies.

Like a shaft from a bow, like a shot from a gun
or a sparrow-hawk in a sparrow-throng
on a March day, I scatter the road-signs,
miles or kilometres what do I care.
Nenagh, Roscrea, Mountmellick,
I pass through them in a daze;
they are only speed limits put there
to hold me up on my way to you.

Through mountain cleft, bogland and wet pasture
I race impetuously from west to east —
a headlong flight in your direction,
a quick dash to be with you.
The road rises and falls before me,
the surface changing from grit to tar;
I forget geography, all I know
is the screech of brakes and the gleam of lights.

Suddenly, in the mirror, I catch sight of the sun
glowing red behind me on the horizon,
a vast blazing crimson sphere like the heart
of the Great Cow of the Smith-God
when she was milked through a sieve,
the blood dripping as in a holy picture.
Thrice red, it is so fierce it pierces
my own heart, and I catch my breath in pain.

I keep glancing anxiously at the dripping sun
while trying to watch the road ahead —
so Sleeping Beauty must have glanced
at her finger after the spindle
of the spinning-wheel had pricked her,
turning it round and round as if in a trance.
When Deirdre saw the calf's blood on the snow
did it ever dawn on her what the raven was?

Oh, I know it's to you that I'm driving,
my lovely man, the friend of my heart,
and the only things between us tonight
are the road-sign and the traffic-light;
but your impatience is like a stone
dropping upon us out of the sky;
and add to that our bad humour,
gaucherie, and the weight of my terrible pride.

Another great weight is descending upon us
if things turn out as expected, a weight
greater by far than the globe of the sun
that bled in my mirror a while back;
and thou, dark mother, cave of wonders,
since it's to you that we spin on our violent course,
is it true what they say that your kiss is sweeter
than Spanish wine, Greek honey, or the golden mead
    of the Norse?

Northern Star

(*i.m. Stewart Parker, 1941–1988*)

Ancestral voices bicker; ghosts
wrestle and dance; indignant hosts
of all persuasions dander down
to throng the lanes of Antrim, Down,
burnished pikes unsheathed from thatch,
sabre and flintlock quick to catch;
still the inspired conspirators
make history in Kelly's Cellars

or at Mac Airt's fort on Cave Hill,
their music above politics still
as starlight shines above a bog
— weaver and printer, ideologue,
children of nature, natural sons
and daughters, trenchant resolutions
echoing in that whin-scented air,
adrift like thistledown elsewhere.

Red dawn, white tide and starry night
dissolve to chaos, heartbreak, 'shite
and lunacy', the severed head,
townlands put to torch and sword,
leaving our souls still incomplete
and white noise of sectarian hate
echoing down the continuous past
in the loved entries of Belfast.

Wee corner shops we used to know,
'close-knit communities', the flow
of generational energy, streams
of consciousness, rain-traffic dreams,
the summer bus from glen to glen —
a common enough existence then,
or nearly, till the story broke
and the whole place went up in smoke.

White noise of gulls at rubbish dumps,
killers and victims both at once,
each blow a self-inflicted wound;
and always the holistic sound
of blackbirds on a summer night
in a world transfigured by starlight
— till all fade oblivionwards
'drowning out any further words'.

Noon at St. Michael's

Nurses and nuns —
their sails whiter than those
of the yachts in the bay, they come and go
on winged feet, most of them, or in sensible shoes.
July, and I should be climbing among stones
or diving, but for broken bones,
from the rocks below.

I try to read
a new novel set aside;
but a sword-swift pain
in the left shoulderblade, the result
of a tumble in Sheridan Square, makes reading difficult
— writing you can do in your head.
It starts to rain

on the sea,
suddenly dark, the pier,
the gardens and the church spires of Dun Laoghaire.
You would think it was suddenly October
as smoke flaps, the yachts tack violently
and those caught in the downpour
run for cover.

But in a few
minutes the sun shines again,
the leaves and hedges glisten as if with dew
in that fragrant freshness after rain
when the world seems made anew
before confusion, before pain;
and I think of you,

a funny-face
but solemn, with the sharpest mind I know,
a thoughtful creature of unconscious grace
bent to your books in the sun or driving down
to New York for an evening on the town.
Doors open wherever you go
in that furious place;

for you are the light
rising on lost islands, the *spéir-bhean*
the old poets saw gleam in the morning mist.
When you walk down 5th Avenue in your lavender suit,
your pony eyes opaque, I am the one
beside you, and life is bright
with the finest and best.

And I have seen,
as you have not, such is your modesty,
men turn to watch your tangle of golden hair,
your graceful carriage and unhurried air
as if you belonged to history
or '*her* story', that mystery.
You might have been

a saint or a great
courtesan, anachronistic now
in some ways, in some ways more up-to-date
than the most advanced of those we know.
While you sit on your sun-porch in Connecticut
re-reading Yeats in a feminist light,
I am there with you.

Galatea

(Ovid, *Metamorphoses*, X, 245-277)

Pygmalion lived for years alone
without a wife to call his own.
Meanwhile, ingeniously, he wrought
a maiden out of ivory, one
lovelier than any woman born,
and with this shape he fell in love.
Alive, she seemed, and apt to move
if modesty did not prevent —
so did his art conceal his art.
He gazed at her in wonderment
and felt her limbs to be quite sure
that she was ivory, nothing more.
Her 'skin' responded to his stroke
or so he thought; and so he spoke,
seized her, imagining his thick
fingers sank into her back,
and looked for bruises on the work.
He whispered gentle, loving words,
brought presents, shells and pebbles, birds
and flowers, things that please young girls;
he clothed her, putting diamond rings
on her white fingers, ropes of pearls
about her neck and breasts. These things
were gorgeous, certainly, although
the naked sculpture even more so.
He laid her down on a bed spread
with sheets dyed a Tyrian red,
called her his lover, propped her head
among soft, feathery pillows as if
a statue might have sensuous life.

Now Venus' feast-day was the date
and Cyprus thronged to celebrate.
Heifers, their spread horns freshly gilt,
had felt the death-stroke to the hilt

in their soft necks, as white as snow,
and the air smoked with incense. Now
Pygmalion, having devoutly laid
gifts on the altar, shyly prayed:
'Gods, if it's true that you can give
anything, grant I may make love — '
Too shy to say 'the maid', he said,
' — to someone *like* my ivory maid!'
But Venus, there in person, knew
what he intended and, to show
that she approved, the altar flames
shot up into the air three times.
Hastening home, the impatient lover
ran to the maid and, leaning over,
embraced her there on her chaste couch.
Her skin seemed warmer to his touch;
his fingers felt her thighs, at which
the ivory grew soft between
his thumbs, as wax melts in the sun
and, gently worked by loving hands,
stretches, relaxes and expands,
responsive even as it responds.

He stood amazed, still doubtful, thought
himself mistaken, and then not;
inflamed, he stroked her thighs again
until the statue blushed! Each vein
fluttered as our protagonist,
pouring out thanks to Venus, thrust
his lips upon live lips at last.
The maid, feeling his kisses, raised
shy eyes to the sun and, in a glance,
saw daylight and his face at once.
The goddess, with her genial presence,
sanctioned the union and in time
a girl, Paphos, was born to them —
from whom the city takes its name.

The Yaddo Letter

(for Rory and Katie)

We are born in an open field and we die in a dark wood.
— Russian proverb

Here among silent lakes and dripping pines
off Route 9P, I write you guys these lines
to ask you what you're up to and what not.
No doubt I'll finish them in my attic flat
in Dublin, if I ever get back there
to the damp gardens of Fitzwilliam Square.
Do you still like your London schools? Do you
still slam the goals in, Rory? Katie-coo,
how goes it with the piano and the flute?
I've a composer in the next-door suite
called Gloria (*in excelsis*), an English novelist,
a sculptor from Vermont, a young ceramist
from Kansas; for we come in suns and snows
from *everywhere* to write, paint and compose.
Sport? We've a pool, closed till the end of May,
a tennis court where no one seems to play;
though there's a horse show, among other things,
starting next week in Saratoga Springs
just down the road — a fascinating place
with spas and concerts and a certain grace . . .
Also a certain measure of renown
since it was here, in an open field north of the town,
that Philip Schuyler clobbered John Burgoyne
in 1777, two hundred and thirteen years ago,
thus helping to precipitate the America we know.
But you're not interested in that kind of stuff;
like me, you'd rather go to the movies for a laugh —
or would you? We talk so infrequently
I hardly know where your real interests lie.
What, for example, are you reading now?
John Buchan? Molly Keane? *Catch-22*?

Nothing too highbrow, time enough for that;
you're better off with a flute or a cricket bat.
You're only (only!) in your middle teens,
too young to be thinking about *seerious* things
like the dream plays and ghost sonatas your
lost father hears and watches everywhere,
especially when he glimpses happy families
a-picnicking among the squirrel trees.
I try to imagine you asleep, at work,
or walking with your mother in Hyde Park
where once we walked each Sunday, hand in hand,
to feed the daffy ducks on the Round Pond,
chucking crumbs to the ones we liked the best,
comical, tufted yellow-eyes, ignoring all the rest.
Remember birthday parties, rockets at Hallowe'en,
bus-rides to Covent Garden to see Eugene?
The day we drove to Brighton? Maybe not.
Summer and winter I would rise and trot
my fingers up your backs like a mad mouse
to wake you chuckling. Now I wake in a silent house
in a dark wood. Once, 'Is it morning time?',
asked Katie waking. Now it is mourning time
in a black heart; but I will not forget
the nooks and corners of our crazy flat,
its dormer windows and its winding stair,
gulls on the roof, its views of *everywhere*!
When Mummy and I split up and I lived in Co. Cork
among the yacht crowd and bohemian folk
I'd wander round the hills above Kinsale
where English forces clobbered Hugh O'Neill
in Tudor times, wrecking the Gaelic order
(result, plantations and the present Border),
or dander down along the Bandon River
wondering when next we'd be together;
then home to a stable loft where I could hear
mysterious night sounds whispering in my ear —

wood-pigeons, foxes, silence, my own brain,
my lamp a lighthouse in the drizzling rain.
After a month of fog a day would dawn
when the rain ceased, cloud cleared and the sun shone;
then magical white wisps of smoke would rise
and I'd think of our own magical London years.
'One always loses with a desperate throw.'
What I lost was a wife, a life, and you.
As for love, a treasure when first it's new,
it all too often fades away, for both, like the morning dew;
yet it remains the one sure thing to cling to
as I cling like grim death to the thought of you,
sitting alone here in upstate New York
half-way to Montreal, trying to work,
lit by Tiffany lamps, Sinéad O'Connor on the stereo.
This above all, to thine own selves be true,
remembering seaside games in stormy Ulster parts
and Sunday lunches at the Chelsea Arts
with lemonade for you in paper cups,
snooker and candlelight for the 'grown-ups'.
Your father (yawn!) has seen enough mischance
trying to figure out the dancers from the dance.
Like Mummy, *some* can dance; I never could,
no more than I could ever see the birches for the wood.
We are *all* children; and when either of you
feels scared or miserable, as you must sometimes do,
look to us, but remember we do too.
I hear the big trucks flashing through the night
like Christmas road-houses ablaze with light,
symbols of modern movement and romance;
but the important thing is permanence —
for you, a continuity with the past
enabling you to prosper, and a fast
forward to where the paradoxes grow
like crocuses in our residual snow;
for me, a long devotion to the art
in which you play such an important part,

a long devotion to the difficult Muse
your mother was, despite our difficulties.
Everything thrives in contrariety — no
thesis without antithesis (and synthesis?); no black
without its white, like a hot sun on the ice of a Yaddo lake.
Children of light, may your researches be
reflections on this old anomaly;
may you remember, as the years go by
and you grow slowly towards maturity,
that life consists in the receipt of life,
its fun and games, its boredom and its grief;
that no one, sons or daughters, fathers, wives,
escapes the rough stuff that makes up our lives.
Equip yourselves in every way you can
to take it like a woman or a man,
respecting values you've long understood
pertaining to the true, the beautiful and the good.
Sorry to sound so tedious and trite.
I'd hoped to be more fun and try to write
you something entertaining as I often try to do;
but this time round I wanted to be *seerious* and true
to felt experience. My love 2U.
Nothing I say you don't already know.
Football and flute, you'll join us soon enough
in the mad 'grown-up' world of Henry James's 'stupid life'.
Write soon and tell me all about your work.
It's time now for your father to be heading for New York,
a city worse than London, rife with confrontation,
much like the one you see on television.
Maybe I'll read this letter at the 'Y'
and tell you all about it by and by.
I hope I haven't bored you stiff already.
Write to me soon in Dublin.

My love, as ever,

— Daddy.

The Hudson Letter

(for Patricia King)

I

Sometimes, from beyond the skyscrapers, the cry of a tug-boat finds you in your insomnia, and you remember this desert of iron and cement is an island.
— Albert Camus, *American Journals*

Winter; a short walk from the 10th St. Pier —
and what of the kick-start that should be here?
The fishy ice lies thick on Gansevoort
around the corner, and the snow shines bright
about your country house this morning: short
the time left to find the serenity
which for a lifetime has eluded me . . .
A rented 'studio' apartment in New York
five blocks from the river, time to think and work,
long-suffering friends and visitors, the bars
where Dylan Thomas spent his final hours,
God rest him; but there's something missing here
in this autistic slammer, some restorative
laid like a magic wand on everything —
on bed, chair, desk and air-conditioner.
I often visualize in the neon slush
that great heart-breaking moment in *The Gold Rush*
where Chaplin, left alone on New Year's Eve,
listens to life's feast from his little shack
and the strains of 'Auld Lang's Syne' across the snow.
Oh, show me how to recover my lost nerve!
The radiators knock, whistle and sing.
I toss and turn and listen, when I wake,
to the first bird and the first garbage truck,
hearing the 'lordly' Hudson 'hardly' flow
to New York Harbour and the sea below.
The lights go out along the Jersey shore
and, as Manhattan faces east once more,

dawn's early light on bridge and water-tower,
Respighi's temperate nightingale on WQXR
pipes up though stronger stations throng the ether —
a radio serendipity to illustrate
the resilience of our lyric appetite,
carnivalesque or studiously apart,
on tap in offices, lofts and desperate 'hoods
to Lorca's 'urinating multitudes'
while I make coffee and listen for the news
at eight; but first the nightingale. Sing, Muse.

II

Out There

Left completely to his own devices, the bachelor's idea of interior decoration is a pyramid of empty beer cans on a window-ledge.
— P. J. O'Rourke, *The Bachelor Home Companion*

Here I was, sitting quietly in my studio
and grading papers with the radio low
as Pascal says we should, when out of the blue
last night, under the fire-escape, some psycho
sends up a stream of picturesque abuse
directed, evidently, at my 4th-floor window,
his reasoning trenchant, complex and abstruse —
one of those paranoids who seem to know
the system's out to get them even so;
for paranoia, of course, is no excuse.
A nervous terrier, left home alone
and maddened, maybe, by the relentless tone,
went crazy, hollering in the flat below;
then it was time for the lunatic upstairs
to shift his desk and re-align his chairs;
a *West Side Story* love-scene on the sidewalk,
whoop of police sirens, car alarms
unanimous as in a California 'quake
while some lay dreaming in each others' arms.
Around five a hand, with Gershwin nonchalance,
shook up the empties in the recycling bin
at the corner, shivering for a drop of gin,
its movements brisk, fastidious and, all at once,
triumphant . . . Dawn; the kick-start as some heroine
draws on her gloves for the Yamaha dream trip
to Provincetown, Key West or Sunset Strip.
Tired vents exhale; cloudy windows condense;
vague vapours pearl fire hydrant and chain-link fence;
and the homeless gaze with satire or indifference

from cardboard boxes on a construction site
as she sets out on her epic expedition.
To each his haste; to each his dreamt occasion.
Nor snow, nor rain, nor sleet, nor gloom of night
stays these swift couriers from their appointed flight.

III

Global Village

This morning, from beyond abandoned piers
where the great liners docked in former years,
a foghorn echoes in deserted sheds
known to Hart Crane, and in our vigilant beds.
No liners now, nothing but ice and grime,
a late flame flickering on Brodsky St. News-time
in the global village — Ethiopian drought,
famine, whole nations, races, evicted even yet,
rape victim and blind beggar at the gate —
the images forming which will be screened tonight
on CNN and *The McNeil-Lehrer News Hour*,
the sense of being right there on the spot —
a sense I get right here that Gansevoort
has 'no existence, natural or real, apart
from its being perceived by the understanding'. Not
that I seriously doubt the reality of the Hudson Bar
and Diner; but the skills of Venturi, Thompson, Rowse
that can make post-modern a 19th-century warehouse
and those of Hollywood *film noir* have combined
to create virtual realities in the mind
so the real thing tells us what we already know
behind the signs. Obviously I don't mean
to pen yet one more craven European
paean to the States, nor would you expect me to,
not being a yuppie in a pinstripe suit
but an Irish bohemian even as you are too
though far from the original 'Ballroom of Romance',
far too from your posh convent school in France.
Out here in the clear existential light
I miss the half-tones I'm accustomed to:
an amateur immigrant, sure I like the corny
humanism and car-stickers — 'I♥NY' —
and yet remain sardonic and un-*chic*,
an undesirable resident alien on this shore,

a face in the crowd in this off-shore boutique
inscribed with the ubiquitous comic-strip blob-speak
— LOVE ONE ANOTHER, RESIST INSIPID RHYME —
exposed in thunderstorms, as once before,
and hoping to draw some voltage one more time.

IV

Waterfront

We shall go down like palaeolithic man
Before some new Ice Age or Genghiz Khan.
— Louis MacNeice,
'An Eclogue for Christmas'

Chaste convalescents from an exigent world,
we come to rivers when we are young or old;
stir-crazy, driven by cabin fever, I choose
the 10th St. Pier and toddle into the cold.
Where once the waters spun to your fierce screws
— *Nieuw Amsterdam, Caronia, Île de France* —
ice inches seaward in a formal dance
where now, adrift with trash and refuse barges,
the photo-realist estuary 'discharges
its footage' into the blind Atlantic snow
where ice confines the crippled *QE2.*
Smoky and crepitant, glacier-spiky, rough
in its white logic, it is a lithograph
from *The Ancient Mariner*, from *Scott's Last Voyage*
or *The Narrative of Arthur Gordon Poe*;
and old Heraclitus might have walked here too.
This morning, though, the throes of a warm snap
so ice cracks far off like a thunderclap
somewhere along Bohemia's desert coast
and puffs drift in the harsh riparian light,
gun-cotton against storm-clouds in the west
that rain infection and industrial waste,
though now we emerge from the industrial night;
and I recall my ten-year-old delight
at the launch of a P & O liner in Belfast,
all howling 'O God, Our Help in Ages Past',
tugs hooting, loose tons of chain thundering into the tide.
I can hear no Jersey blackbird serenade
this rapt friar on the Big Apple side;
yet, having come so far from home,

I try to imagine our millennium
where, in the thaw-water of an oil-drum,
the hot genes of the future seethe. The sun
shines on the dump, not on the *côte d'azur*
and not on the cloistered murals, to be sure.
— SUBVERT THE DOMINANT PARADIGM. GABRIEL 141.

V

'To Mrs. Moore at Inishannon'

> *The sculptor reacted with horror to the prospect of immigrants landing near his masterpiece; he called it 'a monstrous plan'. So much for Emma Lazarus . . .*
> — Mary Gordon, *Good Boys and Dead Girls*

No. 1, 5th Avenue, New York City, Sept. 14th, 1895
— and Mother, dear, I'm glad to be alive
after a whole week on the crowded *Oceanic* —
tho' I got here all right without being sick.
We boarded in the rain, St. Colman's spire
shrinking ashore, a few lamps glimm'ring there
(*'Will the last to leave please put out the lights?'*),
and slept behind the engine for six nights.
A big gull sat at the masthead all the way
from Roche's Point to Montock, till one day
it stagger'd up and vanish'd with the breeze
in the mass'd rigging by the Hudson quays . . .
Downtown, dear God, is like a glimpse of Hell
in a 'hot wave': drunken men, the roaring 'El',
the noise and squalour indescribable.
(Manners are rough and speech indelicate;
more teeming shore than you cd. shake a stick at.)
However, the Kellys' guest-house; church and tram;
now, thanks to Mrs. O'Brien, here I am
at last, install'd amid the kitchenware
in a fine house a short step from Washington Square.
Protestants, mind you, and a bit serious
much like the Bandon sort, not crack like us,
the older children too big for their britches
tho' Sam, the 4-yr.-old, has me in stitches:
in any case, the whole country's under age.
I get each Sunday off and use the privilege
to explore Broadway, the new Brooklyn Bridge
or the Statue of Liberty, copper torch on top
which, wd. you believe it, actually lights up,

and look at the Jersey shoreline, blue and gold:
it's all fire and sunlight here in the New World.
Eagles and bugles! Curious their simple faith
that stars and stripes are all of life and death —
as if Earth's centre lay in Central Park
when we both know it runs thro' Co. Cork.
Sometimes at night, in my imagination,
I hear you calling me across the ocean;
but the money's good, tho' I've had to buy new clothes
for the equatorial climate. I enclose
ten dollars, more to come (here, for God's sake,
they fling the stuff around like snuff at a wake).
'Bye now; and Mother, dear, you may be sure
I remain

yr. loving daughter,

— Bridget Moore.

VI

INSIDER TRADING REPORTS ARE LINKED TO PRICE OF BONDS
NO SOLUTION AT HAND WHILE NUCLEAR WASTE PILES UP
NEW YORK TOUGHING IT OUT TO GET THROUGH THE COLD
QUESTION REALITY DEATH IS BACK NIGHT OWL GABRIEL 141
AT&T BOEING CHRYSLER DUPONT DIGITAL DOW JONES
EXXON GENERAL MOTORS IBM NYNEX SEARS
PARANOIA McCANN ERICKSON AMERICA AFTER DARK
ESCAPED BRONX SEABIRDS SPOTTED IN CENTRAL PARK . . .
. . . On ledge and rail they sit, Inca tern and Andean gull, who
fled their storm-wrecked cage in the Bronx Zoo
and now flap in exhilaration and growing fear
above Yonkers, New Rochelle, Great Neck, Astoria,
Long Beach, Red Hook, Bay Ridge, the whole 'tri-state area',
a transmigration of souls, crazy-eyed as they peer
through mutant cloud-cover and air thick with snow-dust,
toxic aerosol dazzle and invasive car exhaust,
or perch forlorn on gargoyle and asbestos roof,
fine-featured, ruffled, attentive, almost too high to hear
the plaintive, desolate cab-horns on Madison and 5th:
like Daisy's Cunard nightingale, they belong in another life.
They are intrigued, baffled and finally bored stiff
by the wised-up millions lunching far below
but vulnerable too as, askance, they stare
at the alien corn of Radio City, Broadway and Times Square
and up again at the clouds: where on earth can they go?
They 'won't touch garbage'; so where and what will they eat?
If you see one of these nervous birds on ledge or sill
(dark blue, light grey, white head and tail, red bill),
contact the Manhattan Avian Rehab Centre
— (212) 689-3039 — and ask for Clare or Jill;
though, to be frank, their chances are less than fair
nor, to be honest, is our confidence great
that these rare species will be fit to compete
in the fight for survival on the city street
with urban gulls, crows, and other toughs of the air.

VII

The Travel Section

(after Laforgue)

I'm reading about life on the prairie and frontier
when a voice cries: 'Hey, you could live here!'
Outcast from the old world, a desperado
without God or governance, where could I not go?
Out there I'll scalp my European brain,
run wild like a young colt on the open plain —
a sort of post-literate, Huck Finn child of nature
or existential citizen of the future,
an idealistic rustic, rancher, architect,
hunter, fisherman, gambler, prickly autodidact;
and live, buckskin-clad, on whiskey and pot-roast
between Colorado and the Pacific Coast,
sleeping out under pre-Columbian skies
more generous than our bourgeois certainties!
And? A mystique of camp-sites, the 'Lynch' law,
rough diamonds to clutch in my grubby paw,
a gold-rush over the desert at first light,
a poker school around the fire at night . . .
When I grow old, a farm in the sunrise,
a dairy cow, grandchildren at my knees
and, slung from the twin cow-horns over the gate,
a split-pine signboard advertising 'Body Art'.
And if fond memories of the Place Vendôme
or the high hopes of my contemporaries
should tempt me into thoughts of going home
or the rocky buzzard come to symbolize
the infinite, as opposed to the purple sage,
I'll start a new cult of the Golden Age
with its own code based on holistic books,
blithe and post-modern, for the post-pastoral folks.

VIII

Ovid on West 4th

Women are necessarily capable of almost anything in their struggle for survival and can scarcely be convicted of such man-made crimes as 'cruelty'.

— F. Scott Fitzgerald,
Tender is the Night

When his wronged wife Procne sat him down to eat
King Tereus little knew what was on his plate.
(Afternoon now, some silence in the street
till released children dash to bus and swing.)
Pretending this dinner was a traditional thing,
an Athenian feast fit only for a king,
she excused the servants. Throned in his royal seat,
poor Tereus sipped his wine in solitary state
and, forking his own son hot from a covered dish,
called out: 'Hey, send young Itys here to me!'
Procne could barely conceal her wicked glee
and, keen to tell him the ghastly news, replied,
pointing at Tereus' stomach: 'There he is inside!'
'What do you mean?' says Tereus, looking foolish,
'I don't see him.' Then, as he called once more,
fair Philomela appeared, dripping with blood, and flung
Itys' severed head, itself streaming with gore,
right in Tereus' face, as he picked at his own young.
Oh, how she longed then for the use of her tongue!
Nothing would have given her greater pleasure
than to whisper a few harsh words to her ravisher;
as for the king, he nearly had a seizure
to think that he should eat his . . . own son Itys.
Howling, he swept aside the candlesticks
and called the furies from the depths of Styx —
no, howling he overturned the dinner table
and called the furies from the hobs of Hell.
Unhinged to think this flesh of his own flesh

consumed by the viscera where the genes first grew
and he his own son's charnel-house, he drew
his sword to open his own digestive tract
and pluck the chewed-up gobbets from the mush
but turned instead on the two sisters, who fled
as if on wings; and they *were* winged, in fact,
both of them changed in a twinkling into birds
whirring and twittering inches above his head,
swallow and nightingale hovering in mid-air.
One flew to the roof-top, one flew to the woods
where, even today, the nightingale can be heard
descanting in convent garden and Georgian square —
while Tereus, with hair on end and furious sword-bill,
turned into a hoopoe and is furious still . . .
. . . Never mind the hidden agenda, the sub-text;
it's not really about male arrogance, 'rough sex'
or vengeful sisterhood, but about art
and the encoded mysteries of the human heart.

IX

'Nature, not having included me in her plan,
has treated me like an uninvited guest'
— Turgenev, *Diary of a Superfluous Man.*
Uneaten, you call home while I take a rest.
It's 9.00 p.m. London time when your mother
picks up the phone 3,000 miles away
in Shepherd's Bush. Dinner is nearly over
perhaps, and the BBC on the news-box
(Soviet disintegration, 'Anglo-Irish' talks)
as it used to be, while on the sofa lie
new fiction, Jacobean drama, philosophy,
the *Observer* magazine and the *Daily Mail.*
— I'm guessing . . . Tell me, son, do you recall,
ten years ago now, when our 'little platoon'
would march round Barrie's pond each afternoon?
Here early for the World Cup and having a ball,
you talk to your sister now in that lost domain
describing how, holed up in a brownstone
on St. Luke's Place, and painting the house in lieu
of rent, you're goofing off tonight to a party below Canal
with friends in the film scene and the grunge rock milieu;
then on I come ('Hi, Katie') with my banal
'Happy Birthday' and 'Happy St. Valentine's Day'
and my lame excuses for not being able to pay
your school fees this time round; and I feel,
all of a sudden, like the worst kind of heel.
Sometimes, as I sit in the pub or stand up there
in Columbia University like Philby in Red Square,
I blush like a traitor; but what kind of a traitor?
A traitor to the past? To a country not our own?
To the land of fiscal rectitude and spiritual desolation?
The 'family values' brigade? The conservative task-force?
The gene militia? The armies of the unborn?
I know 'our loyalty to unhappiness', of course,
'the feeling that this is where we really belong';
and yet, across 3,000 miles of water
and five time-zones, my own prayer for my daughter

would be, not innocence and ceremony
exactly, but a more complicated grace,
the sort of thing you play when you're alone
in the House of Atreus, something slow and meditative,
some rich myth of reconciliation
as if a statue moved and began to live —
for I like to think all this is a winter's tale.
A precocious feminist, already at the age of five
contemptuous of your raggedy dolls, derisive
yet *seerious*, I know you'd take a pretty satirical view
of the daft cards and naff hearts in the stores right now
— 'Be Mine', you know what I mean, 'I Dream Only of You' —
yet at American dusk, if I catch, as I sometimes do,
a TV-lighted, nuclear-family glimpse
of pillows, home computers and Noguchi lamps,
it sets me thinking of old times and how,
too busy growing up myself, I failed to watch you grow.
Sometime soon you must visit this musical city
to hear Purcell in Carnegie Hall, an American string quartet,
Eartha Kitt at the St. Regis, *Il Trovatore* at the Met.
I've had neither the authority nor the opportunity
to tell you about the things you need to know,
as your mother will: how not to rely on looks
only, but on acquired skills and the wisdom found in books —
up to a point, of course . . . You were a scream,
therefore a born artist, but even the *being* is an art
we learn for ourselves, in solitude, on our very own,
listening to the innermost silence of the heart,
prolonging the inconsequence of a gaze
and dreaming at all times our uninterruptible dream
of redemptive form. I saw a film recently,
Glenn Gould playing Bach to the Canadian wilderness,
the great chords crashing out into empty space,
the music of the planet, the glorious racket
with which we explain ourselves in perpetuity
to our hi-tech geological posterity
at the frozen outer reaches of the galaxy.

It's ridiculous but just do it, as they say here;
make noise without embarrassment or fear. Take it
from the top, Katie; yours is the sound we want to hear!

X

St. Mark's Place

Auden, floppy-slippered bear of St. Mark's Place,
I seem to glimpse your cheesy limestone face
as you stand at your dirty window, gin in paw,
on a hot evening during the great Cold War
where the young Trotsky published *Novy Mir*.
Joseph the druggist, Abe in the liquor store,
Maurice the mailman and Marianne Moore
are the happier for your grumpy love; for, funny
in Hobbit T-shirt and dubious Levi's, you
were a victim of nothing but irony, Gramsci's new
'disease of the interregnum'; and to castration-
and-death phone-threats replied without hesitation:
'I think you've the wrong number.' Lord of martini
and clerihew, so insistent on your privacy,
who so valued personal responsibility,
what would you make now of the cosmic *pax
Americana*, our world of internet and fax,
an ever more complex military-industrial complex,
situational ethics, exonerative 12-step programs,
health fascism, critical theory and 'smart' bombs?
While we hole up in our bath-houses and catacombs,
votaries of Eros if not always of Aphrodite,
I see you ride at rush-hour with your rich pity
and self-contempt an uptown train packed to the doors
with 'aristocratic Negro faces', not like ours,
or reciting 'The Unknown Citizen' at the 'Y'.
When will she — Gaia, Clio — send downpours
to silence the 'gnostic chirrup' of her calumniators?
When will we hear once more the pure voice of elation
raised in the nightwood of known symbol and allusion?
Oh, far from Mother, in the unmarried city,
you contemplate a new ode to Euphrosyne,
goddess of banquets; and in the darkest hours
of holocaust and apocalypse, cheap music and singles bars,

you remind us of what the examined life involves —
for what you teach is the courage to be ourselves,
however ridiculous; and if you were often silly
or too 'prone to hold forth', you prescribe a cure
for our civilization and its discontents
based upon *agapè*, baroque opera, common sense
and the abstract energy that brought us here,
sustaining us now as we face a more boring future.

XI

Chinatown

> *The wind of the common people whirls from lanes and alleys, poking the rubbish, stirring up the dust . . .*
> — Hsiang Ch'u, 3rd c.

. . . and whips the pagodas of Confucius Square.
GABRIEL 141. DEATH IS BACK. FIND THE CURE.
A rackety sunset under a storm-lit sky
where we sit, uncool dad and laconic son,
amid the festive clatter of Son Low Kee,
dining on midnight mussels and sesame prawn
torn from the hairy darkness of the sea.
A crackle of firecrackers all over the ward
for the Chinese New Year, Gambino and Genovese
having moved on. 'Where the broom fails to reach,'
said Mao, 'the dust won't clear of its own accord';
but we like it here in this ethnocentric refuge
under the fairy lights of Brooklyn Bridge
where the quiet or chattering families sit at board.
We're one of the quiet tables as we review
your temporary job, tonight's occasion.
You're listening to Guns 'n' Roses, Simple Minds, U2
and reading *Moby Dick*, according to you;
but I recognize your strategies of evasion
for I too was young and morose, in youth
a frightful little shit, to tell the truth,
a rancorous paragon of bile and sloth
in the days of nihilism and alienation,
though housetrained by your mother later on:
in any event, those ancient days are gone
like the T'ang Dynasty and the shoes of 1941.
We are all lost boys, or so we like to imagine —
each sprung, like Gatsby, from his own self-conception;
whereas, of course, there's not much you can do
about the odd parents who conceived of you

and being young, I remember it well, is tough:
will the last bus be gone, her light be on or off?
I wouldn't do it again for all the tea in Taiwan;
but, now that you've reached the age of rock and soccer,
road-movie dreams, and I the age of 'serious medicine',
let me, Polonius of the twilight zone,
offer you some belated, functional succour.
I need hardly speak to you in praise of women
since you grew up amongst them. (So did I
but there's a tale will keep indefinitely.)
Be thou familiar but by no means vulgar; shun
the fatuous rectitude of received opinion,
newspeak and euphemism. Don't 'stick up for your rights'
or worry about your self-esteem; contrive
your own life and live it by your own lights
where such considerations don't apply.
Costly thy habit as thy purse can buy.
Be sceptical but wholehearted; don't be shy;
avoid spirits and nicotine; read Stendhal on love;
trust your own instincts, even the most fugitive;
and welcome to *la condition humaine*.
Cheer up, son; oh, and above all disbelieve
the cynic who tries to tell you how to behave
for, as Confucius said, fine words are seldom humane.

XII

Alien Nation

These chronic homeless are mostly single adults who have given up seeking help because they feel the 'system' has given up on them and is largely unresponsive to their needs. Many are substance abusers . . . Getting high or drunk may be the only way they know of alleviating their pain and disappointment.

— *What You Can Do to Help the Homeless*
(Simon and Schuster 1991)

RX GOTHAM DRUG GAY CRUISES SONY LIQUORS MARLBORO
ADULT VIDEO XXX BELSHAZZAR FIND THE CURE
IGLESIA ADVENTISTA DEL 7MO. DIA . . .
. . . We come upon them in the restless dark
in the moon-shadow of the World Trade Centre
with Liberty's torch glimmering over the water,
glued to a re-run of *The Exterminator*
on a portable TV in a corner of Battery Park
(some have park views, others sleep in the park),
and think how sensible the alternative polity
beneath the ostensible, pharaonic city
glimpsed through rain or dust from an expressway —
the old clothes, packing cases and auto trunks
seen everywhere from here to the South Bronx,
its population growing by the week, by the day,
oblivious to our chaos theories and data banks,
from the Port Authority Bus Terminal to JFK
and farther afield, in freight-yard and loading bay,
gull-screaming landfill, stripped trailer and boxcar,
the gap increasing between the penthouse tower
and the desert of cinderblock and razor wire
watered by truck-stop rainbow and sun-shower,
or behind the Ritz-Carlton and Holiday Inn.
We are all survivors in this rough terrain;
I know you and you me, you wretched buggers,
and I've no problem calling you my brothers

for I too have been homeless and in detox
with BAAAD niggaz 'n' crack hoes on the rocks
and may be there again, for all I know,
roaming the streets at neon-fingered dawn.
Blown here like particles from an exploding sun,
we are all far from home, be our home still
a Chicago slum, a house under the Cave Hill
or a caravan parked in a field above Cushendun.
Clutching our bits and pieces, arrogant in dereliction,
we are all out there, filling the parks and streets
with our harsh demand: 'Sleep faster, we need the sheets!'
Now off to your high loft in the disco night,
young faces glittering under trippy light,
smoke red and yellow where the doctor spins
high-octane decks among the boogie bins.
An ocean breeze, wild-flower-scented, soft and warm,
blows downtown where we part in the night air;
a Haitian driver, mordant as Baudelaire,
whisks me up Hudson St. in a thunderstorm.

XIII

Sappho in 'Judith's Room'

What is important now is to recover our senses; in place of a hermeneutics we need an erotics of art.

— Susan Sontag,
Against Interpretation (1964)

The reed-voiced nightingale has been my guide,
soft-spoken announcer of spring, whose song I set
against a cult of contention I decried —
except, of course, for 'the fight to be affectionate'.
A corps of men, a list of ships? Give me instead
my non-violent girls — Cydro, Gongula — and particularly
our glamorous Anactoria somewhere over the sea
whose eyes' mischievous sparkle remains to me
a finer sight than Homeric bronze; for now,
like the moon rising at sunset, casting its glow
on the waves, on evening meadows of brine and dew,
she climbs the night sky, and perhaps her heart too
is heavy with recollection, perhaps out there she hears
the wind among the reeds, and calls, so the soft-petal'd ears
of darkness hear her, and the dividing sea.
Aphrodite, weaver of intrigue, revisit my heart
as so often before in your dove-drawn chariot.
Nothing was alien to me, nothing inhuman:
what did I teach but the love of women?
Soon, when the moon and Pleiades have gone,
in the vast silence of the night I shall lie alone
or sit, 'tenth Muse', in this American bookstore
relishing the historical ironies in store
and the 'homeless flow of life' beyond the door.
The authors are all women, and I myself
am represented on the poetry shelf
(miraculously, I hold here in my hands
stanzas exhumed from the Egyptian sands);
for if harsh nature made me short and dark
she picked me out to do immortal work

and grades my stature, slight though I seem to be,
in lines of verse that are still read even here
and not just by my own Sapphic coterie.
Sure I've been down to the dead kingdom to hear
the grim statistics, and seen with my own eyes
women and children in their extremities
but, beyond speech and the most inclusive song,
my theme is love and love's *daimonic* character,
a site of praise and not of grievances
whatever the torment — which we meet, if wise,
in our best festive and ingenious guise.
Let of old Plato frown the eye austere,
before the *cafeneion* I'd sit when young
in sea-girt Mytilene of the dirty dances
making eye contact with new acquaintances
and relishing our sweet Aeolian tongue;
and, now that I exceed in fame our fine
Alcaeus, the laureate of politics and wine
whose high style was more 'serious' than mine,
the bad girls of my cult, an ardent choir
whose shafts shivered their music in my lyre,
votaries of Aphrodite, a thoughtful crowd,
still gather here to hear me read aloud;
and if I cling still to an old favouritism
or fall for a younger man from time to time
I'm happiest here in a place like Judith's Room
with Djuna, Janis, Gloria, Brooke and Kim.
Girls all, be with me now and keep me warm —
didn't I *say* we'd live again in another form?

XIV

Beauty and the Beast

> *'I don't know any stories; none of the lost boys know any stories.'*
> *'How perfectly awful', said Wendy.*
>
> — J. M. Barrie,
> *Peter Pan*

I go night-shopping like Frank O'Hara I go bopping
up Bleecker for juice, croissants, Perrier, ice-cream
and Gitane filters, pick up the laundry, get back
to five (5!) messages on the answering machine
from Mary K. and Eliza, Louis, Barry and Jack,
and on TV sixty channels of mind-polluting dreck.
Thank God for the VCR. Now at last I can screen
the old movies I haven't seen since I was young —
A Night to Remember, Rear Window, High Noon,
The Man Who Never Was, A King in New York . . .
Tonight, for example, tickled to bits, I stick on
the 'original, uncut' version of *King Kong*:
childish, perhaps, but a cultural critic's dream.
I re-wind, fast-forward, and replay the scene
where Kong instals Fay Wray screaming on the high rock
where he lives, and she's attacked by a gryphon, roc,
velociraptor, hoopoe, some such creation,
a thousand feet above the Indian Ocean,
wherever, and you can see the little freighter
waiting far out there on the sparkling water.
Sensitive Kong doesn't interfere with her sexually
though he does *paw* and sniff his fingers, actually,
eyes bright with curiosity; then the entire cast
come tough-talking through the primeval rain forest,
chivalrous Robert Armstrong sets her free
and they run off together down to the shore,
indignant Kong chasing them with a roar
because the poor sap really loves her, do you see.

I sit here like an old child with a new toy
or a creature from outer space, Saturn perhaps,
admiring the ingenuity of the planet of the apes
when (look!) the huge gorilla, the size of a fly
('Eighth Wonder of the World', says the publicity),
climbs up, like Batman, the side of the Empire State,
a black speck outlined against the morning sky
clutching Fay, said Noël Coward, 'like a suppository'.
It's all inconsistent, of course, and disproportionate,
he's too small there and too big on the street, *I know,*
but it makes no difference, it's a magnificent show.
. . . The little bi-planes come gunning for him now
and Kong, by Jove, knocks one of them out of the sky
with a hairy hand. They wear him out, of course,
and he falls to extinction among the crowds below.
And Fay??? She screams but she's safe; it might've been worse.
I breathe again and zap, lord of the universe,
the credits. Semiotician, couch potato,
I've had them all here in my room on video —
Leigh, Grahame, Taylor, Kelly and Monroe;
but why so few poems for the women I know?
Because these things used to be open to innuendo?
Fay, born in Alberta, you were also in *Dirigible*
and 'existed most forcefully when faced with terror'
says *Video Guide* — like most of us, probably. Well,
Kong and I dedicate this one to you, old girl,
wherever you are; pushing 90 and hanging in there,
we want you to know we love you and root for you still.

(*for Fay Wray*)

XV

Domnei

Now that we all get laid and everyone swings,
who needs the formal continence of *l'amour*
courtois and the hang-ups of a provincial clique
before innocence died at Béziers and Montségur?
Still, in the brisk heart a faint voice will speak,
in a starlit corner of the soul there sings
to an enclosed loved one the intense troubadour
in his quaint language, and his rondeau rings
resiliently on the vineyards, streams and rock-
strewn hillsides of 12th-century Languedoc;
still in her forest tower under the wide rain
of Poitiers, Limoges, Dordogne or Aquitaine
there sleeps the remote, enfamilied chatelaine
or she herself (Marie de Ventadour,
Iseult de Capio) writes to another man —
while Riquier, Bornheil, Vidal and Uc St.-Cir,
the accomplished amateur and the shivering boy
render, beneath her window, a 'chaste' homage.
The sun goes down beyond the known world's edge
and a crescent moon climbs an incurious sky;
as to the kind of love we mean, they say,
one must be patient, such is its quality —
nor is there place here for the coward, bluffer
or those rhymers who, mingling lies with truth,
corrupt the wife, the husband and the lover.
Perhaps all this was a deplorable thing,
a vicious fiction or a coercive myth —
but when the earth renews itself in spring
and whitethorn flowers to hear the blackbird sing
I too sing, although she whom I admire
finds little to her taste in what I write.
I praise not only her clear skin and fine eyes
but also her frank speech and distinguished air;
so dumbstruck am I on her visiting days

I can find no words to speak of my desire
yet, when she leaves me, my composure flees.
No one I know can hold a candle to her
and when the world dims, as it does tonight,
I see the house she goes to blaze with light.

XVI

Key West

our little wooden northern houses
— Elizabeth Bishop

Somewhere along Route 1 — Plantation, Tavernier —
cloud-splitting Angie broke over the Keys last year
in June, the earliest ever, bringing torrential rains,
though it wasn't one of those really *terrible* hurricanes
you hear about, that wreck 'homes' and wreak atrocities
on isolated farms, snug harbours, close communities,
but a swift cloud-stream of premonitory showers
that waltzed off in the direction of New Orleans
irrigating pine and cedar, lemon groves and sandbars
while the Bahamas heaved in still-turbulent seas.
The outskirts of Key West, when we got there,
you driving, your new sunglasses in your hair
and Satchmo growling from the car radio,
were still where they were supposed to be, and calm
between downpours red poinciana, jasmine, palm
and the white frame-houses built a century ago
by tough skippers against cyclone and tornado
whistling in from the Gulf of Mexico.
The town gasped in a tropical heatwave
and I recalled old Mr. Temple's narrative
in *Key Largo*, the great nameless storm of 1935
that killed 800 people (it did too) and blew
the East Coast Railroad into the ocean — true,
the bridges are still standing, but that was the last train.
Suave mari magno turbulantis aequora ventis
e terra magnum alterius spectare laborem:
it's cool, when gale-force winds trouble the waters,
to watch from shore the tribulations of others!
. . . Uh-oh, before dawn it came round again,
fat drops hitting on storm lanterns, demented budgies
screeching beyond the pool and the churning trees;
and I pictured the vast turmoil undersea,

a mute universe of sponge and anemone,
of conch and snapper, octopus and algae,
odd fish of every stripe in their coral conservatories,
while counting the chimes of St. Mary's, Star of the Sea.
Later, exhausted hens on the telephone lines,
disheveled dogs in the flooded Bahamian lanes:
chaos, *triste tropique* — till, mauve and rose,
flecked with pistachio cloud, a new kind of day arose
and I saw why once to these shores came *other* cold
solitaries down from the north in search of love and poetry
— the mad sailor, the stuffed bullfinch blue and gold,
the shy perfectionist with her painter's eye —
to sing in the crashing, galaxy-lit sea-porches.
It was one of those far-out, raw mornings, the beaches
littered with dreck, and a derelict dawn moon,
mountains and craters in visible cameo, yearned
close to the earth as if murmuring to return,
milk of what heavenly breast, dew drenching the skin —
a wreckers' morning, with everyone a bit lost
as if landed from Senegal or the Ivory Coast.
Why so soon in the season? Newspapers and TV
spoke of 'El Niño', the fabulous, hot tide-thrust
born in December off Peru like the infant Christ
sea-changing *all* with its rough magic; and advised
of hurricanes to come, so that one feared not only
for the Cuban cabin and the gimcrack condominium
but for the 'sleek and effortless vacation home'
featured in the current issue of *Key Design*,
the 'storm-resistant' dream house with its 'vinyl membrane',
a bait-fridge and 'teak sailfish-fighting chair';
for roads and bridges, lighthouses, any structure
presumed permanent; towns and cities everywhere
vulnerable to a trickle of sand, to a breath of fresh air;
and thought of the fragility of all architecture,
the provisional nature even of aerospace.
I keep on my desk here a coarse handful of Florida sea-moss

and remember, this wintry night, that summery place —
how we strolled out there on the still-quaking docks
shaken but exhilarated, turned to retrace
our steps up Caroline St., and sat in Pepe's
drinking (rum and) Coke with retired hippies
who long ago gave up on the land and settled among the rocks.

XVII

Imbolc

A roof over my head, protected from the rain,
I'm reading, pilgrim father, your letters to your son
and wondering if, unlike you, I should head for home.
Escaping the turbulence of this modern Rome
in a flurry of skyline views and exploding foam,
I can see that 747 in flight over Nova Scotia,
over Shannon and Limerick, snoring back to the future,
to that land of the still-real I left in '91,
of Jennifer Johnston and Seosaimhín Ní Gabhráin;
I can see the old stormy island from the air,
its meteorological gaiety and despair,
some evidence of light industry and agriculture,
familiar contours, turfsmoke on field and town;
I can even hear the cabin crew's soft '*fáilte*'
and the strains of 'My Lagan Love' as we touch down.
A recovering Ulster Protestant like you from Co. Down,
I shall walk the Dublin lanes as the days grow shorter,
I who once had a poem in *The New Yorker*,
and spend old age, if any, in an old mac
with the young audibly sneering behind my back,
deafened by seagulls and the playground cries
of children — ourselves, once — by perilous seas.
Now, listening to the *rus-in-urbe*, spring-in-winter noise
of late-night diners, while the temperatures rise
and the terrible wind-chill factor abates, I realize
the daffodils must be out in ditch and glen
and windows soon flung wide to the 'small' rain;
and marvel how, a figure out of the past,
an old man in a hurry, you stuck it here to the last,
negotiating the icefields of 8th Avenue
to die on West 29th of the Asian flu.
. . . But first you met by chance at the riverside
a young woman with a sick child she tried to hide
(not out of shame, you felt, but anguished pride),

soft-spoken, 'from Donnybrook', amid the alien corn.
'*It pained me that her bright image should fade.*'
Thus your epiphany, and you wrote to explain:
'The nightingale sings with its breast against a thorn,
it's out of pain that personality is born'.
Things you understood: children, the human face,
'something finer than honesty', the loneliness
of beautiful women, the priority of the real.
Things that puzzled you: economy, fear,
the argument from design, the need to feel secure,
the belief in another world besides this one here.
Despite your rationalism, did it ever appear
that the universe might be *really* 'magical', sir,
and you yourself a showing-forth of that soul?
'Art is dreamland.' When you rejoined the whole
what glimpse was given to you in the black hole?
Now, to 'Yeats, Artist and Writer', may we add
that you were at home here and in human nature
but also, in your own words, lived and died
like all of us, then as now, 'an exile and a stranger'?

XVIII

The Small Rain

I do hate people who come knocking late.
— Eartha Kitt

Once upon a time it was let me out and let me go —
the night flight over deserts, amid cloud,
a dream of discipline and fit solitude.
Now, drifters, loners, harsh and disconsolate,
'inane and unappeased', we come knocking late;
and now it's take me back and take me in.
So take us in where we set out long ago,
the enchanted garden in the lost domain,
the vigilant lamplight glimpsed through teeming rain,
the house, the stove in the kitchen, the warm bed,
the hearth, *vrai lieu*, ranged crockery overhead —
'felicitous space' lost to the tribes. I lodge
one window slightly open to let in the night air
— 10° below, these nights, on average —
thus heating the street, the clouds, the stratosphere,
and peer down through the fire-escape. It's broad
day all night on the 24-hr. film-set,
kliegs bright on stadium and construction site;
but a civilization based on superfluous light
concedes no decent dark, so we create
with blinds and blankets our own private night
to keep the glare out. Searchlights and dead stars
pick out the Trump Tower and the United Nations,
the halls of finance, the subway walls of the brain,
the good, the bad, the ugly and the insane,
the docks and Governor's Island; and the bars
where the lost and the disappointed feel no pain
are empty except for the all-night populations
with no homes to go to but their eternal one.
This is the hour of the chained door and the locked gate,
harsh blues of the rowdy and the unfortunate,

and the fetishes are wakeful in their places —
lamp, chair, desk, oil-heater and bookcases
brisk with a bristling, mute facticity
connecting them to the greater community
of wood and minerals throughout the city.
When the present occupant is no longer here
and durables prove transient, as they do,
all will survive somehow; the pictures too,
prints, posters, reproductions, such as they are:
Botticelli's sea-born, shell-borne Aphrodite,
Dunluce, 'The Doors of Dublin', Whitman in a suit,
Monet skiffs on the Seine, a window by Bonnard,
Leech's convent garden, a Hopper light,
Hokusai's wave, Lichtenstein's *ingénue*
shedding a tear ('B . . . but, Jeff . . .') beside the door
and (look!) my favourite, over there on the right,
picked up at a yard-sale in Connecticut,
Kroyer's *Women on the Beach*, a hazy shore,
their footprints in the sand to the waterline,
the human presence since we live here too —
all primal images in their different ways
watching for springtime and the lengthening days.
Jequirity, monkshood, nightshade, celandine;
the friends and contemporaries begin to go
— Nina Gilliam, Eugene Lambe, and others too.
'A dry soul is best'; and at night to lie
empty of mind, the heart at peace; *and thou,*
dark mother, cave of wonders, open now
to our languor the interior of the rose
that closes round volition, and disclose
your secret, be it Byzantium or the sphere
all centre, no circumference . . . I pretend
you're here beside me; guardian angel, best friend,
practitioner of tough love and conservation,
I'd say make all safe and harmonious in the end
did I not know the voyage is never done

for, even as we speak, somewhere a plane
gains altitude in the moon's exilic glare
or a car slips into gear in a silent lane . . .
I think of the homeless, no rm. at the inn;
far off, the gaseous planets where they spin,
the starlit towers of Nineveh and Babylon,
the secret voice of nightingale and dolphin,
fish crowding the Verrazano Bridge; and see,
even in the icy heart of February,
crocus and primrose. When does the thaw begin?
We have been too long in the cold. — Take us in; take us in!

The Yellow Book

(Context: Baudelaire)

Chastely to write these eclogues I need to lie,
like the astrologers, in an attic next the sky
where, high among church spires, I can dream and hear
their grave hymns wind-blown to my ivory tower.
Chin in hand, up here in my apartment block,
I can see workshops full of noise and talk,
cranes and masts of the ocean-going city,
vast cloud-pack photographs of eternity.
I watch a foggy star open and shine
in the azure sky, a lamp at a window-pane,
smoke rising into the firmament like incense,
the moon dispensing its mysterious influence.
I watch for spring and summer, autumn too;
and when the winter comes, with silent snow,
I shut the shutters and close the curtains tight
to build my faerie palaces in the night
and think of love and gardens, blue resorts,
white fountains splashing into marble courts,
birds chirping day and night, whatever notion
tickles the infantile imagination . . .
Rattling the window with its hoarse burlesque
no mob distracts me from my writing desk;
for here I am, up to my usual tricks —
evoking springtime on the least pretext,
extracting sunlight as my whims require,
my thoughts blazing for want of a real fire.

I

Night Thoughts

One striking post-war phenomenon has been the transformation of numerous countries into pseudo-places whose function is simply to entice tourists.

— Paul Fussell, *Abroad*

Night thoughts are best, the ones that visit us
where we lie smoking between three and four
before the first bird and the first tour bus.
Once you would wake up shaking at this hour
but now, this morning, you are a child once more
wide-eyed in an attic room behind the shore
at some generic, gull-pierced seaside town
in war-time Co. Antrim or Co. Down —
navies aglow off Bangor and Whitehead,
dark sea, Glenn Miller's 'Moonlight Serenade',
huge transport planes thundering overhead.
Each white shoe you can remember, each stair-rod,
each streaming window on the Shore Road,
a seaside golf-links on a summer night,
'pale sand-dunes stretching away in the moonlight'.
A horse-drawn cab out of the past goes past
toward Leeson St. Night thoughts are best and worst.
My attic window under the shining slates
where children slept in the days of Wilde and Yeats
sees crane-light where McAlpine's fusiliers,
site hats and brick-dust, ruin the work of years.
The place a Georgian theme-park for the tourist,
not much remains; though still the first of dawn
whitens a locked park, lilac and hawthorn
dripping in wintry peace, a secret garden
absorbed since the end of summer in its own
existence, gulls driven inland by sea-mist.
Soon crocus, daffodil, air-brake and diesel-chug,
those rain-washed April mornings when the fog

lifts and immediate 'coaches' throng the square,
even in the bathroom I hear them shouting out there —
aliens, space invaders clicking at the front door,
goofy in baseball caps and nylon leisurewear.
. . . Sententious solitude, ancient memory, night
and silence, nobody here; but even as I night-write
blind in a bedside notebook, 'impersonal moonlight
audible on steps, railings, sash window and fanlight',
my biro breaks the silence and something stirs.
Never mind the new world order and the bus tours,
you can still switch on the fire, kick off your shoes
and read the symbolists as the season dies:
Now for the coughing in school dormitories,
the hot drink far from home. November brings
statistics, albums, cocoa, medicine, dreams,
windows flung wide on briny balconies
above an ocean of roofs and lighthouse beams;
like a storm lantern the lonely planet swings.

II

Axel's Castle

A mature artist takes the material closest to hand.
— George Moore

Rain all day; now clouds clear; a brief sun, the winds die;
a wan streak of bilious light in the sky before dark;
'the attic study and the unfinished work'.
Only at dusk Minerva's owl will fly;
only at dusk does wisdom return to the park.
On winter evenings, as the cars flash by,
what hides there in the kingdom of mould and bark?
Beyond the iron railings and the little gate
only a worm stirs, and dead leaves conflate
in a dried-up fountain crisp-packet and matchbox,
the bright pavilion silent in its nook;
dead leaves up here too, lamplight night and day.
Commuters hustle home to Terenure and Foxrock
while I sit in the inner city with my book
— *Fanny Hill, À Rebours, The Picture of Dorian Gray* —
the pleasures of the text, periphrasis and paradox,
some languorous prose at odds with phone and fax.
The psychiatrist locks up and puts out the light
above desk and couch in his consulting rooms.
It's cold up here in the city of litter and drums
while fires glow in the hearths of suburban homes;
I have no peacocks, porphyries, prie-dieux,
no lilies, cephalotis, nepenthes, 'unnatural' vices,
yet I too toil not neither do I spin, I too
have my carefully constructed artificial paradises.
A foxy lady slips into her shoes
and leaves me words of wisdom; when she goes
I sit here like Domitian in a hecatomb of dead flies,
an armchair explorer in an era of cheap flight
diverted by posters, steamer and sea-plane
at rest in tropical ports. I read where your man

transforms his kitchen into a quarterdeck
to simulate ocean travel and not get sick.
I get sea breezes in my own galley all right,
particularly before dawn when, war in heaven, I hear
remote winds rippling in the stratosphere
and regret never having visited Rio, Shanghai,
Haiti, Singapore or the South Seas; though why
travel when imagination can get you there in a tick
and you're not plagued by the package crowd? A mature
artist takes the material closest to hand;
besides, in our post-modern world economy
one tourist site is much like another site
and the holy city comes down to a Zeno tour,
the closer you get the more it recedes from sight
and the more morons block your vision. Beyond
the backlit tree-tops of Fitzwilliam Square
a high window is showing one studious light,
somebody sitting late at a desk like me.
There are some die-hards still on the upper floors,
a Byzantine privacy in mews and lane,
but mostly now the famous Georgian doors
will house a junk-film outfit or an advertising agency.
The fountain's flute is silent though time spares
the old beeches with their echoes of Coole demesne;
foreign investment conspires against old decency,
computer talks to computer, machine to answering machine.

III

At the Shelbourne

(Elizabeth Bowen, Nov., 1940)

Sunrise in the Irish Sea, dawn over Dublin Bay
after a stormy night, one shivering star;
and I picture the harsh waking everywhere,
the devastations of a world at war,
airfields, radio silence, a darkened convoy
strung out in moonlight on a glittering sea.
Harsh the wide windows of the hotel at daybreak
as I light up the first ciggie of the day,
stormy the lake like the one in Regent's Park,
glittering the first snow on the Wicklow hills.
Out back, a precipitous glimpse of silent walls,
courtyards, skylights of kitchen and heating plant,
seagulls in rising steam; while at the front
I stand at ease to hear the kettle sing
in an upper room of the Kildare St. wing,
admiring the frosty housetops of my birthplace
miraculously immune (almost) to bomb damage.
Sun through south-facing windows lights again
on the oval portrait and the polished surface
where, at an Empire writing-table, I set down
my situation reports for the Dominions Office,
pen-sketches of MacEntee, James Dillon and the rest,
letters to friends in Cork or in Gower St.,
— Virginia, Rosamond and the *Horizon* set —
bright novelistic stuff, a nation on the page:
'. . . *deep, rather futile talks. It is hard afterwards*
to remember the drift, though I remember words,
that smoke-screen use of words! Mostly I meet
the political people; they are very religious.'
There is nothing heroic or 'patriotic' about this;
for here in this rentier heaven of racing chaps,
journalists, cipher clerks, even Abwehr types

and talkative day-trippers down from Belfast,
the Mata Hari of the austerity age,
I feel like a traitor spying on my own past.
It was here the ill-fate of cities happened first —
a cruiser in the Liffey, field-guns trained on the GPO,
the kicking-in of doors, dances cancelled, revolvers
served with the morning tea on silver salvers,
a ghostly shipboard existence down below,
people asleep in corridors as now
in the London Underground, mysterious Kôr,
a change of uniforms in the cocktail bar
though the bronze slave-girls still stand where they were,
Nubian in aspect, in manner art-nouveau.
I must get the Austin out of the garage,
drive down this weekend to Bowen's Court
if I can find petrol, and back for the Sunday mail-boat —
though this is home really, a place of warmth and light,
a house of artifice neither here nor there
between the patrician past and the egalitarian future,
tempting one always to prolong one's visit:
in war, peace, rain or fog you couldn't miss it
however late the hour, however dark the night.

IV

'shiver in your tenement'

You might have thought them mature student, clerk
or priest once, long ago in the demure '60s
before the country first discovered sex —
Cathal O'Shannon, Harry Kernoff, Austin Clarke
arriving by bus at noon in search of roguery
from Howth, Raheny, Monkstown or Templeogue,
some house by bridge or woodland *à l'usage*
of the temporal, of the satiric or lyric Muse.
Gravely they strolled down Dawson or Grafton St.,
thoughtful figures amid the faces, the laughter,
or sat among the race-goers and scroungers
in Sinnott's, Neary's, the Bailey, the Wicklow Lounge —
pale, introspective almost to the point of blindness
or so it seemed, living the life of the mind,
of European *littérateurs*, their black Quartier hats
(all purchased from the same clerical outfitter)
suggestive of first editions and dusty attics.
They sipped watery Jameson — without ice, of course —
knew London and Paris but preferred the unforced
pace of the quiet city under the Dublin mountains
where a broadsheet or a broadcast might still count.
Those were the days before tourism and economic growth,
before deconstruction and the death of the author,
when pubs had as yet no pictures of Yeats and Joyce
since people could still recall their faces, their voices;
of crozier-wielding bishops, vigilant censors,
pre-conciliar Latin, smoke pouring from swung censers;
of sexual guilt, before French letter and Dutch cap,
fear muttered in the dark of dormitory and side-chapel.
There was much dark then in the archdiocese
though some, like you, had found a gap of brightness —
now, of course, we live in a blaze of tropical light
under a green pagoda sunshade globally warm
like the slick glass on a renovated farmhouse.
Mnemosyne, mother of nine, dust at St. Patrick's,

labour 'accustomed to higher living', poverty old hat,
does art benefit from the new dispensation?
What, in our new freedom, have we left to say?
Oh, poets can eat now, painters can buy paint
but have we nobler poetry, happier painting
than when the gutters bubbled, the drains stank
and hearts bobbed to the clappers in the sanctuary?
Has art, like life itself, its source in agony?
Nothing to lose but our chains, our chains gone
that bound with form the psycho-sexual turbulence,
together with those black hats and proper pubs,
at home now with the ersatz, the pop, the phony,
we seldom see a young nun, a copy of *An Phoblacht*
or love and hate, as once, with a full heart.
Those were the days; now patience, courage, artistry,
solitude things of the past, like the love of God,
we nod to you from the pastiche paradise of the post-modern.

V

Schopenhauer's Day

The recent past always presents itself as if destroyed by catastrophes.
— Adorno

What does the old bastard see when he looks down?
A creature of habit like everyone in this town,
he has lived up there above the promenade
for more than twenty years, and every day
observed the same deliberate formulae
now second nature: up at dawn, just one
mug of his favourite Java before work
— mind-body problems — flute practice (K.299),
the Pan-pipes in honour of a previous life;
then lunch with students at the Englischer Hof
and reads till four, when he goes for the daily walk —
two hours, neither more nor less, hail, rain or shine.
At six to the library and a magazine,
a thicket of fiddle-bows in the Kaisersaal,
a solitary supper at the Stork Hotel,
home by ten and early to bed: a routine
perfected over the years and one designed
to release from trivia the aspiring mind.
Cabs and coaches clash and squeal in the square,
the money-making craze is everywhere;
but a fire of pine or spruce keeps out the cold.
A pedestrian, mildly valetudinarian bachelor,
he stares from the window at his idea of the world,
its things-in-themselves, the sun rising once more
on bridge and embankment, baroque edifice, Gothic spire,
freight barges crunching ice down to the Rhine
and the innocent flower-gardens of the south shore
beaming with self-delight, churning with worms:
the earth and he were never on intimate terms.
Minerals rage, base metals dreaming of gold
in the hills, while St. Bartholomew chimes the hour;

plants, water, citizens, the very stone
expand with a sulphurous purpose of their own;
the very viruses scream to the higher forms.
Tat tvam asi; these living things we are
but only in the extinction of our desire,
absorption of the knower in the known.
There are perceptual difficulties, the *trompe-l'oeil*
of virtual reality; for what is real really?
Often we think what we see is not what we think we see;
he too is a mere appearance dreamt by another system,
he can't get through to the world nor the world to him.
As the Buddhists do, he tries to concentrate
on a faint chime (say) or on the idea of 'white'
while knowing these exercises cannot mitigate
life's guilt or the servitude of love and hate.
The only solution lies in *art for its own sake*,
redemption through the aesthetic, as birds in spring
sing for their own delight, even if they also sing
from physical need; it comes to the same thing.
'No rose without a thorn, many a thorn without a rose.'
Bring out the poets and the artists; take
music, the panacea for all our woes,
the heartfelt calculus of Bach and Mozart
or the calm light of Dutch interior art;
and yet, he says, he fears for the fate of those
born in a later era, as if our bleak
and pitiless whoring after the sublime,
implying conflict as sublimity does,
bequeathed some frightfulness to a future time:
'Through the cortex a great melancholy blows
as if I'd seen the future in a dream —
Weimar, a foul Reich and the days of wrath,
a *Vogue* model in the dead dictator's bath;
and the angel of history, a receding 'plane
that leaves the cities a rubble of ash and bone
while black soldiers tap-dance on my gravestone.'

VI

To Eugene Lambe in Heaven

— University Rd., Belfast, 1961; etc.

It's after closing-time on a winter's night
in Smoky Joe's café a generation ago —
rain and smoke, and the tables are packed tight
with drunken students kicking up a racket,
exchanging insults, looking for a fight
since there's nothing to do and nowhere else to go;
and the sad Italians (parents, daughter, son)
who own the place and serve these savages
of the harsh north their chips and sausages
look up and grin with relief as you come in,
their baffled faces lighting up at once
at your quaint 'whisker' and velvet smoking-jacket,
your manner that of an exiled Stuart prince
transfiguring tedium . . . Next year you appeared
in the same gear and spread Tolstoyan beard,
our ginger man, in Trinity's front square
you called the 'playground' once; and it was here
in pub and flat you formed the character
we came to love, colloquial yet ornate,
one of those perfect writers who never write,
a student of manners and conversation straight
from the pages of Castiglione or Baudelaire:
'*a form of pride rare in this generation,*
stoical, spiritual even, resistant to the trite;
the Protestant countries lack gallantry and devotion . . . '
Not that you read much, you had no need to read
so flunked your courses; destined for the law
took up, instead, interior decoration,
installing yourself wherever the calling led
and awaiting the 'rush of gold' you never saw.
There you were, in the fine house of a friend,
a citrous gin or herbal tea to hand,

young women in attendance, an abashed host constrained
to listen patiently while you explained
the iniquity of ownership; for you had no ambition
save for the moment, of will-power not a whit
since nothing could measure up to your idea of it.
Dublin in the '60s! — Golden days
of folk revival, tin whistle and *bodhrán*,
ecology, yin and yang, CND, late-century blues,
Gandolf's Garden, *Bananas* and *Peace News*;
then London, Covent Garden, quit the booze
but dreamed the hashish poem on opera nights,
De Quincey's 'infinite ecstasies, infinite repose',
while living above the market unknown to the old fogies
ensconced in the Garrick with their port and stogies
and the hacks in the Coach & Horses, *laudatores*
temporis acti, unregenerate Tories
shut out for ever from your generous insights.
At a time of drag and Pop Art, hair and clothes,
Beardsley prints, floral design and rainbow hues,
of Quant and Biba, Shrimpton and Twiggy, lurid tights,
gratuitous gesture, instant celebrity, insolent pose,
yours was a sociable life but a lonely one,
your castle of indolence a monastic den
where you sat up late to contemplate the din
of Leicester Square, Long Acre and Drury Lane,
vocations entertained but never followed through.
A job, a house, a car, perhaps a wife,
financial panic, the 'normal' sort of life
so many know, such things were not for you
who made the great refusal but remained
philosophical with your dwindling flow of visitors,
chivalrous with women, ceremonious with waiters,
noble in exile, tragic in the end,
and died dancing . . . But hip went out of fashion
in an age of sado-monetarism, and the game
now is to the 'oeconomists and calculators' —

the new harshness must have wounded you to the heart.
We always knew you had too big a heart,
we always knew about the heart condition
you nursed with a vegetarian regime
of rice and nuts. You were a saint and hero
to the young men and girls we used to know
once in the golden age; and now it's closing-time
in the condemned playgrounds that you loved, Eugene,
in Davy Byrne's and Smoky Joe's. The scene
is draggy now in these final days, and with
everyone famous for fifteen minutes, few
survive except those, like you, the stuff of myth.
Oft in the stilly night I remember our wasted youth.

VII

An Bonnán Buí

A heron-like species, rare visitors, most recent records referring to winter months . . . very active at dusk.
— Guide to Irish Birds

A sobering thought, the idea of you stretched there,
bittern, under a dark sky, your exposed bones
yellow too in a ditch among cold stones,
ice glittering everywhere on bog and river,
the whole unfortunate country frozen over
and your voice stilled by enforced sobriety —
a thought more wrenching than the fall of Troy
because more intimate; for we'd hear your shout
of delight from a pale patch of watery sunlight
out on the mud there as you took your first
drink of the day and now, destroyed by thirst,
you lie in brambles while the rats rotate.
I'd've broken the ice for you, given an inkling;
now, had I known it, we might both be drinking
and singing too; for ours is the same story.
Others have perished — heron, blackbird, thrushes —
and lie shivering like you under whin-bushes;
but I mourn only the bittern, withdrawn and solitary,
who used to carouse alone among the rushes
and sleep rough in the star-glimmering bog-drain.
It used to be, with characters like us,
they'd let us wander the roads in wind and rain
or lock us up and throw away the key —
but now they have a cure for these psychoses
as indeed they do for most social diseases
and, rich at last, we can forget our pain.
She says I'm done for if I drink again;
so now, relieved of dangerous stimuli,
at peace with my plastic bottle of H_2O
and the slack strings of insouciance, I sit
with bronze Kavanagh on his canal-bank seat,

not in 'the tremendous silence of mid-July'
but the fast bright zing of a winter afternoon
dizzy with head-set, flash-bulb and digifone,
to learn the *tao* he once claimed as his own
and share with him the moor-hen and the swan,
the thoughtless lyric of a cloud in the sky
and the play of light and shadow on the slow
commemorative waters; relax, go with the flow.

VIII

Hangover Square

The snowman infants from the nursery school
devised from the first fall of January
stares back from a far corner of the square —
a selfish giant made to freeze and rule
the garden as if self-generated there,
his abstract mien and cold, bituminous eye
proclaiming a different order of reality
from the bright children who gave rise to him.
When they go there to play at mid-morning
their primary colours seem to prefigure spring,
the deliquescence of each rigorous thing;
but the ex-child at the window watching them,
specs on his nose and winter in his eyes,
knows himself outcast from the continuum
and draws his curtain against darkening skies . . .
A long time since the hearties and the aesthetes,
imperious questors and saint-faced degenerates,
old boys of Yeats's 'tragic' generation
in cricketing blazers and inept bow-ties
who ate the altar rails, pawned pride for drinks
or tumbled from high stools in the Rose & Crown.
Those desperate characters of the previous '90s,
slaves of the Siren, consorts of the Sphinx
like Dowson, Johnson, Symons and Le Gallienne
were heroes, though, compared with our protagonist,
a decadent who lived to tell the story,
surviving even beyond the age of irony
to the point where the old stuff comes round again;
and this is the sin against the Holy Ghost,
the cynicism that views with equanimity
the enemies of promise, *les amours jaunes*,
the organism dark with booze and nicotine.
Today is the first day of the rest of your life?
— tell that to your liver; tell that to your ex-wife.

Owning like them 'an indolent, restless gift',
fitful, factitious and at best makeshift,
burning without warmth or illumination,
each verse co-terminous with its occasion,
each line the pretext for a precious cadence,
I keep alight the cold candle of decadence.
A rueful veteran of the gender wars,
in 'the star-crowned solitude of [mine] oblivious hours'
I remember London twilights blue with gin
sub regno Cynarae, the wine and roses
where 'She-who-must-be-obeyed', furs next the skin,
drove us to celibacy or satyriasis.
'Nothing, of course, not even conventional virtue
is so provincial as conventional vice'
— Symons, *The Symbolist Movement in Literature*.
The most of what we did and wrote was artifice,
rhyme-sculpture against the entangling vines of nature —
a futile project since, in the known future,
real books will be rarities in techno-culture,
a forest of intertextuality like this,
each one a rare book and what few we have
written for prize-money and not for love.
No doubt I should invest in a computer
but I'm sticking with my old electric typewriter,
its thick click, black ink on the white pages,
one letter at a time, fur round the edges.

IX

At the Gate Theatre

(for Dearbhla Molloy)

'. . . Ah, what new pain must I now undergo?
What monstrous torture have I yet to know?
All I've endured, the madness and the fear,
self-pity, rage, humiliation, self-hate,
the insult of rejection, even, were mere
ripples of the approaching storm . . . ' Not many
in the trade now can decently impersonate
the great ones of the tragic repertoire
— Medea, Cleopatra, Gruoch Macbeth —
much less achieve the famous 'diamond edge'
of the doomed Phaedra's lightning-inviting rage,
her great apostrophes to love and death;
so here am I, like any stage-door Johnny,
to call your playing-out of Phaedra's agony,
your bright contralto, stringed and starlit vertigo
of outrage and despair from head to toe
not only wonderful but actually sublime
in the old sense of resistance overcome,
articulate terror, storm answered with storm,
a heaven-splitting performance. When she cries
defiance to the gods, the wings, the quivering flies,
we know we are in the presence; but we know too
a whole theatrical tradition is in crisis —
this play peaked and exhausted all at once
an entire genre; for its fierce eloquence
yielded in no time to the *comic* Muse,
the death of tragedy and the Birth of the Blues.
Backstage tonight, I glimpse the ghostly faces
of Micheál and Hilton, Geraldine and Siobhán
amid the festive racket of make-up and paint-sprays,
Hedda Gabler, The School for Scandal, Happy Days,
moonlit revels and laughter in the dark,
the thrill of envenom'd chalice and poisonous book;

for tragedy too, of course, is enormous fun
though now we've no use for the tragic posture.
When the mad queen conducts her futile strife
with the blank forces of inhospitable nature
we see that the problem is not death but life —
the only cure for tragedy, the one
sure antibiotic against original sin.
The Greeks followed tragedies with satyr plays;
and look at the old age of Euripides
who, after a lifetime struggling with new ideas,
sent out his Bacchae to the woods and glens
to dance devotion to the god of vines
under the rocks, under the moonlit pines.
Bring on ivy and goatskin, pipe and drum,
for Dionysus son of Semele is come
to release us from our servitude to the sublime,
no further resistance offered by the medium,
the whole history of creative tension a waste of time.

X

The Idiocy of Human Aspiration

(Juvenal, *Satires*, X)

No one in his right mind would want to be
a big fish gobbling up the smaller fry;
it's the big fish who attract hostility
like Seneca and the rest in Nero's day.
You're better off to sit tight in your room
than be conspiring in the rising steam
among the towels of the baths and gym;
take change if you go out walking after dark,
avoid the war-zones and the periphery
and keep your wits about you in the park
where a knife gleams behind each shadowy tree.
All pursue riches in our modern Rome,
gardens, a coach-house and a 'second home'
bought with the revenue from untaxed income
at Capua, Aquinum, Trevignano or Tivoli;
but poison's seldom served in wooden cups.
Beware the crystal glass and golden bowl,
be careful when you raise wine to your lips
dining with colleagues on the Palatine hill
or old 'friends' in the Caffè Giovenal'
on swan and flamingo, antelope and stuff.
So which philosopher would we rather know
— the one who, staring from his portico,
laughs, or the one who weeps? Easy to laugh,
if we started weeping there'd be no end to it.
Democritus would shake with continual mirth,
even in *his* primitive times, at life on earth
and showed that stoicism spiced up with wit,
some candour and good sense, can mitigate
even the thick air of a provincial city.
Binge sex and fiscal heroin, discreet
turpitude flickering in a brazier light —
all anyone does now is fuck and shit;

instant gratification, infotainment, celebrity
we ask, but mumbling age comes even so,
the striking profile thick and stricken now,
the lazy tackle like a broken bough,
the simian features and the impatient heir.
What else can you expect from your white hair,
your voice like cinders under a kitchen door?
What use to you the glittering cleavages,
the best box in the house above the stage
when blind and deaf? Now fever and disease
run riot through our waste anatomies,
the old mind dithering in its anecdotage,
the joints all seizing up with rheumatism,
seek guidance of the heavenly gods who treasure
our lives more than we do ourselves. Subdued
by protocol and the fear of solitude,
you wed in haste and now repent at leisure
even as your hands shake in their final spasm.
Ask for a sound mind in a sound body
unfrightened of the grave and not demented
by grief at natural declension; study
acceptance in the face of fate; and if
you want to worship mere materialism,
that modern god we have ourselves invented,
I leave you to the delights of modern life.

XI

At the Chelsea Arts Club

Everywhere aspires to the condition of pop music,
the white noise of late-century consumerism —
besieged by Shit, Sperm, Garbage, Gristle, Scum
and other raucous trivia, we take refuge
from fan migrations, police presence, road rage,
spy cameras, radio heads, McDonald's, rowdytum,
laser louts and bouncers, chat shows, paparazzi,
stand-up comedian and thug journalist,
TOP TORIES USED ME AS THEIR SEX TOY
and Union-jacquerie at its most basic
in shadowy, murmurous sanctuaries like this
beside Whistler's Thames, once 'clothed in evening mist
where the buildings lose themselves in a dim sky,
the great chimneys become campanili
and warehouses are palaces in the night'.
Now both embankments gleam with exhausted chrome
revving at funeral pace, with the home team
up in the league and quoted on the exchange
and interest in the game at fever pitch,
we treasure the more those symphonies in white,
those nocturnes consecrating wharf and bridge.
Elsewhere the body art, snuff sculpture, trash aesthetics,
the video nasties and shock computer graphics;
but here you still might meet with 'significant form' —
indeed, the interior illustrates the term
with its retro mode and snooker table, piano,
'the whole place rather like a studio',
shirts by Jekyll & Hyde, the wine and roses,
the sniftery dandies at their studied poses,
the eyepatch woman and the monocle man,
Caroline and Georgina, Sophie, Fanny,
Oxfam and Savile Row, Versace, Armani,
garden and sky rose-red and Dufy-blue.
Maybe I'm finally turning into an old fart
but I do prefer the traditional kinds of art,

respect for materials, draughtsmanship and so on —
though I'm in two minds about Tank Girl over there,
the Muse in chains, a screw-bolt in one ear,
the knickers worn over the biking gear . . .
Best in the afternoon when the bar is shut,
the smoking room, an empty Chekhov set,
stained ochre, yields to silence, buttery light,
euphoria and nostalgia; so let me write
in praise of yellow while it is still bright,
of crocus and freesia, primrose and daffodil,
the novels of Huxley, Rimbaud's missing vowel,
yahoos, yippies, yuppies, yoga, yoghurt, Yale,
bananas, Danaë's golden shower, baby clothes and toys,
prohibition, quarantine, caution, cowardice, buoys,
lamplight, gaslight, candlelight, illness, fog,
pencils, *I Ching*, golf, 'radio-active', bubonic plague,
illuminated scripture, Klimt and Schiele, Kafka's Prague,
Aladdin's lamp and genie, mechanical earth-movers,
treason, deceit, infection, misery, unhappy lovers,
a night wake, magic realism, Gnosticism, Cabbalism,
guilt and grief, conspiracy theories, crime,
the back pages, dangerous liaisons, journalism,
charity, sunlit smoke, delight and shame,
angels and archangels, cherubim and seraphim,
the earliest buses, the Congo, Manhattan taxis,
cottage doors, the old *telefón* boxes,
failure, the word 'curious', the word 'screech'
and the little patch of brick Swann liked so much.

XII

Aphrodite's Pool

I dive and rise in an explosion of spindrift
and drift to a turtle-faced inflatable raft —
evening, Cyclades, one cloud in the azure,
a brain-scan light-show swarming on blue tiles,
a flickering network of vague energies
as on dolphin murals and docked caïque bows,
a murmuring hosepipe where the pool fills,
snatches of music from a quiet house,
the pump-house like a temple to the Muses;
on a marble slab flipper and apple core,
straw hat and wristwatch in a deckchair,
sandal and white sock. Nymphs have been here;
water nymphs have been here printing the blind
nap-time silence with supernatural toes
and casting magic on the ruffled water
still agitated by a dry seasonal wind.
Donkeys chew the roses, swifts skim the ripples,
a last plane fades beyond the glittering sound,
its wild surf-boards and somnolent fishing-boats,
as the air fills with cicadas and mosquitoes,
the sky with sunset and astronomy; goats
and ravens nod in the god-familiar hills
among spaceship vertebrae and white asphodels.
The prone body is mine, that of a satyr,
a fat, unbronzed, incongruous visitor
under the fairy lights and paper frills
of a birthday party I was too late to attend.
Aloof from the disco ships and buzzing bikes
the pool ticks faintly among quiet rocks;
rose petals on the surface and in the air,
mimosa and jasmine fragrance everywhere,
I flirt like some corrupt, capricious emperor
with insects dithering on the rim; for this
is the mythic moment of metamorphosis
when quantitative becomes qualitative and genes

perform their atom-dance of mad mutation . . .
I climb out, shower off chlorine and sun-lotion,
and a hot turquoise underwater light
glows like Atlantis in the Aegean night;
network, stars-of-the-sea, perpetual motion,
a star-net hums in the aphrodisiac sea-lanes.

XIII

Dusk

(*after Baudelaire*)

Night now, bewitching night, friend of the evil-doer,
sneaks up like an accomplice; like a boudoir
the sky closes; and men, mild in themselves,
change into ravening vampires and werewolves.
Soft night, desired by the unfortunate ones
whose limbs articulate with aches and groans
a day of servitude; night that relieves
those victims sacrificed to arduous lives —
the driven thinker with his ashen face,
the cleaning-woman who can know release.
Unwholesome spirits in the atmosphere
wake stupidly, meanwhile, like businessmen
and, cruising bat-like through the evening air,
flap at the door-post and the window-pane.
Under the lamplight that the wind teases
the whores light up outside the whorehouses
like ants pouring out of their black holes;
insurgents waiting for the word to strike,
they fan out everywhere through dark defiles
in diseased organs of the body politic
like flies that buzz around an open sewer.
You can hear a kitchen whistle here and there,
a playhouse laugh, a concert thump and blare;
the new rich, loud with bubbly and cigars,
fill up the restaurants and cocktail bars
and gangsters without pity or remorse
will soon be at their dirty work, of course,
privily forcing bureau drawer and strong-box
to stuff their face and clothe their mistress' backs.
Be still, my soul, at this unearthly hour
and stop your ears to its incessant roar,
for now the sufferings of the sick increase.
Night takes them by the throat, their struggles cease

as one by one they head for the great gulf;
the wards fill with their cries, who soon enough
will come no more to sup the fragrant broth
with a loved one, at dusk, by a known hearth —
for some of us have never known the relief
of house and home, being outcast in this life.

XIV

Rue des Beaux-Arts

There is only one thing . . . worse than being talked about, and that is not being talked about.
— Oscar Wilde

The new art is everywhere with its whiplash line
derived from pre-Raff ivy and twining vine,
its biomorphic shapes, motifs of cat and moth;
base metals and industrial design,
outside and inside, in themselves uncouth,
aspire to the carnal life of pond and bower —
and you yourself, old trendy that you are,
have exchanged the silvery tinkle of champagne
for muddy clouds of absinthe and vermouth,
bitter herbs self-prescribed to make you whole.
As you said, a yellow-journalism survivor
has no need to fear the yellow fever;
but it's mid-July and nature has crept back
to the rue des Beaux-Arts and the rue du Bac,
the humid side-streets of the Latin quarter
with its rank plants and warm municipal water,
its fiery pavements scorching feet and soul;
'the whole body gives out a silent scream'.
Deep in the silent pharmacy of your room
you doze most of the day with curtains drawn
against the hot-house light of afternoon,
rising at agate Paris dusk to take
your walk by the twilit river, *quai des brumes*,
visit a church to chew the altar rail
(what ever happened to the Greek ideal?)
and check with the sales people at Galignani's
on the latest magazines; and more than once
you've mixed with tourists in the Luxembourg
to watch schoolchildren under the stony gaze
of Anne de Bretagne and Marguerite de Provence
and listen to infants piping in the Coupole,

your Babylonian features raised in reminiscence.
'Art's mainspring, the love of life, is gone;
prose is so much more difficult.' The morgue
yawns, as it yawned too for Verlaine, Laforgue,
nor will you see your wife and sons again.
Gestures, a broken series; performance strain;
judge by appearances and what you get
is an old windbag. Still full of hot air,
still queer as fuck and putting on the style,
you spout in the Odéon given half a chance
for yours is the nonchalance of complete despair.
'The thing now is to forget him; let him go
to that limbo of oblivion which is his due' —
though the *Daily Chronicle* and the *St. James' Gazette*
are gone, while you are talked of even yet.
Backlit by sunset, a great trench of sky
glows like a brazier; grotesque tableaux,
unprecedented animals are engraved there
in angelic purple-and-gold photography
and the stars shine like gaslight. Gazing west
you can just make out the tip of Finistère
where the last rock explodes in glistening mist.
'They will not want me again in airy mood;
they would like me to edit prayers for those at sea.'
Job with a skin-rash and an infected ear,
Oisín in the real world of enforced humility,
you pine still for the right kind of solitude
and the right kind of society; but it's too late
to benefit from the astringency of the sea
or come to terms with the nature you pooh-poohed;
for you, if anyone, have played your part
constraining nature in the name of art,
surviving long enough for the birth-knell
of a new century and a different world.
Go sup with the dead, the party's life and soul:
'The greatest men fail, or seem to have failed.'

XV

Smoke

Bone-idle, I lie listening to the rain,
not tragic now nor yet 'to frenzy bold' —
must I stand out in thunder yet again
who have *thrice* come in from the cold? Sold
on sobriety, I turn to the idea of nicotine,
my opium, hashish, morphine and cocaine,
'Turkish on the left, Virginia on the right',
my cigarette a lighthouse in the night.
Autumn in Dublin; safe home from New York
I climb as directed to our proper dark,
five flights without a lift up to the old
gloom we used to love, and the old cold.
Head in the clouds but tired of verse, I fold
away my wind-harp and my dejection odes
and mute the volume on the familiar phone
('. . . leave your number; speak after the tone')
to concentrate on pipe-dreams and smoke-clouds.
Skywards smoke from my last Camel rises
as elsewhere from our natural resources
and the contagious bonfire of the vanities
like pillars of cloud. I was with Xenophon
in Persia, I was with the discoverers
when first they landed on American shores
in search of a trade-route to the Orient
and found instead, to their bewilderment,
a sot-weed continent in the western ocean.
Now closing time and the usual commotion,
crowds and cars as if to a revolution;
blue in the face behind my veils of smoke
I try to recapture pool dreams or evoke
aesthetic rapture, images of felicity,
the mist on Monet's nebulous nenuphars
or the dawn vision of a subsiding city
'rising like water-columns from the sea',

everyone crowding to the rail to see
the Tiepolo ceiling in the Gesuati,
clouds of glory, Elysian yellows and blues.
Geared up by Klein and Nike, Banana Republic, Gap,
we are all tourists now and there is no escape;
smoke gets in your face, in your eyes, up your nose
but offers inspiration, aspiration, hope,
lateral thinking, 'pure speculative ether',
an a-political sphere above the weather.
26. *INT. RICK'S. A night-club, expensive, chic*
with an air of sophistication and intrigue
and everybody puffing; those were the days
of legendary nuance, 'drift', lavender haze
and the frightful things of which we cannot speak.
No puffing now, not even on death row,
even in the electric chair tobacco is taboo.
. . . What *use* is it, you ask, as we exhale
clouds of unknowing with our last gasp. Well,
it suggests alternatives to the world we know
and is to that extent consoling; also
'a man should have an occupation of some kind'.
Raleigh, for instance, spent his time in Youghal
weighing cigars against cigar ashes to find
the weight of smoke, perhaps even of the soul;
and Bakhtin under siege, no soap, no supper,
used his own manuscripts as cigarette paper.

XVI

America Deserta

High in the air float green-blue copper roofs like the tips of castles rising from the clouds in fairy tales and cigarette advertisements.

— Zelda Fitzgerald,
Harper's Bazaar, 1929

Often enough you've listened to me complain
of the routine sunshine and infrequent rain
beyond the ocean blue; and now, begod,
where once it never drizzled but it poured,
in dirty Dublin and even in grim Belfast
our cherished rainfall is a thing of the past,
our climate now that of the world at large
in the post-Cold War, global-warming age
of corporate rule, McPeace and Mickey Mao.
Imitative in all things, we mimic now,
as nature art, the general new-age weather,
a smiley-face of glib promotional blather;
anxious not to be left behind, we seize
on the dumb theory and the prescribed disease
who were known once for witty independence
and valued things beyond the world of sense;
subscribing eagerly to the post-modern kitsch
we shirk our noble birthright as the glitch
in the internet, the thorn in the side, the pain
in the neck and the (holy) ghost in the machine.
An alien among aliens during my New York time
spying for the old world in the new, thought-crime
grown secretly like a windowbox of cannabis
in the shocking privacy of a book-lined space,
I valued above all our restful evening walks
to the West Side pierheads and the desolate docks
under a sunset close-encounter blaze
to watch the future form from the heat-haze

in the garbage mouth of the Hudson. We never hung
with the fast cocaine crowd or the surfing young
or spent our nights at Chaos, Traffic, Trapeze
with the Lindas, Bridgets, Kates and Naomis
but glimpsed from cloudy helicopter heights
the neon-fingered dawns and laser nights,
knew leaves show-cased in ice, the sick limo,
the virtual park and lamp-post in the snow,
those retro scenes beloved of Sam Menashe
and the hard-drinking, chain-smoking Eurotrash —
'ecstatic agents of the sublime superstate'
you catch in a red-eye café-society photo-flash.
What ever happened to the critical spirit,
real jazz, *film noir* and grown-up literate wit?
The earth belongs to the living; life imitates art
with palaces in the air, each one a fort
in a medieval city gripped by plague —
a nightmare, said Neruda, of corruption and fatigue,
mergers and acquisitions, corporate raiding,
'casino features in program and index trading' . . .
Oh, mile-high sex is fine but does it excuse
monopoly capitalism and global image control?
Back home now with my 20th-century blues
I surf the radiant icon for world news
and watch with sanctimonious European eyes
Whatever, American Evil, Born to Kill,
the continuing slave narrative, people in chains,
stick children, tanks, where once again warplanes
emerge from rain-clouds with a purposeful growl
as in the depths of Nostradamus' water-bowl;
drought, famine, genocide, frustrated revolution
and the silent roar of 'ant-like' migration.
Not long from barbarism to decadence, not far
from liberal republic to defoliant empire
and thence to entropy; not long before
the great money scam begins its long decline

to pot-holed roads and unfinished construction sites,
as in the dark ages a few scattered lights —
though it's only right and proper we set down
that in our time New York was a lot of fun.
I think of diner mornings in ice and thaw,
the Lion's Head, renamed the Monkey's Paw,
the heavens on the ceiling of Grand Central Station;
you wildly decadent in forbidden furs
in the shadow of the Bobst or the Twin Towers,
the skyline at your back, the pearl-rope bridges
and a nation singing its heart out in the business pages.

XVII

The World of J. G. Farrell

It was, after all, only the lack of perspective that
made it seem he would be swept away.

(*for Lavinia Greacen*)

A huge house (*Troubles*) at the water's edge
whistling and groaning in the wind from the sea,
blind windows, flying slates, whole days of reverie,
'the cemetery of all initiative and endeavour',
outbuildings, tea-gold streams, a heathery road
where the hero comes to claim his dying bride,
a yellow vintage 'motor' in the garage,
crows bickering high up in a foggy wood,
vegetable encroachments, intestinal shapes,
the click and ripple of exhausted pipes,
a creeper twining around a naked light
while a young man, inspected by binoculars,
harangues a restive crowd from a watery rock;
hill stations deserted (*Siege*), impenetrable foliage,
long bars empty (*Grip*) in tropical heat,
pools afloat with matchboxes and driftwood,
fly-blown verandahs, ceiling fans at rest,
carnivorous plants entangling gates and fences,
the coercive empire an empire of the senses,
of rustling organisms and whispering rain forest,
a dripping silence after torrential rain,
the fluttering butterfly that starts the hurricane.
Whisper, immortal Muse, of the insanity of the great,
the futility of control, the proximity of the pit,
of babies in the dust, smoking rubbish, a circling kite.
The girls from Goa, in silk and satin and boa,
have boarded the last ship out of the opium war
while Gurkha riflemen parade at the aerodrome
to a skirl of bagpipes and the 'Skye Boat Song'
leaving to the Chinese, if they so desire,

the investment banks and polo fields of Hong Kong,
the Coke and Marlboro ads; they're going home.
Everyone's going home now, those with homes to go to;
the bugles blow and the Union Jack comes down
in the West Indies and the Antarctic soon,
Bermuda, Antigua, South Georgia and Pitcairn
and even, who knows, Gibraltar and Ulster too.
The big-game trophies and lion skins have gone
from the cold interiors of northern Europe
while the consular derelict with his jungle juice
and perpendicular terror of the abyss
can take the cure and start to live in hope.
Better a quiet life, the moon in a bucket of water
with nobody there to hear though the stars do
and a bedside book like the teachings of Chuang Tzu —
type of the unselfconscious thinker who,
never a slave to objective reality, knew
our vital unity with the rest of nature;
disdained, of course, utilitarian method;
like Echo, answered only when called upon
in bamboo cage or palace of white jade.
We have lost our equilibrium, he said;
gaze at the world but leave the world alone.
Do nothing; do nothing and everything will be done.

XVIII

A Bangor Requiem

We stand — not many of us — in a new cemetery
on a cold hillside in the north of Co. Down
and stare at an open grave or out to sea,
the lough half-hidden by great drifts of rain.
Only a few months since you were snug at home
in a bungalow glow, keeping provincial time
in the chimney corner, *News-Letter* and *Woman's Own*
on your knee, wool-gathering by Plato's firelight,
a grudging flicker of flame on anthracite.
Inactive since your husband died, your chief
concern the 'appearances' that ruled your life
in a neighbourhood of bay windows and stiff
gardens shivering in the salt sea air,
the sunburst ideogram on door and gate,
you knew the secret history of needlework,
bread-bin and laundry basket awash with light,
the straight-backed chairs, the madly chiming clock.
The figure in the *Republic* returns to the cave,
a Dutch interior where cloud-shadows move,
to examine the intimate spaces, chest and drawer,
the lavender in the linen, the savings book,
the kitchen table silent with nobody there.
Shall we say the patience of an angel? No,
not unless angels be thought anxious too
and God knows you had reason to be; for yours
was an anxious time of nylon and bakelite,
market-driven hysteria on every radio,
your frantic kitsch decor designed for you
by thick industrialists and twisted ministers
('Nature's a bad example to simple folk'); and yet
with your wise monkeys and 'Dresden' figurines,
your junk chinoiserie and coy pastoral scenes,
you too were an artist, a rage-for-order freak
setting against a man's aesthetic of cars and golf
your ornaments and other breakable stuff.

Visible from your window the sixth-century
abbey church of Colum and Malachi,
'light of the world' once in the monastic ages,
home of antiphonary and the golden pages
of radiant scripture; though you had your own
idea of the beautiful, not unrelated to Tolstoy
but formed in a tough city of ships and linen,
Harland & Wolff, Mackie's, Gallaher's, Lyle & Kinahan
and your own York St. Flax Spinning Co. Ltd.;
daft musicals at the Curzon and the Savoy,
a bombing raid glimpsed from your bedroom window.
Beneath a Castilian sky, at a great mystic's rococo tomb,
I thought of the plain Protestant fatalism of home.
Remember 1690; prepare to meet thy God —
I grew up among washing-lines and grey skies,
pictures of Brookeborough on the gable-ends,
revolvers, RUC, 'B' Specials, law-'n'-order,
a hum of drums above the summer glens
shattering the twilight over lough water
in a violent post-industrial sunset blaze
while you innocently hummed 'South of the Border',
'On a Slow Boat to China', 'Beyond the Blue Horizon'.
. . . Little soul, the body's guest and companion,
this is a cold epitaph from your only son,
the wish genuine if the tone ambiguous.
Oh, I can love you now that you're dead and gone
to the many mansions in your mother's house;
all artifice stripped away, we give you back to nature
but something of you, perhaps the incurable ache
of art, goes with me as I travel south
past misty drumlins, shining lanes to the shore,
above the Mournes a final helicopter,
sun-showers and rainbows all the way through Louth,
cottages buried deep in ivy and rhododendron,
ranch houses, dusty palms, blue skies of the republic . . .

XIX

On the Automation of the Irish Lights

We go to the lighthouse over a golf-course now,
not whins and heather as we used to do,
though we loved golf a generation ago
when it was old sticks and rain-sodden sand —
the sea breeze and first-morning-springy turf,
the dewy, liminal silence of the rough,
the little club-house with its tin roof,
steamers and lightships half a mile from land,
an old sea civilization; but now, unmanned,
the wave-washed granite and limestone towers stand
on the edge of space untouched by human hand,
a routine enlightenment, bright but abandoned.
So long from Alexandria to Fastnet and Hawaii,
to Rathlin, Baily, Kinsale, Mizen, Cape Clear.
These are the stars in the mud, the moth's desire,
the cosmic golf that guides us *ab aeterno*
to 'a little cottage with a light in the window';
like Ptolemy and Ussher the mind creates
its own universe with these co-ordinates
marked out by beacons of perpetual fire
from the centuries of monastic candle-power
to the new technologies and the solar glow —
we are star water; as above, below.
Think (i) of evening light and tower shadow,
the families living in the toy buildings there
beneath that generalized, impartial stare,
the children 'abstract, neutral and austere',
star-clustering summer dusk, a single bird;
and (ii) rock keepers. Imagine them off-shore
in their world of siren-song, kelpie and mermaid,
listening to the wind and short-wave radio
and exercising as best they can in tiny
gardens above the sea. Think finally (iii)
of tower lights rising sheer out of the sea
where after gales a grumbling boulder knocks,

shaking the whole place, at igneous rocks.
Wind high among stars, solstice and equinox
will come and go unnoticed by human eye —
no more solitude, dark nights of the soul;
the new noisy knowledge replaces the midnight oil.
Now the ivory towers will be 'visitor centres'
visited mostly during the long winters
by sea-birds — gannet, puffin, kittiwake —
and their quartz lenses' own impersonal stroke.

XX

Christmas in Kinsale

After the fairy lights in seaside lounge and bar
the night walk under a blustery Advent sky,
sidereal frost systems money will never buy,
one gull on a night wave, one polished star,
crane-light at the quayside, a dark harbour-mouth.
Stars in the spars, Spar closing, Quinnsworth
and Super Valu shut, the oracles are dumb,
the blow-ins drinking for the thirst to come
on the estuary we swam once like the Bosphorus,
moonlight on ripples like flecks of phosphorus,
pausing at mid-stream for a shooting star,
wild gas we transit, the crushed dirt and ice,
a heavenly multitude, rock storms of space,
a circling camera, wandering screwdriver —
already rock stars have their names out there
in post-obituary orbit for all time.
The young are slouching into Bethlehem
as zealots turn out for the millennium
on Sinai and Everest, Patmos and Ararat,
container bodies, gaze fixed on the night
for a roaring wind and the promised meteorite
of fire and brimstone; Druid and Jacobite
will be there watching for the swords of light,
the *aisling* and the dreamt apocalypse
between an earthquake and a solar eclipse.
. . . Wind-chimes this morning as in younger years
from the Church of Ireland and the Carmelite friars,
smoke rising like incense from a chimney-pot.
Once, angels on every branch, scribes in the trees,
'a continuous chorus of divine praise'.
Does history, exhausted, come full cycle?
It ended here at a previous *fin de siècle*
though leaving vestiges of a distant past
before Elizabeth and the Tudor conquest —

since when, four hundred years of solitude,
rainfall on bluebells in an autumn wood . . .
Holed up here in the cold gardens of the west
I take out at mid-morning my Christmas rubbish.
Sphere-music, the morning stars consort together
in a fine blaze of anticyclone weather
cradling the calm inner, the rough outer harbour,
the silence of frost and crow on telephone lines,
the wet and dry, the garbage and the trash,
remains of rib and chop, warm cinders, ash,
bags, boxes, bulbs and batteries, bathroom waste,
carcases, tinfoil, leaves, crumbs, scraps and bones —
if this were summer there would be clouds of flies
buzzing for joy around the rubbish bins.
The harsh will dies here among snails and peonies,
its grave an iridescence in the sea-breeze,
a bucket of water where the rainbow ends.
Elsewhere the cutting edge, the tough cities,
the nuclear wind from Windscale, derelict zones;
here the triumph of carnival, rinds and skins,
mud-wrestling organisms in post-historical phase
and the fuzzy vegetable glow of origins.
A cock crows good-morning from an oil-drum
like a peacock on a rain-barrel in Byzantium;
soap-bubbles foam in a drainpipe and life begins.
I dreamed last night of a blue Cycladic dawn,
again the white islands shouting, 'Come on; come on!' . . .

Night and Day

(*after Ariosto*)

Brighter and clearer to me than mere daylight
are crafty night-for-day and day-for-night
when sun and stars, conspiring with the dark,
relax their vigilance and fade to black.
Cloud cover, shadow; the world goes to bed
and leaves two lovers only wide awake,
one caped and hooded down a colonnade
furtively flitting on invisible wings
where a door opens with a faint squeak
audible only to the intent sex maniac.
I'm still not sure if I'm imagining things
when your hand guides me to a secret spot
where hips and thighs like vines reticulate,
I quench my thirst in your wide-open mouth,
we gasp the quick rush and exchange of breath
and tremble in the metaphysical love fight.
These images will persist until life cease,
exploding like the sulphurous candlelight
which showed us clearly what was taking place,
pre-coital fever and post-coital peace,
consensual chiaroscuro and thumping heart.
No love can be complete with the light out
— so much better to have the gaze rest
on gaze, flesh tones and cherishable breast,
the speaking ears, the flickering and the moist
and the rose-petal lips unknown to thorn,
so satisfying the senses that each one
comes into play and none is left forlorn.
So precious the night-time and so brief,
and so severe the hardships of this life
when day breaks, banishing your dozy lover,
can we not live in a world of love for ever?

After Michelangelo

I

How can it be, as long experience shows,
the image present in the calcium carbonate
lasts longer, lady, than the artist does
who turns to dust again as at the start?
The cause yields to the outcome and withdraws;
nature is conquered once again by art
and, proving this, my very sculpture knows
death and time, faced with the work, depart.
A long life to the pair of us I can give
in either medium, whether in paint or stone,
to keep our living countenances alive
so people centuries after we have gone
will see your beauty and my wretched plight
and know in loving you I got it right.

II

Certain of death, though not yet of the hour,
I know my short life to be largely done;
to live on earth is for the senses fun
while the soul wishes only to retire.
The world is blind, and profit-driven verbiage
silences any superior thought; the age
of chivalry is dead, the lights are gone,
bluff triumphs and the truth cannot emerge.
Lord, when will the great event occur
your saints expect? A long anticipation
foreshortens hope and finds the soul unfit —
what use your promise of so great a light
if death comes, meanwhile, freezing everyone
for ever at the place it strikes us down?

A Dirge

(*Giovanna, Duchess of Amalfi, 1490-1520?*)

I

'I live here on this harsh and lonely cliff
like a mournful raven who avoids the life
of green branch and clear water, at a remove
from the world I know, from the friends I love
and from my very self, while my thoughts fly
to him, the one I venerate and deify,
whirling and shrieking until I put them right
and they flock to one bright corner of the sky.

'I am by now so tired of these long waits,
so worn out with frustration and desire
and the blithe disregard he demonstrates
while I sit here frantic at his non-return
I call for relief upon the silent moon
whose blade freezes the world with its white fire
and cuts the naked body to the bone,
so crushingly does grief reduce my spirits;

'but she turns a deaf ear to my plaintive cries
ignoring thoughts she does right to despise
even as he our long-hoped-for reunion —
and so, with the tears pouring from my eyes,
I invoke the pity of these waves and seas
and him at ease there in his high dominion
who answered closely to my amorous leisure
and made my bitter life a life of pleasure.'

II

Your ruined prison belvedere looks down
from its high cliff on a thriving tourist town
in siren land, the sea-front strung with light.
I wonder does your ghost walk here at night
as we like to think, a lantern in one hand,
its grave-clothes rippling in a south wind,
insisting still in your resilient voice
on your right to take the lover of your choice?

The high-pitched chatter of the ubiquitous cricket
shatters the sunset with its imperious racket;
sometimes on the horizon a cruiser shines,
the emerald coastline echoes with warplanes.
Harshness is global, cosmic; even as I write
dumb bombs have been 'delivered' during the night
— symptoms persist, and our sententious theatre
still flatters our perverse and turbulent nature.

No more apricots, no more chargeable revels,
you are brought down by inexplicable evils
and that body of yours, that witty face
buried by owl-light in an unknown place.
Even so we revel in the infection, flirt
with the corruption of a provincial court,
seduced by scheming web and flowery skull
and dazzled by 'I am Duchess of Malfi still'.

Exposing gleefully your strange disdain
to the weird violence of vengeful men,
a morbid cleric and a choleric duke,
your poet comes with his demented book —
and I too who climb to your hill-top
not, like the wolf, to find and dig you up
but to do homage in our own violent time
to one who lights time past and time to come.

A Siren

(*after Saba*)

Anyone watching you in the water would think: 'A siren!'
Winner in the women's swimming event, you seem
strange on the screen of my inglorious life.
While you smile in triumph I tie a thread,
a thin unbreakable thing, to your toe
but you stride past without noticing me.
Your friends, young like yourself, crowd round
and make a noise in the bar; and then
just for a moment cloud-shadow, a grave
motherly shadow shivers down from your
eyebrows to the proud, beautiful chin

and joins your rising to my own setting sun.

Ghosts

We live the lives our parents never knew
when they sang 'Come Back to Sorrento':
driving west in the evening from Pompeii,
its little houses sealed up in a tomb
of ash and pumice centuries ago
and now exposed to the clear light of day,
we found an old hotel with a sea view
and Naples' lights reflected in the bay
where, with a squeal of seagulls far below,
white curtains blew like ghosts into the room.

from *'Gramsci's Ashes'*

(after Pasolini)

There's nothing May-like in this toxic air
which further darkens or with blazing light
blinds the dark garden of the foreigner
and nothing May-like in the soapy cloud
casting its veil on the vast amphitheatre
of yellow attics ranged beside the mud
of the Tiber and among the purple pines
of Rome. Autumnal spring spreads mortal peace,
though disabused like all our destinies,
over the ancient stones, exhausted now,
and finished ruins where the strong
ingenuous impulse to start life anew
crumbled; and now silence, hot but hard,
where a motorbike whines off into the blue.
A boy in that far spring when even wrong
was at least vigorous, that Italian spring
our parents knew, vital with earth and song
and so much less distracted, when the place
united in fanaticism, you drew
already, brother, with your skinny paw
the ideal society which might come to birth
in silence, a society not for us
since we lie dead with you in the wet earth.
There remains now for you only a long
rest here in the 'non-Catholic' cemetery,
a last internment though this time among
boredom and privilege; and the only cries
you hear are a few final hammer-blows
from an industrial neighbourhood which rise
in the evening over wretched roofs, a grey
rubble of tin cans and scrap metal where
with a fierce song a boy rounds out his day
grinning, while the last rain falls everywhere.

Roman Script

Nel rifiuti del mondo nasce un nuovo mondo.
— Pasolini

I

Rain in the night; now cock-crow and engine-hum
wake us at first light on the Janiculum
and we open the shutters to extravagant mists
behind which an autumn sun hotly insists
on parasol pine, low dove and glistening drop,
bright lemon, jonquil, jasmine and heliotrope —
the Respighi moment, life mimicking art again
as when the fiddles provoke line-dancing rain.

II

Turn back into the room where sunlight shows
dim ceilings, domino tiles, baroque frescoes,
a scenic interior, a theatrical space
for Byronic masquerade or Goldoni farce,
vapours and swordsmanship, the cape and fan,
the amorous bad-boy and the glamorous nun,
boudoir philosophy, night music on balconies,
the gondola section nodding as in a sea breeze.

III

Rome of conspiracy theories and lost causes,
exiles have died here in your haunted palaces
where our own princes, flushed with wine and hope,
they say, and the squeal of a lone bagpipe
torn from the hazy, restless western ocean,
dreamed up elaborate schemes of restoration —
a world more distant now than Pompeiian times
with the shipyards visible from the nymphaeums.

IV

Type up the new stuff, nap between four and five
when for a second time you come alive
with flies that linger in November light
and moths not even camphor puts to flight;
listen with them to sepia furniture
and piano practice from the flat next-door;
watch where the poplar spires of evening thin
to smoke-stains on the ochreous travertine.

V

Now out you go among the *botteghe oscure*
and fluttering street-lamps of Trastevere,
over the bridge where Fiat and Maserati
burn up the race-track of the eternal city,
floodlit naiad and triton; for at this hour
the beautiful and damned are in Harry's Bar
or setting out for pit-stops, sexy dives
and parties, as in the movie of our lives.

VI

Here they are, Nero, Julia, Diocletian
and the grim popes of a later dispensation
at ease in bath-house and in Colosseum
or raping young ones in the venial gym —
as the prophet said, as good a place as any
to watch the end of the world; to watch, at least,
the late mutation of the romantic egotist
when the knock comes at last for Don Giovanni.

VII

Snap out of your art fatigue and take a trip
to church and basilica, forum, fountain and frieze,
to the Sistine Chapel's violent comic-strip
or the soft marble thighs of Persephone; seize
real presence, the art-historical sublime,
in an intricate owl-blink Nikon moment of time,
in a flash-photography lightning storm above
Cecilia's actual body, Endymion's actual grave.

VIII

Mid-morning noise of prisoners playing hard
in the Regina Coeli's echoing exercise yard —
for even the wretched of the earth are here
with instructions to entertain the visitor;
and we walk in reality, framed as virtuality,
as in a film-set, Cinecittà, a cinema city
where life is a waking dream in broad daylight
and everything is scripted for our delight.

IX

Others were here, *comunque*, who dreamed in youth
of a society based on hope and faith —
the poet of internment, solitude, morning sea,
of the lost years when we used to fall in love
not with women themselves but some commodity,
a hat, a pair of shoes, a blouse, a glove
(to him death came with the eyes of a new age,
a glib post-war cynicism restyled as image);

X

and the poet of poverty, ash on the night wind,
starlight and tower blocks on waste ground,
peripheral rubbish dumps beyond the noise
of a circus, where sedated girls and boys
put out for a few bob on some building site
in the cloudy imperium of ancient night
and in the ruins, amid disconsolate lives
on the edge of the artful city, a myth survives.

XI

His is the true direction we have lost
since his corpse showed up on the beach at Ostia
and life as we know it evolved into imagery,
production values, packaged history,
the genocidal corporate imperative
and the bright garbage on the incoming wave
best seen at morning rush-hour in driving rain:
'in the refuse of the world a new world is born'.

XII

(*A Rewrite: Metastasio*)

I invent dreams and stories, and even as I outline
dreams and romances on the unwritten page
I enter into them with so soft a heart
I weep at evils of my own design.
I've more sense when not deceived by art;
the creative spirit is quiet then and rage,
love, genuine emotions, spring for once
from real life and from felt experience.

Ah, but words on the page aren't the whole story
for all my hopes and fears are fictions too
and I live in a virtual fever of creation —
the whole course of my life has been imagination,
my days a dream; when we wake from history
may we find peace in the substance of the true.

'Shapes and Shadows'

— William Scott, oil on canvas,
Ulster Museum

The kitchens would grow bright
in blue frames; outside, still
harbour and silent cottages
from a time of shortages,
shapes deft and tranquil,
black kettle and black pot.

Too much the known structures
those simple manufactures,
communion of frying pans,
skinny beans and spoons,
colander and fish-slice
in a polished interior space.

But tension of hand and heart
abstracted the growing art
to a dissonant design
and a rich dream of paint,
on the grim basic plan
a varied white pigment

knifed and scrubbed, in one
corner a boiling brown
study in mahogany;
beige-biscuit left; right
a fat patch of white,
bread and milk in agony.

Rough brushwork here, thick
but vague; for already
behind these there loom
shades of the prehistoric,
ghosts of colour and form,
furniture, function, body —

as if to anounce the death
of preconception and myth
and start again on the fresh
first morning of the world
with snow, ash, whitewash,
limestone, mother-of-pearl,

bleach, paper, soap and foam,
top-of-the-milk cream,
to find in the nitty-gritty
of surfaces and utensils
the shadow of a presence,
a long-sought community.

A Swim in Co. Wicklow

The only reality is the perpetual flow of vital energy.
— Montale

Spindrift, crustacean patience
and a gust of ozone,
you come back once more
to this dazzling shore,
its warm uterine rinse,
heart-racing heave and groan.

A quick gasp as you slip
into the hissing wash,
star cluster, dulse and kelp,
slick algae, spittle, froth,
the intimate slash and dash,
hard-packed in the seething broth.

Soft water-lip, soft hand,
close tug of origin,
the sensual writhe and snore
of maidenhair and frond,
you swim here once more
smart as a rogue gene.

Spirits of lake, river
and woodland pond preside
mildly in water never
troubled by wind or tide;
and the quiet suburban pool
is only for the fearful —

no wind-wave energies
where no sea briar grips
and no freak breaker with
the violence of the ages
comes foaming at the mouth
to drown you in its depths.

Among pebbles a white conch
worn by the suck and crunch,
a sandy chamber old
as the centuries, in cold
and solitude reclines
where the moon-magnet shines;

but today you swirl and spin
in sea water as if,
creatures of salt and slime
and naked under the sun,
life were a waking dream
and this the only life.

The Dream Play

What night-rule now about this haunted grove?

The spirits have dispersed, the woods
faded to grey from midnight blue
leaving a powdery residue,
night music fainter, frivolous gods
withdrawing, cries of yin and yang,
discords of the bionic young;
cobwebs and insects, hares and deer,
wild strawberries and eglantine,
dawn silence of the biosphere,
amid the branches a torn wing
— what is this enchanted place?
Not the strict groves of academe
but an old thicket of lost time
too cool for school, recovered space
where the brain yields to nose and ear,
folk remedy and herbal cure,
old narratives of heart and hand,
and a dazed donkey, starry-eyed,
with pearls and honeysuckle crowned,
beside her naked nibs is laid.
Wild viruses, Elysian fields —
our own planet lit by the fire
of molten substance, constant flux,
hot ice and acrobatic sex,
the electric moth-touch of desire
and a new vision, a new regime
where the white blaze of physics yields
to yellow moonlight, dance and dream
induced by what mind-altering drug
or rough-cast magic realism;
till morning bright with ant and bug
shines in a mist of glistening gism,
shifting identities, mutant forms,
angels evolved from snails and worms.

Stanzas for Mary Stuart

The written, verse or prose, was of no consequence —
what counted was the flesh and its intensities,
your physical presence in the hunt or dance,
the white neck, chestnut hair and hazel eyes,
a madcap royal circus, mermaid uproar
bodied forth in performance and caricature.

Castle to castle with your box of mysteries
— Ridolfi, Babington — the exotic rout
descends through England under abstract skies
remembering fountain-blow, herb garden,
readings from Ovid, Petrarch and Ronsard
at the court of the sick boy-king; oboe, lute;

thin northern spires shining through smoky rain,
the Scots lords at your feet, Knox in his place,
golf in the blowing heather, cards and dice,
the charcoal braziers of your draughty palace,
deer bristling like a wood on the skyline,
the astral magic of your vanished reign.

I want to take this opportunity to apologize
for stupidity and unchivalrous dispraise
in hard times; we've no excuse, I know,
but the harsh love endemic here, although
even ironists for whom miraculous cures
are visionary can still believe in yours.

I have a bone to pick with your strange son
under whose auspices my own thorny region
received the benefits of reformed religion,
inheriting from generation to generation
a great wrong, a contentious imagery
and a squabble about the nature of reality.

We who looked to the future in earlier phases
look back now where the extinct futures died,
zone out and lie low with the lost causes
in urban attic or 'unspoilt' countryside,
somewhere invisible from the remote control
to raise a resistance for the endangered soul —

as if we could escape from the global market
and the benefits of cultural hegemony,
the multinational protection racket,
the world singing in perfect harmony
at ev'ning from the top of Fesole . . .
How can we know what you were like really
who respond only to electronic stimuli?

Porphyria, piety, plague, a mysterious texture —
we drive in a grave silence from glen to glen
remembering bagpipe music in the rain,
a biscuit tin and a speckled fountain pen.
Word to the kitchen, beyond script and scripture,
Donne's Imagery, The Elizabethan World Picture
and the oil-rigs creaking in the arctic north:
a chopped head wrapt in its billiard cloth,
we host your image to the iconic future
already figured in your theatrical death.

St. Patrick's Day

No wise man ever wished to be younger.
— Swift

I

Down the long library each marble bust
shines unregarded through a shower of dust
where a grim ghost paces for exercise
in wet weather: nausea, gout, 'some days
I hardly think it worth my time to rise.'
Not even the love of friends can quite appease
the vertigo, sore ears and inner voices;
deep-drafted rain clouds, a rock lost in space,
yahoos triumphant in the market-place,
the isle is full of intolerable noises.

II

Go with the flow; no, going against the grain
he sits in his rocking chair with a migraine,
a light in the church all day till evensong,
the sort of day in which a man might hang.
No riding out to bubbling stream and weir,
to the moist meadow and white belvedere;
on tattling club and coffee-house a pox,
a confederacy of dunces and mohocks —
scholars and saints be d-mn'd, slaves to a hard
reign and our own miniature self-regard.

III

We emerge from hibernation to ghetto-blasters
much better than our old Sony transistors,
consensual media, permanent celebration,
share options, electronic animation,
wave motion of site-specific daffodils
and video lenses in the new hotels;
for Niamh and Oisín have come to earth once more
with blinding breastplate and tempestuous hair,
new festive orthodoxy and ironic icon,
their faces lit up like the Book of Kells.

IV

Defrosting the goose-skin on Bridget's daughters
spring sunlight sparkles among parking meters,
wizards on stilts, witches on circus bikes,
jokers and jugglers, twitching plastic snakes,
pop music of what happens, throbbing skies,
star wars, designer genes, sword sorceries;
we've no nostalgia for the patristic croziers,
fridges and tumble-driers of former years,
rain-spattered cameras in O'Connell St.,
the sound mikes buffeted by wind and sleet —

V

but this is your birthday and I want to recall
a first-floor balcony under a shower of hail
where our own rowdy crowd stood to review
post-Christian gays cavorting up 5th Avenue,
wise-cracking dialogue as quick and dry
as that in *The Big Sleep* or *The Long Goodbye*;

for we too had our season in Tír na nÓg,
a Sacred Heart girl and a Protestant rogue,
chill sunshine warming us to the very bone,
our whole existence one erogenous zone.

VI

. . . A vast opaque body obscured the sun,
rising and falling in an oblique direction,
bright from the sea below, one even plate
above the clouds and vapours, smooth and flat,
adorned with figures of the moon and stars,
fiddles and flutes, the music of the spheres.
The king can deprive them of the dews and rains,
afflicting them with drought and diseases;
or drop stones, against which no defence,
directly upon their heads whenever he pleases . . .

VII

Borneo, Japan; night breezes, and while they breathe
hawthorn and bluebell of Armagh and Meath
a mouse watches where, beside confining quays
in a dirty-windowed website computer loft,
brain circuits off in the dark hovercraft,
he inhales the helium of future centuries,
the new age of executive science fiction,
flying islands in focus, no lateral vision,
the entire universe known, owned and reified
except for a tiny glitch that says to hide.

VIII

I now resign these structures and devices,
these fancy flourishes and funny voices
to a post-literate, audio-visual realm
of uncial fluorescence, song and film,
as curious symptoms of a weird transition
before we opted to be slaves of fashion
— for now, whatever our ancestral dream,
we give ourselves to a vast corporate scheme
where our true wit is devalued once again,
our solitude remembered by the rain.

IX

The one reality is the perpetual flow,
chaos of complex systems; each generation
does what it must; middle age and misanthropy,
like famine and religion, make poor copy;
and even the present vanishes like snow
off a rope, frost off a ditch, ice in the sun —
so back to the desk-top and the drawing board,
prismatic natural light, slow-moving cloud,
the waves far-thundering in a life of their own,
a young woman hitching a lift on a country road.